LONDON'S SECRET HISTORY

London's smallest police-station? Trafalgar Square

Peter Bushell

LONDON'S SECRET
HISTORY

'I love a little bit of *secret* history.'

Samuel Johnson

Constable · London

This book is dedicated to

MAGGIE

With deep love and admiration

First published in Great Britain 1983
by Constable and Company Limited
10 Orange Street London WC2H 7EG
Copyright © 1983 by Peter Bushell
ISBN 0 09 464730 5
Reprinted 1983
Set in Linotron Plantin 11pt by
Rowland Phototypesetting Ltd
Bury St Edmunds, Suffolk
Printed in Great Britain by
St Edmundsbury Press
Bury St Edmunds, Suffolk

Contents

List of Illustrations

Introduction

Any bookshop browser who happens upon this volume is entitled to ask: 'Why another book on London?' The short answer is that most guide-books restrict themselves to facts and dates and buildings – by any standard a dull diet. This book deals with *people*.

In the course of several years as a guide-lecturer, I was confronted again and again by the frustrated readers of those other guide-books. Without exception they all asked me the same question: 'Where is the *real* London and why can't we find it?'

This sense of unfulfilment – of having swallowed more of the shadow of London than the substance – is natural enough. But it need not be so. It is true that no city reveals all its secrets in a week or plays all of its cards face up; but armed with the right kind of book an astounding number of them can be winkled out in a very short time.

What I have endeavoured to do is to produce a book which, through a series of loosely-linked anecdotes, deals with the *secret*, sometimes bizarre and often amusing aspects of the metropolis. 'For me there is nothing more effective to recall the past – and that is what I want from history – than the significant anecdote' wrote Bernhard Berenson. I am sure the principle is a sound one. While I know that Robert Peel founded the police force, it was not until I read that his smile was like 'a silver-plate on a coffin' that he ceased to be merely a historical personage and took on the aspect of real flesh and blood. Every schoolboy knows that Constable was a painter, very possibly a great one, but Constable the man was a closed book, at least to me, until I learned that he was such a ditherer that even in donning a pair of trousers 'he was apt to lose time in deciding which leg should go in first'. Florence Nightingale is a remote, rather austere heroine: but the fact that she had for a pet a miniature owl which she carried with her everywhere in one of her pockets not only softens that image but very effectively draws her a little out of Time's shadow.

As a result of my researches I have come to think of London as a giant's Monopoly board – the inhabitants being both counters and players. People buy and sell individual properties, wax fat or thin on the proceeds and are in time replaced at the table (through death or bankruptcy or plain *ennui*) by other players. Some, like the Tichborne Claimant will produce documents authorising them to throw by proxy. Others, like Horatio Bottomley, will attempt to talk their colleagues into curious deals, over-reach themselves and go to jail. Some, like Stanley Baldwin, will take every throw seriously and scowl at those such as John Gay and Philip Sassoon, who do not.

Certain names – the quintessential satellites of London – appear again and again: Dr Johnson, Pepys, 'Old Q', and Sydney Smith. To the tourist who asks: 'Are there any such men left and if so why are we always going to the wrong places to meet the wrong people?' I can only say: 'Read on'.

What follows is necessarily an individual account and if more space has been devoted to Pepys than to Evelyn, to ghosts than to politics, that is simply because Pepys and ghosts are my personal preference. By the same token, it was not my brief to draw moral or sociological conclusions. In fact, in deciding to write this book I was motivated by nothing more high-minded or profound than a desire to create a sense of continuity with the past: to view not only the office block but the tavern which it dispossessed.

In consequence, what follows is *not* strictly a guide-book. It is that curious anomaly – a light-weight reference book which endeavours to amuse. I hope it will serve equally well as a bedside compendium which can be dipped into for a few minutes and then safely laid aside with no great loss of continuity. Those readers who prefer to consume books in one sitting may feel that it is often haphazard and disjointed. I can only sympathise and plead that London itself is haphazard and disjointed and terrain of necessity must mould its cover.

P.B.
London
December 1982

Acknowledgements

No work of this nature could possibly be encompassed without help. Among those to whom I am indebted for reading proofs and offering constructive criticism are Peter Emery, Keith St John Foster, Jeremy Ward, Lord Longford, Michael Fabian, Peter Hale, Ted Collinson, Brian Russell and the Very Reverend Edward Carpenter, Dean of Westminster Abbey. I also owe a further debt to Brian Russell for his advice on the legal aspects of publication. In administrative matters I am obliged for the sympathy and understanding shown to me by Betty Cowell and John Marriott. I extend my sincere thanks to the various librarians with whom this work has brought me into contact, but especially to Brian Claughton, Grahame Buchelle, Paul Mainwaring and Brian Merrick, all of whom proved unstinting in their efforts to keep me supplied with necessary works of reference. It is no exaggeration to say that without their benevolence (and occasional flashes of ingenuity) this book would never have been written. If you seek their monument, look no further than the bibliography.

It is also necessary to testify to the kindness of Stan Stovell and Brian Clark. Nor can I overlook Maisie Fitzpatrick, who valiantly shouldered aspects of vital research at a time when I was unable to do so myself. For her friendship and her consistent moral support I am also deeply grateful to Lynette Duff. Her readiness to undertake numerous and what must sometimes have seemed tiresome commissions, often at short notice, has significantly eased my burden. It would be the basest ingratitude if I did not also thank Helen Forsyth and Eva Hanagan, both of whom sustained me over many months and talked on my behalf in all the right quarters. My thanks must also go to the staff of Messrs Constables, my publishers, and especially to their Editorial Director, Elfreda Powell, who guided me through the uneasy months leading up to publication.

Of the nearly 400 books listed in the bibliography, the majority were actually read rather than merely consulted. They have all made a significant contribution, although my most constant sources of reference have been:

John Timbs: *Curiosities of London*
William Kent: *Encyclopaedia of London*
Arthur Mee: *London: The City and Westminster*
H. B. Wheatley: *London Past & Present* (3 vols)
G. G. Williams: *Guide to Literary London*

Finally, I am profoundly indebted to Sir Edward Marsh's little-known memoir *A Number of People* (1939). In addition to being one of the very best 'inconsequential' auto-biographies, it contains many excellent anecdotes which cannot be found elsewhere. I first read it in 1971, while living in Spain, and in a roundabout fashion it inspired me to attempt the present work.

1

Mayfair: The Grand Parallelogram

That greatest of all Regency wits, Sydney Smith, once described the parallelogram bounded by Oxford Street, Piccadilly, Regent Street and Hyde Park as containing 'more intelligence and human ability – to say nothing of wealth and beauty – than the world has ever collected in such a space before'.

Provided that we possess the specialised eye-sight to behold it, that secret world of Mayfair still survives. Its day may have gone but it has not ceased to exist. For me, the elegant creatures of the past have left an indelible imprint on London's time and space; and in some fifth dimension, some historical time-warp, they continue to function. Behind the wall-eyed mansions of Grosvenor Square – all anonymous offices now – plump butlers still wait unseen upon royal dukes and their dames; half-mad society hostesses still preside over glittering throngs in smooth-floored salons; the painted wheels of an infinity of chariots and chases still clatter soundlessly round the squares and streets; and, illuminated by the winking light of candles, jaundiced aristocrats dine with members of that dubious tribe of young women which somehow managed to *kiss* its way into polite society.

There is much to discover in Mayfair's past that is good and gay – nobility, humour, charm and more than a little gold. There is also a dark sediment of scandal and intrigue, of falsehood, pride and humbug, of cruelty, mayhem and mischief. In short, Mayfair is a microcosm of all the merits, vices and absurdities known to man.

Today, Mayfair's western extremity is marked by the great

humming turnpike of Park Lane; all wheels, roar and confusion. But if much of its elegance has faded, several of its
buildings cannot be ignored. The first of these is Brook
House, which stands on the corner with Upper Brook Street.
The seventh floor was London's first penthouse and formerly
belonged to Lord and Lady Mountbatten. It has thirty rooms
including eighteen bedrooms. Earl Mountbatten's own
sleeping quarters, which were relatively spartan, were modelled on a captain's cabin aboard a warship – a small bunk-
bed, a ship's brass clock, screw-down furniture and windows
resembling portholes. The apartment's most intriguing
accessory, however, was the lift, which was capable of
making the journey from the ground to the seventh floor in
four seconds. With the aid of a stop-watch, Earl Mountbatten calculated the exact time a caller would need from the
moment he rang the street bell to the moment at which the
lift would deposit him opposite the entrance to the penthouse
– and then trained his footmen to fling open the door at the
precise moment the caller was reaching out to knock on
it.

Old Brook House, which occupied this site until 1931, was
the London home of the banker, Sir Ernest Cassel, Lady
Mountbatten's grandfather. Despite his wealth, Sir Ernest
was not a happy man. He said he had only experienced real
enjoyment twice: 'Each time with the Pytchley Hunt'. His
treasures were mere investments and when he was away from
home they were locked up in steel cases in the house's
subterranean vaults. Nonetheless, he constantly worried
about them, as indeed he worried about every aspect of his
fortune. During the Great War he stopped sending his
waistcoats to be laundered because he considered the charge
of 1s 6d excessive. He died at Brook House in 1921 leaving a
fortune of six million pounds. He was found by his secretary,
slumped across his desk in a library lined with first editions
none of which he had ever read. He was buried in a coffin of
pure silver.

Beyond Brook House lies Culross Street, in all probability

Sir Ernest Cassel of old Brook House, Upper Brook Street, said to
have enjoyed himself only twice in his life

named after Viscount Colville of Culross. In his memoirs, the
sixth Duke of Portland recalled that Viscount Colville invariably wore a small gold ball as a watch-fob. As it was
hollow, society disputed for some years whether or not it
contained anything. One night, at dinner, Culross was per-

suaded by a pretty young woman to open it. Inside was his
spare glass eye.

As its eastern end, Culross Street is bisected by Park
Street, once the domicile of the Prince Regent's greatest
friend, Lord Alvanley. He was as great a 'beau' in his way as
his friend, George Brummell, but twice as prodigal. 'There is
no reason because you have no money,' said he, 'that you
should not have anything else', and indeed he managed to
live the best part of his life on credit. His greatest idiosyn-
crasy was to refuse to blow out candles. He was fond of
reading in bed but always doused the light by flinging it into
the centre of the room or smothering it beneath his pillow.

In 1848, shortly after his marriage, the art critic, John
Ruskin, came to live at number 31 Park Street. The union
did not long survive. Ruskin was out of sympathy with
women. In fairness, it should be said that women were often
out of sympathy with him. Lady Waterford said she could
forgive him looking like a 'wizened rat'; 'but it is his jokes
I cannot bear, they make me so sorry and miserable for
him.'

At right-angles to Park Street is Upper Grosvenor Street, a
sad little thoroughfare because it was here, in 1965, that the
American statesman, Adlai Stevenson, collapsed and died.
Twice a candidate for the Presidency, he is now best remembered for his sharp wit. He once defined an editor as 'a person
who separates the wheat from the chaff and prints the chaff';
and classified Richard Nixon as 'the kind of man who would
cut down a redwood, then mount the stump for a speech on
conservation'.

Upper Grosvenor Street leads us into Grosvenor Square
which takes its name from the principal private landlords of
London, the Grosvenor family, Dukes of Westminster.

The novelist, Sir Edward Bulwer-Lytton, spent his last
five years at number 12 Grosvenor Square. He believed
himself to be omnipotent, and one morning, while some
guests were eating breakfast at his country retreat, he
astonished them by entering the room, unkempt and wearing

only a dressing-gown. Without acknowledging their presence, he shambled round the table and peered intently into each face by turn. His wife murmured: 'Don't take any notice. He thinks he is invisible.'

Lord Lytton's marriage had not been a happy one. But he was dearly loved by his children, who were always thinking up ways to please him. One evening they set up a costume drama depicting the return of a crusader from the Holy Land. After the knight had been recounting his exploits for some time, his 'wife' suddenly produced a string of 'babies' and uttered the immortal line: 'I, too, my Lord, have not been idle.'

Lord Lytton's near neighbour, at number 15 Grosvenor Square, was the evangelist, Laura Bell. In 1887 her husband, Mr Thistlethwaite, died here. Being afraid of burglars he was in the habit of keeping a loaded pistol on a table near the bed. Late on the evening of 9 August he suffered a fainting fit whilst undressing. As he fell he overturned the table, dislodged the gun and was shot. His death was viewed with some suspicion by the police, but as he and Laura had been happily married for thirty-five years they eventually concluded that it had been nothing more than a freakish accident.

Although such matters had long ceased to be the subject of polite conversation, Laura had at one time been the most expensive courtesan in London. In 1850, two years before she met her husband, she had charged the Nepalese prime minister £250,000 for the privilege of spending the night with her.

A little south of Grosvenor Square is Farm Street, the only famous resident of which was the American actress, Tallulah Bankhead. She occupied number 1 in 1926 when she was twenty-three. She once confessed to being 'as pure as the driven slush'; and when someone informed her that Shirley Temple had been photographed through gauze, she replied: 'Then they ought to photograph me through linoleum.'

Opposite St George's Primary School, Farm Street merges

into South Street. Florence Nightingale died in a house on the site of what is now number 10 in 1910 at the age of ninety. She had long suffered from a wide variety of ailments, most of them imaginary, and much of her life from middle-age was spent as a bed-ridden recluse. Within three years of her return from the Crimea, Miss Eden was writing to Lady Theresa Lewis: 'every breath she draws may be heard through closed doors'. Yet she wheezed on very comfortably for more than half a century after that. By an administrative oversight the Order of Merit, conferred in 1907, was not presented until she was dying. She whispered: 'Too kind . . . too kind', and never spoke again.

Where Park Lane joins Curzon Street is the now defunct Playboy Club. The previous building which stood here was modelled on a French château and was built at the end of the last century for the eccentric South African millionaire, Barney Barnato. Although he never lived in it, Barnato adorned the façade with his portrait and decorated the roof with a series of hideous statues, identified by the wits as his petrified creditors. A cigar-puffing tycoon of the old school, his visiting-cards were engraved with the motto: 'I'll stand any man a drink but I won't lend him a fiver.' His beginnings were mysterious and the source of his great wealth surrounded by speculation. At the Savoy on one occasion, he was asked whether it was true that he had started life as a circus clown. He said: 'No' – then walked twice round the room on his hands.

In June 1897 Barnato was lost overboard from the 'Scot' en route from South Africa to London. While taking a turn on deck one afternoon he suddenly turned to his nephew and enquired the time. When the youth said: 'Three-fifteen', he walked to the side of the ship and threw himself over. His body was never recovered.

Barnato's Park Lane home eventually passed to Sir Philip Sassoon, an exquisite young man who implemented a number of 'essential' reforms. To mask the ugliness of the drainpipes he had them covered in gold leaf. The flowers in

Florence Nightingale with her pet owl, Athena, c. 1850. Much of her later life was spent in a house in South Street. Drawing by Parthenope Lady Verney.

each room were dyed to match the colour of the curtains. When the Union Jack was found to clash with the evening sky he had it struck and replaced with 'something less garish'. Philip was never a social lion himself, but he greatly enjoyed the company of those who were. One Easter a malicious acquaintance sent him an anonymous telegram which read: 'Christ is risen. Why not ask Him to lunch?'

Connecting the southern end of Piccadilly with Park Lane is the quiet little backwater of Old Park Lane. Here can be found the Londonderry Hotel. It commemorates old Londonderry House which stood on this site until 1962. The home of the Earls of that name, it was so vast that when a footman attached a pedometer to his ankle he found that he walked in the course of his duties an average of eighteen miles a day. Some of the rooms in Londonderry House lay forgotten for decades. One such belonged to the son of the sixth Marquess, a keen amateur photographer, who died before attaining his majority. For more than a hundred years his dark-room lay undisturbed, gathering dust. When someone did at last look into it they discovered a pathetic souvenir in the form of a crutch lying among the jumbled stacks of glass plates. It was darkly rumoured that the deformity of the hip which had made the crutch necessary had been induced by the sixth Marquess who, on learning that he was not the child's father, dashed him in a rage to the floor.

There are no certain grounds for believing this story; but the sixth Marchioness, Theresa, was certainly on very friendly terms with Edward VII who drove over from Buckingham Palace to see her almost every day. One morning, after the King had departed, Theresa returned to the room in which they had been talking and discovered a housemaid trying all the chairs by turn. She immediately divined what the girl was at and, pointing to one of the seats, said: 'That is the chair the King sat in. Go and have a good sit in it.'

Turning right from Park Lane into Curzon Street we come to Leconfield House, situated on the corner with Chesterfield Gardens. It is named after a former resident, the second Baron Leconfield. He lived here in dread of contracting typhoid and refused to touch London water under any circumstances. Every day a cart arrived at his door bearing fresh spring water from his Sussex estate at Petworth. However, as Sophocles has pointed out, fate has on occasion an inexorable purpose which 'no fort will keep out and no ship outrun'. Despite the Baron's precautions, the typhoid got him in the end. He contracted it after drinking a glass of water . . . while on a visit to his Sussex estate at Petworth.

Chesterfield Street, the next turning on the left, was once the domicile of George 'Beau' Brummell. He lived at number 4. Like most dandies he abhorred ostentation and wore only the most conservative clothes. 'If John Bull turns round to look after you', he said, 'you are not well dressed, but either too stiff, too tight or too fashionable.'

Nonetheless, Brummell was extremely fastidious about his appearance and his toilette was an involved affair. To give them the perfect shine, his boots were polished in champagne; and to ensure the perfect fit of his gloves, one establishment was commissioned to cut the thumbs and another the fingers. Hours were sacrificed to the remorseless pursuit of the perfectly tied cravat. One morning a visitor met Brummell's valet bearing away a pile of these accessories, clean but crumpled. As they passed on the stairs the servant murmured in a sepulchral voice: 'Our failures'.

Notwithstanding that his own grandfather had been a valet, Brummell was hard on servants and the maid who fetched a coarse dish with a handle in mistake for Corfe's edition of Handel would not long have survived at number 4. When Brummell contracted a chill he laid the blame squarely on his valet: he said the fellow had forced him to go into a room containing a damp stranger.

Running parallel with Curzon Street is Charles Street, formerly the home of the popular Irish actress, Dorothea Jordan. The mistress of the Duke of Clarence – afterwards William IV – she lived at number 20, producing ten children by him in ten years. When William endeavoured to reduce her allowance she quietly handed him a slip of paper which at that date was attached to all play-bills. It said: 'No money refunded after the rising of the curtain.'

Another woman of wit who lived in Charles Street was the society hostess, the Honourable Mrs Ronnie Greville. She occupied number 18, decorating the walls of her sitting-room in eighteen-carat gold. She had a sharp satirical tongue and in 1940, when her rival, Alice Keppel, was holding half of London in thrall with a dramatic account of her escape from France, one jump ahead of the advancing Germans, Mrs Greville said: 'To hear Alice talk you would think she had swum the Channel with her maid between her teeth.'

Berkeley Square, which junctions at its south-western corner with Charles Street, was begun in about 1740. Sadly, the nightingale's association with the Square is at best ironic. It first made its appearance in 1923 in Michael Arlen's short story: 'A Nightingale Sang in Berkeley Square'. Its song was contrived as a sour counterpoint to the desultory sound drifting across the Square from an open window of a husband and wife quarrelling in the presence of the woman's lover.

The great collector and memoirist, Horace Walpole, lived eighteen years at number 11 Berkeley Square and died there in 1797. One of his descendants later lost the house on the turn of a card to the banker, Henry Baring. Another was a notorious xenophobe who, when the Prince Consort died, put on his brightest clothes and openly went about rejoicing that there was now one foreigner less in the world.

Number 44 Berkeley Square is probably the finest remaining example of a Georgian terrace house in central London. It was built in 1744 for Lady Isabella Finch who appears to have had an overpowering desire to be married. When Lord Bath returned a loan of half-a-crown she insinuated, rather archly, that she would willingly forgo *half-a-crown* if she might aspire to a *coronet*. His Lordship seems not to have heard the remark, although it was several times repeated. Her home is now the Clermont Club and commemorates a later resident, the Earl of Clermont, whose principal claim to fame is that he was once accidentally shot by George IV. He was squatting behind a bush at the time with the result that '23½ grains of Number Four Shot' were subsequently removed 'from Lord Clermont's bum'.

Due to the many and spectacular phantoms which are said

to inhabit the building, number 50 Berkeley Square is known as 'the most haunted house in London'. Although nothing untoward has been seen here now for almost forty years, the legend persists and there is an old story that the house is so charged with psychic tension that it is only necessary to touch the exterior brickwork in order to receive a tingling sensation at the base of the spine. The three most common manifestations are: a small unhappy child; a mad woman; and a rather melodramatic girl who clings by her fingers to a high window-ledge in a last desperate endeavour to evade the lewd attentions of an old man, thought to be her guardian.

In the mid-Victorian era the house's unsavoury reputation ensured that it remained empty for long periods; but a wealth of activity continued behind the blank windows. Bells rang, lights flashed and the air was intermittently rent by the sound of disembodied screams, moans and thuds. Late at night, passing pedestrians heard sounds reminiscent of a body being dragged across the floor; and the measured footfalls of someone in a deep reverie pacing back and forth across the bare floorboards.

One foggy night, looking for somewhere to sleep, two stranded sailors broke into the house only to be confronted by a hideous, formless creature with a gaping black hole for a mouth. One sailor, in his terror, flung himself from the middle window of the top floor and was impaled on the railings below. His gibbering companion was found wandering about nearby by a patrolling policeman.

Number 53 Berkeley Square also has a ghost, the figure of an old gentleman dressed in seventeenth-century costume who occasionally manifests at a first-floor window. The story goes that he had a cherished daughter who eloped but left a note promising to return and visit him after the wedding, a promise she broke. From time to time this sad old shade comes to stare forlornly out of the window, searching among the bustle of the modern Square for an undutiful daughter who never came and who now will never come.

If there are other ghosts connected with Berkeley Square

they are less well authenticated and we would anyway do well to remember that not every nocturnal bump has a super- natural genesis. Sometimes the explanation is even more bizarre, as witness the story told by Augustus Hare of the lady

who awoke in the night with the disagreeable sense of not being alone . . . and soon felt a thud upon her bed. There was no doubt that someone was moving to and fro in the room, and that hands were constantly moving over her bed. She was so dreadfully frightened that at last she fainted. When she came to herself it was broad daylight, and she found that the butler had walked in his sleep and laid the table for fourteen upon her bed.

In nearby Fitzmaurice Place is the Savage Club, most esteemed, it is said, by those who do not belong to it. J. B. Priestley called it 'the place where dirty stories go when they die'. George Grossmith, father of the author of *Diary of a Nobody*, was a regular at the Club's musical evenings – and one night dropped dead during the course of one of them. As he did so moments after requesting the pianist to play 'The Dead March in Saul', he was at first suspected of having perpetrated a rather tasteless Pooteresque joke.

Clarges Street, which runs south from Curzon Street to Piccadilly, has had several famous residents. The actor, Edmund Kean, spent eight years at number 12 in the company of a tame puma; and during the Victorian era Robert Bristowe lived at number 22 – so incapable of assert- ing himself that, rather than undertake the unpleasant task of dismissing a brace of troublesome servants, he bought a jaguar to frighten them away. On entering the hall he turned the animal loose, barricaded himself in the parlour and rang the bell. But the servants – who may have divined some sort of trap – refused to answer the summons. Faced with the prospect of starving to death, Bristowe cut a hole in the door and shot the beast with his revolver.

Until 1979 Clarges Street was also the home of the fabulously wealthy oil millionairess, Olga Deterding. She shared her penthouse with several stuffed sheep. Due to her habit of sprinkling raisins on the carpet behind them more than one visitor came away believing them to be real.

Piccadilly, that 'magic mile' which runs from Hyde Park Corner to Piccadilly Circus, probably commemorates a seventeenth-century draper who lived hereabouts and who made his money from a type of support for the Elizabethan ruff, known as a pickadil.

The first building of note here is Norman Shaw's Piccadilly Hotel, built in 1908 for a wealthy cut-price tailor named Mallaby-Deeley. Sir Harry Mallaby-Deeley was an astute man who made a curious 'compact' with a young aristocrat named Edward Fitzgerald. In 1919 Fitzgerald – who was heir to the Dukedom of Leinster – had brought himself through his spendthrift ways almost to the brink of bankruptcy when he was contacted by Sir Harry who made him a very strange proposal. He offered to pay him a lump sum of £60,000, in return for which young Fitzgerald was to 'sell' him his inheritance. This meant that from the day he succeeded as Duke, until the day of his death, Edward would be able to enjoy neither the possession of his property nor the disposal of its income, then estimated at £80,000 a year. He also agreed to do nothing to shorten his life – a life which Sir Harry took the additional precaution of insuring for £30,000.

Lord Edward, believing that the benefits to himself were tangible and immediate, whilst those he was assigning were dubious and speculative, accepted. He was only five years younger than the sixth Duke – his brother, Maurice – and there was no reason for supposing that Maurice would die young.

But in 1922, just three years after the signing of the agreement, Maurice did die, of a brain tumour, and Mallaby-Deeley entered into 'his' inheritance. For more than fifty years he and his family lived in the Leinster mansions, enjoying all the benefits of Ireland's premier dukedom and accumulating more than four million pounds in estate revenue; while Edward lived for the most part in a succession of seedy bed-sitters and poky council flats, ekeing out an existence on twenty pounds a week, the amount of a pension which in later years the Mallaby-Deeleys were grudgingly prevailed upon to grant him. In his old age Edward ran a tea-shop at Rye, in Sussex, with his fourth wife. He died in 1976 aged ninety. His estates then reverted to his son – who found them so despoiled as to be practically worthless.

Two hundred yards west of the Piccadilly Hotel we come to perhaps the most 'secret' of all Piccadilly's buildings: Albany, a set of exclusive residential chambers for single gentlemen set back behind a discreet courtyard. The building has known many famous residents and at the height of the General Election campaign in 1966 Mr Edward Heath was photographed in his Albany bedroom balancing on a skateboard.

Pursuing her nine-month infatuation with Lord Byron, Lady Caroline Lamb tricked her way into his Albany chambers one day in 1812 disguised as a page-boy. Finding him out, she wrote the words 'remember me' on the fly-leaf of one of his books. This invasion of his privacy so enraged Lord Byron that he at once sat down and penned a vituperative poem which ended:

> Remember thee! Aye, doubt it not,
> Thy husband too shall think of thee,
> By neither shalt thou be forgot,
> Thou false to him, thou fiend to me!

From 1804 to 1807 Jane Austen's brother, Henry, ran his bank from rooms adjacent to Albany; and close by the front entrance another banker, the miserly old Meyer de Rothschild one day dropped a penny. He spent a deal of time vainly searching for it only to find upon straightening up that somebody had relieved him of his watch.

On the corner with Berkeley Street is a car salesroom. Of

no consequence in itself, it stands on an historic site. It was formerly occupied by Devonshire House, the London mansion of the Dukes of Devonshire, built in 1735 for the third Duke, a man of such scrupulous principle that Dr Johnson once said of him that if he had promised you 'an acorn and none had grown that year in his woods . . . he would have sent to Denmark for it.' His grandson, the fifth Duke, was an ill-featured, slovenly creature who affected in public an air of weary detachment. He never permitted anything to put him out of countenance and when, as a guest at a ball, his lounging against a valuable glass ornament caused it to fracture, he merely stared at it for a moment and said: 'I wonder how I did that.' Intent on discovering the secret he went and lolled against another and broke that also, saying: 'This is singular enough.' His son, the sixth Duke, was a conservative man who resisted change wherever he found it. When the railways first began to thrust northwards he refused to sell a single acre of his Derbyshire estates for fear that the trains would unsettle his pheasants. He thus extended the journey to Wick by forty miles.

By far and away the most amusing of the Devonshire Dukes was the eighth, known to his friends as 'Harty Tarty'. He seems to have spent much of his life being bored and once had to be reprimanded by Queen Victoria for picking his nose at her dinner table. In the House of Lords, when someone inadvertently woke him up during a debate he pulled out his watch and grumbled: 'Good heavens! what a bore! I shan't be in bed for another seven hours.' He is said to be the only peer who ever dreamed that he was making a speech to the House of Lords – and woke up to discover he was. An enthusiastic huntsman, but a poor shot, 'Harty Tarty' once killed a pheasant and his gun-dog and inflicted flesh-wounds on two bystanders with a single cartridge. One of the wounded was his chef, who, said his Lordship graciously: 'is the last person I would wish to kill'.

His son, the ninth Duke, was cast in a similar mould. During a by-election campaign in 1931, Stanley Baldwin launched a virulent attack upon the Press which, he claimed, was aiming 'at power without responsibility – the privilege of the harlot'. At this the Duke of Devonshire blanched visibly and muttered: 'That's done it. He's lost us the tarts' vote.'

Piccadilly has long been a street of clubs and for many years one of the most exclusive was the Turf. It was following a meal at the Turf that Maurice Baring unwittingly caused great distress to a waiter by complimenting him on the service. The man burst into tears, saying: 'I have been employed here man and boy for forty years, sir, and that's the first kind word I have ever had.'

Number 94 Piccadilly is the Naval and Military Club, known from the traffic signs at its two approaches as the 'In and Out'. The house previously belonged to Lord Palmerston who died here aged eighty-one in 1865 after a residence of nine years. A week before his death he was seen to scramble rather furtively over the area railings. Taking great pains to ensure that he was not observed, he then scrambled back again. His last illness come upon him suddenly and he entirely refused to believe that it would prove fatal. His last words were full of unconscious irony: 'Die?', he said. 'Why, my dear Doctor, that is the last thing I shall do.'

Number 127 Piccadilly is occupied by the Cavalry Club. Some of its rules are idiosyncratic and at one time to display any kind of official papers here was a crime punishable by instant expulsion. Among the Club's mementoes are some pressed flowers gathered from the 'valley of death', down which the Light Brigade made its historic charge in 1854.

A few doors away from the Cavalry, at number 148 Piccadilly, the banking family de Rothschild had their London home. The penny-dropping Meyer de Rothschild we have already encountered. His youngest son, James, enormously increased the family wealth by dressing as a woman and smuggling gold ingots across the enemy lines to finance the Duke of Wellington in his Peninsular Campaign. Gronow relates that 'the mother of these mighty capitalists attained the age of ninety-eight'. When she knew she was dying she pleaded with her doctor to help her. 'Madame,' he said. 'What can I do? I cannot make you young again.' The lady said she did not wish to be young again. 'But I want to continue to grow old.'

On the western side of Duke Street and Piccadilly is Fortnum and Mason, the grandest of all provision merchants. It was founded, in all probability, by one of George III's footmen in about 1770. Charles Dickens was a regular customer and Queen Victoria ordered from here a consignment of concentrated beef-tea to send to Florence Nightingale in the Crimea. The present Queen is the twelfth crowned-head to patronise the store.

Regrettably, Fortnum's ceased to be a family concern some years ago. It is now a subsidiary of Associated British Foods, a former chairman of which was the Canadian, Garfield Weston. A widower, he met his second wife when she was employed here as a waitress in the tea-rooms.

Close to Green Park underground station is the first of several northern tributaries of Piccadilly worth exploring: Stratton Street, once the home of the banker, Thomas Coutts. In 1815, when he was eighty, Thomas married the actress, Harriot Melon, a woman more than forty years his junior. At his death he left her a fortune of almost a million pounds. After five years of widowhood Harriot remarried, taking for her second husband the ninth Duke of St Albans. As she was then a portly woman of fifty and her husband a mere stripling of twenty-six, society dubbed them 'Lord Noodle and Queen Dolabella'.

The Duke of St Albans had first proposed to Harriot in 1826, but at that date she refused him. A year later, when he applied a second time, by letter, she despatched a servant with a note refusing him again. He had not long set out, however, when Harriot had a change of heart and sent a second messenger off on horseback to overtake and recall him.

Harriot's family – quite wrongly – suspected the Duke of being a fortune-hunter and on the eve of the wedding her relatives sat up all night in an attempt to dissuade her from the match. But Harriot was set on it. Her husband was amiable and more than passably good looking. She also knew that as his Duchess she would be admitted to a rank of society which, as the wife of a mere banker, had previously been denied her.

Although the Duke needed all his qualities of amiability on his wedding night – Harriot insisting on bringing to bed the pillow on which her first husband had died – 'Lord Noodle and Queen Dolabella' remained happily married for ten years. Only as her own end approached did Harriot ask to be carried once more to her old home in Stratton Street. At her specific request she was put into the bed where her first husband had died. Again the old pillow was brought out and she lay clutching it, convinced that before she breathed her last Thomas would come to her, as he had promised to do, in the guise of a small bird, and serenade her from the window-sill.

'For two months before her death', says *London Past and Present*, 'she lay in the great dining-room towards Piccadilly, without pain but weak and tranquil'. On the morning of 6 August 1837 her breathing became very shallow. She looked towards the window and saw, on the other side of the glass, a robin. She ordered the window opened. As soon as this was done, the bird fluttered to the foot of her bed and began to sing. A few moments later, Harriot died. She left sufficient gold sovereigns to carpet twenty-four square miles.

The bulk of Harriot's sovereigns passed to Thomas Coutts' granddaughter, Angela Burdett-Coutts who, because she was now the richest young woman in England, received a quite astonishing number of marriage proposals. Notwithstanding that she was very tall and not the least good looking, no man could stand to be alone with her for five minutes without proposing. One of her greatest friends was Lord Houghton who believed that Angela liked him:

because I never proposed to her. Almost all the young men

of good family did: and those who did their duty by their family *always* did. Mrs Browne [Miss Coutts' companion] used to see it coming and took herself out of the way for ten minutes; but she only went into the next room and left the door open, and then the proposal took place, and immediately it was done Miss Coutts coughed and Mrs Browne came in again.

When Mrs Browne fell ill – perhaps from sitting too often in rooms with the door open – a nurse was hired. This lady proved markedly eccentric and 'when so dispoged' would take deep draughts from a bottle which she kept on 'the chimley-piece'. When her nose itched she rubbed it vigorously on the fender. The two ladies were so diverted by her antics that they described them in some detail to their good friend, Charles Dickens, who afterwards used her as the model for 'Sairey Gamp' in *Martin Chuzzlewit*.

Another of Piccadilly's tributaries is Berkeley Street, once the site of the famous brothel run by the procuress, Mrs Porter. She it was who engineered an introduction for the Duke of Wellington to the beautiful demi-rep, Harriette Wilson, when that lady first became the rage of the town. Unfortunately, Harriette was not much struck with the 'Iron Duke'. She said he looked 'very like a rat-catcher'. For his part, the Duke was hopelessly tongue-tied in Harriette's presence and when he did attempt a conversational canter she promptly squelched him. One day, after a silence longer than usual, he said: 'I was thinking of you last night after I got into bed.' Harriette replied: 'How very polite to the Duchess.' Some years later, when she was ill and penniless, Harriette attempted to blackmail the Duke – as she attempted to blackmail half of London – by offering to leave him out of her memoirs in exchange for a suitable sum of money. The 'rat-catcher's' retort has become famous: 'Publish and be damned!'

In its own quiet way, Brown's, at number 21 Dover Street, is one of the most elegant hotels in London. Opened by a former butler to Lord Byron in the year of Queen Victoria's accession, it has known many eminent guests. In the 1870s Alexander Graham Bell made the first telephone call from Brown's; and Kipling was removed from here to hospital five days before his death in 1936. During the Second World War, the Dutch Government in Exile declared war on Japan from the hotel.

Harriette Wilson, famous courtesan, of Berkeley Street. She found the Iron Duke 'very like a rat-catcher'

A less well known Dover Street hostelry was Batt's. When the exceedingly eccentric Sir George Sitwell became a resident, Ada Leverson remarked to his son, Osbert, 'I see your father's changed belfries.'

Beyond Dover Street is Old Bond Street where, 'at the silk bag shop' in 1768, Laurence Sterne breathed his last. He murmured: 'Now it is come,' and then 'put up his hand as if to stop a blow and died in a minute'. His servants rifled his possessions and made off with everything they could carry. It is said that even his body was stolen. It was dug up by the Resurrection Men, at dead of night, and sold to an anatomist. While it was in the process of being dissected, the anatomist was joined by a colleague. As luck would have it, he was one of Sterne's life-long friends. He glanced at the corpse and fainted.

Another anatomist, the seventeenth-century physician Sir William Petty lived for some years in nearby Sackville Street. A peace-loving man he once – through no fault of his own – found himself challenged to mortal combat by the ferocious Sir Heiron Sankey. The chronicler, John Aubrey, said of this: 'Sir William is extremely short-sighted, and being the challengee, it belonged to him to nominate place and weapon: he nominates for the place a dark cellar; and the weapon to be a great carpenter's axe. This turned the knight's challenge into ridicule, and so it came to naught!'

Forming the eastern boundary of Mayfair is Regent Street, famous for the grand sweep of its façade and for the Café Royal, founded in the middle of the last century by a Frenchman named Daniel Nicols on a borrowed capital of £5. With its huge mirrors and gilded caryatids the Café Royal became in the 1890s the haunt of many eminent artists and men of letters. Jerome K. Jerome wrote part of *Three Men in a Boat* at one of the marble-topped tables; and Oscar Wilde frequently dined here with Lord Alfred Douglas.

A less well known habitué was T. W. H. Crosland, whose visiting cards were engraved with the legend: 'Jobbing Poet –

Funerals Attended'. The target of an anonymous squib, *The Unspeakable Crosland* (which it later transpired he had written himself) he was at heart a rather sad man. He wrote his own epitaph and it is worth repeating:

> If men should say ought of me
> After I die;
> Say there were many things he might have bought
> And did not buy.
> Unhonoured by his fellows he grew old,
> And trod the path to Hell.
> But there were many things he might have sold,
> And did not sell.

Marie Lloyd once chased the head-waiter round the grill room of the Café Royal with a hat-pin; and Dylan Thomas was temporarily barred in 1935 for scraping his tongue with the menu and presenting the detritus to another diner. Leonard Pawle used to confound guests by sticking matches in his cheeks and setting light to them.

The greatest exhibitionist of them all, however, was the Black Magician, Aleister Crowley, who used to stalk to his table wrapped in a cloak which he believed rendered him invisible. He was only once persuaded to take it off – when he was seen to be wearing nothing but a beautiful bronze butterfly, its wings extended to cover his loins, which he had stolen from Epstein's nude statue of Oscar Wilde. It is not known whether he ever returned it, but he still owes the Café Royal a hundred pounds.

Parallel to Regent Street is Savile Row, the traditional home of English bespoke tailoring. Sheridan lived for a time at number 14, stopping his rattling windows with banknotes; and died in a front bedroom of number 17 in 1816, muttering: 'Tell Lady Besborough that my eyes will look up at the coffin lid as brightly as ever.' Sadly, his debts pursued him even beyond the grave. Masquerading as a mourner, a bailiff gained access to the room in which his corpse was lying, impounded it on behalf of a creditor and refused to release it for burial until the sum had been paid.

A few hundred yards north of Savile Row is the church of St George's, Hanover Square, built in 1724. The church has long been a venue for smart weddings and Shelley, Disraeli, 'George Eliot', Buchan and Galsworthy were all married here. On at least one occasion P. G. Wodehouse's faint-hearted hero, Bertie Wooster, narrowly avoided matrimony at St George's. His intended was Honoria Glossop, a girl whose laugh has been compared to 'a squadron of cavalry charging over a tin bridge'.

A less respectable character associated with the church is George Joseph Smith who began his career of bigamy here just before the Great War. From his *modus operandi* he is remembered as 'The Brides in the Bath' murderer. After tricking lonely women into going through a form of marriage with him, he swiftly robbed them of their savings and drowned them in their baths, making it look like an accident. He was a sanctimonious creature who sped the soul of his last victim on its way with a wet-handed rendition of 'Nearer My God to Thee' played on a broken-down harmonium. When he saw that the judge's summing-up was not to be in his favour, he shouted: 'I am not a murderer – though I may be a bit peculiar.' Faced with the prospect of the gallows, his courage deserted him and he had to be carried to the execution shed by four burly warders.

Running from the north-west side of Berkeley Square to New Bond Street is Bruton Street. It has a special place in the nation's affections because in 1926 the present Queen was born at number 17, the home of her maternal grandfather, the Earl of Strathmore. The house has since been replaced by a bank, but its history was an interesting one. After the death of the ninth Earl of Strathmore his widow, Mary, remarried. Her second husband was a brutish man who maltreated and even imprisoned her. Lady Mary eventually escaped and made her home in Bruton Street once more; but she developed a morbid fear that a similar fate would overtake her daughters and in consequence kept them as closely confined as she had once been kept herself. One of the girls, Lady Anna Bowes, nonetheless contrived to fall in love with a lawyer living in the house opposite. When her mother refused to sanction their union she escaped to his chambers by traversing a wooden plank which he extended from his top-floor window. The marriage was celebrated the same day – but, alas, both parties lived to regret it.

Taking the second turning on the left out of Old Bond Street we find ourselves in Grosvenor Street. Between the wars Alice Keppel, last mistress of Edward VII, lived at number 16. During the 'season' she let the house to wealthy foreigners endeavouring to break into society. One of the more amusing of these was the parvenue Mrs Laura Corrigan (formerly a telephonist from Chicago) who attempted to negotiate a rental which would have entitled her to an introduction to all of Alice's friends.

Crossing Grosvenor Street at right angles is Davies Street, which commemorates the heiress, Mary Davies, who in 1677 married the 21-year-old Sir Thomas Grosvenor. She was very young, probably not more than thirteen, but her dowry included vast tracts of Mayfair. In middle age, Mary lost her reason and, after the death of her husband, fell under the influence of an unscrupulous Jesuit priest, Lodowick Fenwick. Convinced that she could fly, she attached feathers to her arms and talked of casting herself down from a high place. Fenwick – who had reasons of his own for wishing to keep her intact – subdued her by sprinkling powdered opium on her poached eggs.

A little further north is Brook Street, which takes its name from the now subterranean Tye Bourne (Tyburn) brook, which crosses it. George Frederick Handel lived for almost forty years at number 25 and there wrote the 'Messiah' in twenty-four days without once stirring out of doors. Until very recently number 53 Brook Street was the home of the Bath Club, the Committee of which always considered itself something of an arbiter in swimming matters. It once censured the American 'Tarzan', Johnny Weismuller, for 'failing to swim like a gentleman'; and there is an old but apocryphal story that when a sample of the water from the swimming-pool was sent for analysis the jar was returned marked: 'This horse has diabetes.'

At Oxford Street we come to what is arguably one of the most fascinating shopping areas in the world. Yet most of its 'secret' associations are picaresque. On the far side of Adam and Eve Court is the Old Kentucky Palace, a café-restaurant not quite as ancient as its name would suggest. The site was formerly occupied by Messrs Attenborough, a firm of pawnbrokers, and it was here, in 1910, that Hawley Harvey Crippen, that mildest of poisoners pawned his dead wife's jewels for £195.

West of Poland Street is the emporium of Messrs Marks and Spencer, one of the most ubiquitous and popular chain stores in England. It has been calculated that on any given day eight out of every ten people will be wearing at least one item manufactured under their brand name; and that two out of three women will be wearing a 'St Michael' bra. Jeffrey Jackson, who as British Ambassador to Uruguay was held captive for some months by guerillas, wore a Marks and Spencer vest throughout his ordeal and presented it to the firm on his release. The site of the store was formerly occupied by a chemist's shop from which Thomas de Quincey made his first purchase of opium.

Nearby is the Oxford Street branch of the Bata Shoe Company, unique in having once pioneered a climbing-boot for nudists. These were fitted with small side pockets so that the wearers might have somewhere to stow their more portable possessions.

Until recently, one of the most impressive of the Oxford Street department stores was Marshall and Snelgrove, built in the style of a French château. Mr Snelgrove was very much a town man, while James Marshall preferred the semi-rural charms of Mill Hill, commuting to the store each day by train. His standing in the community was such that he was not only permitted to select the site for the station but also granted the freedom to flag down anything passing through it.

Lady Florence Paget, known as 'the Pocket Venus', caused something of a sensation as the result of a trip to Marshall and Snelgrove's. Shortly after her engagement to Harry Chaplin she went there to buy her trousseau. But instead of doing so she left her carriage at the Oxford Street entrance as a decoy, walked the length of the store and passed out through the Vere Street exit. Waiting for her there was the dissolute Marquis of Hastings who carried her off to a nearby registry office where they were married the same day by special licence.

Lady Florence seems to have been assailed by doubts as to the wisdom of her choice as early as the first morning of her honeymoon, when she discovered that her husband's idea of a perfect breakfast was kippers boiled in gin. Lord Hastings further alienated his wife by churlishly baiting his former rival. Both men were prominent breeders of blood-stock and in 1867 Lord Hastings wagered an enormous sum of money that his horse, 'Marksman', would beat Mr Chaplin's 'Hermit' in the Epsom Derby. On the morning of the race 'Hermit' was so lame that he had to travel to the course with one foot in a bucket of ice. Nonetheless, he triumphed over 'Marksman' by a neck. Lord Hastings lost £120,000, three-quarters of it to Mr Chaplin. He died a ruined man soon afterwards. Harry Chaplin always showed his widow exemplary kindness. It is probable that he also assisted her financially. Ten years after the elopement outside Marshall and Snelgrove's he married another. The union was a very happy one and the couple survived many years.

2

Soho and its Environs

The area of Soho – which for our purpose extends eastwards to St Giles and south as far as St Martin's Place – has been the principal foreign quarter of London since 1685 when the revocation of the Edict of Nantes sent French Protestants fleeing to England *en masse*. As much as such things are possible it remains resistant to change and John Galsworthy's description of it, a hundred years ago, as being: 'Untidy, full of Greeks, Ishmaelites, cats, Italians, tomatoes, restaurants, organs, coloured stuffs, queer names and people looking out of windows,' is almost as true today as it ever was.

Walking east from Oxford Circus and taking the first turning on the right, we find ourselves in Argyll Street. It takes its name from the site of the former town-house of the Dukes of that name, whose reputation for thoughtfulness, at least among their Scottish tenants, was a byword. They erected on their estates scratching posts for the cattle; and in consequence it is still a tradition in the West Highlands for locals to mutter 'God bless the Duke of Argyll' when scratching themselves.

Situated at the point where Argyll Street runs into Great Marlborough Street is the home of the great eighteenth-century eccentric, Henry Cavendish. His timidity and reclusiveness were legendary. Any servant who intruded upon his privacy was instantly dismissed. He ordered his meals by means of notes left on the hall table; and his heir was allowed to visit him once a year for thirty minutes. In his *English Eccentrics & Eccentricities* John Timbs recalls:

His great income was allowed to accumulate without

attention. The bankers . . . finding they had in hand a balance of £80,000, apprised him of the same. The messenger was announced, and Cavendish, in great agitation, desired him to be sent up; and, as he entered the room . . . cried: 'What do you come here for? What do you want with me?'

'Sir, I thought it proper to wait upon you, as we have a very large balance in hand of yours, and we wish your orders respecting it.'

'If it is any trouble to you I will take it out of your hands. Do not come here to plague me!'

'Not the least trouble to us, sir, not the least, but we thought you would like some of it to be invested.'

'Well, well, what do you want to do?'

'Perhaps you would like forty thousand pounds invested?'

'Do so, do so! and don't come here to trouble me or I'll remove it!'

At his death in 1810 Cavendish left a fortune of two million pounds and was the largest holder of bank-stock in England.

South of Great Marlborough Street is Carnaby Street, famous in the 'Swinging Sixties' as a Mecca of young fashion. If that tide has since ebbed, and the fashionable are today conspicuous by their absence, the myth survives, enshrined within a pedestrian precinct patronised mainly by tourists. It is dominated by expensive, garish shops playing deafening rock music.

Turning right into Beak Street and taking the second turning on the left, we come to Warwick Street, once the domicile of the artist, Capitsoldi. An ingenious man – but a poor one – finding himself without furniture 'he proceeded to paint chairs, pictures and window-curtains on the walls of his sitting-room'. These were so 'admirably executed that, with an actual table and a couple of real chairs, he was able to entertain on occasion a friend in an apartment that appeared adequately furnished'.

Close to Beak Street is Brewer Street, which takes its name from a brewery which in the seventeenth century stood on the site of what is now Lex garage. For a short time the street was the home of that strange character, the androgynous Chevalier D'Eon. He first came to England in 1762 as an undercover agent for Louis XV, who was then contemplating an invasion of England. The invasion came to nought; but the Chevalier stayed on – thereby providing London with a source of amusement and enquiry which diverted it for many years. The problem was that nobody could ever quite determine whether the Chevalier was a man or a woman. His features were beautiful rather than handsome, and his figure undeniably curvaceous; but he was a heavy drinker, a great smoker of cigars, an accomplished rider and a fearsome duellist. The truth only emerged after his death, in 1810, when he was eighty-two. A post-mortem revealed that in essence the good Chevalier was male. In every other respect his body was female.

Just off Brewer Street is Golden Square. The most interesting resident here was Vladimir de Pachmann, of all players of Chopin's works the greatest. Every day until his death in 1933 he used to walk around the boundaries of the Square, a fortune in precious stones concealed in the lining of his battered old hat.

From Golden Square a short walk brings us to Shaftesbury Avenue, a bustling thoroughfare named after the renowned nineteenth-century factory reformer and philanthropist, Anthony Ashley Cooper, seventh Earl of Shaftesbury. Today this street is dominated by theatres, the most interesting of which is the Globe, designed by W. R. Sprague in 1906. The joint venture of the American impresario Charles Frohman and the English actor-manager Sir Edward Seymour-Hicks, it was indirectly responsible for Frohman's death. Learning that the American had taken the liberty of installing a lift in the building without first obtaining permission, the landlord threatened to sue. When this news reached Frohman in New York, he boarded the first liner sailing for England. As

ill-luck would have it, the year was 1915 and the vessel was
the *Lusitania*. In mid-Atlantic it was torpedoed by a German
submarine. Shortly before the ship went down, Frohman
turned to a friend, smiled and quoted a line from *Peter Pan*:
'To die will be an awfully big adventure.'

In its long career the Globe has produced two minor
sensations. It was the first British theatre in which an actress
appeared on stage wearing pyjamas. And on 12 April 1950
the Duke of Argyll brought Mrs Charles Sweeney here to see
a production of Anouilh's *Ring Round the Moon*. At the final
curtain, discovering the door to their box was jammed, he
took advantage of the situation to propose. Mrs Sweeney
accepted. Some years later they were divorced in an action
which has passed into legal history as perhaps the most lurid
ever to come before a British court.

Running parallel to Shaftesbury Avenue on its southern
side is Dansey Place. Until recently it possessed a gas-lamp of
the type known as 'Webb's Patent Sewer-Gas Destructor',
which operated on what the Metropolitan Water Board call
'the gases of putrefaction' piped up from the sewers below.
Known to scientists as CH_4, and to engineers as 'firedamp',
methane gas is a veritable power-house of energy, the daily
'end-product' of a single cow being sufficient to produce
enough fuel to meet all the heating and lighting needs of an
average household for twenty-four hours. It also has more
sinister uses; and during the Second World War there was
even a limited production of sewage-methane bombs.
Weighing thirty pounds, they produced on contact an enormous bang and sent flames shooting into the air to a height of
twenty feet.

In contrast to the quietness of Dansey Place, Gerrard
Street, to its south, is a busy exotic street, now the heart of
London's Chinatown. Plagued by a shrewish wife, John
Dryden lived the last fourteen years of his life at number 43;
and when the good lady complained that he paid her no
attention, and heartily wished herself a book, he said: 'Pray,
my dear, if you do ever become a book let it be an almanack,

for then I shall change you every year.' Their relationship is best summed up by the epitaph he composed for her:

Here lies my wife: here let her lie!
Now she's at rest, and so am I.

Another very dominant female who lived in Gerrard Street for a time was the actress, Fanny Kemble. The greatest 'Juliet' of her day, in private life she was insensitive, despotic, scathing and contemptuous. She enjoyed using her matured powers to inflict gratuitous slight on people smaller than herself; and on one occasion, in New York, when a dress-shop manager – wishing to ascertain the address to which her purchases were to be sent – ran after her down the street and was sufficiently injudicious as to try to attract her attention by touching her lightly on the sleeve, she turned on him with such fury, screwed her features into a mask of such outrage, screamed 'Unhand me, villain!' with such force and command, that the poor man's hair is said to have turned white overnight.

A second member of the theatrical profession who not only lived in Soho but was also born in the same year as Fanny Kemble was Edmund Kean. As a boy he lived at number 9 Lisle Street, the home of his uncle, Moses Kean, who took him in after he was orphaned. A wild and unruly child, he was for ever running about the by-ways of Soho and could so seldom be found that his uncle eventually forced him to wear a brass collar engraved: 'This boy belongs to number nine Lisle Street, Leicester Square, please bring him home.'

South of Lisle Street is Coventry Street. Half way along it and hardly noticed today by the relentless press of tourists which mills between Piccadilly Circus and Leicester Square at all hours, is a set of inconspicuous glass doors. They give on to a short but steep flight of steps leading down to the red-velvet heart of the Café de Paris, one of London's most famous dance halls. The place has a tragic history which the superstitious attribute either to the fact that it stands on the site of a Tudor bear-pit or to the architect's injudicious modelling of the ballroom on the one aboard the *Titanic*.

In its early days the Café de Paris was a popular society rendezvous. David Niven met his first wife here and Norah, Lady Docker worked for a time in the ballroom as a dancing partner. At the height of the Blitz, on the evening of 8 March 1941, the place was crowded. Couples were shuffling on the tightly-packed dance floor to the music of Ken 'Snakehips' Johnson and his band. An air-raid was in progress and during the pause between numbers it was just possible to distinguish the dull thud of exploding bombs and the rhythmic reply of the anti-aircraft batteries as they filtered through from the 'real' world up above. But although there was a rumour that Buckingham Palace had been hit – a rumour which subsequently proved to be true – nobody paid much attention to the bombs.

Shortly before ten o'clock, however, two 50-kilo landmines smashed through the ceiling of the Rialto cinema above. They continued on their downward course and although one of them failed to explode, the other detonated in front of the rostrum, killing eighty people instantly, including 'Snakehips' Johnson. In the ensuing darkness and confusion people stumbled about in a daze, half-blinded by the smoke and the settling dust and rubble. One young man, hideously wounded, swayed, laughed shakily and said: 'Oh, well, it's not everybody who can say they've been cut in on by the Luftwaffe.' It was an oblique, atavistic response to catastrophe rooted deep in the English character: a response almost as fine as that of the East-ender who surveyed the smoking ruins of her house and muttered: 'If 'itler carries on like this he'll get 'iself disliked.'

The dead were carried upstairs and laid out in the lee of the Rialto cinema. Passers-by stopped to stare down at the sawdust-covered bodies in silent shock. Among them was the author, Anthony Jacobs, who felt that the sawdust invested

The Café de Paris, Coventry Street, where on 8 March 1941 eighty
people died in the Blitz

the corpses with 'a kind of unreal sheen, they looked like
beautiful dolls that had been broken and the sawdust come
out . . . Whenever I go down Coventry Street now I remember that dream, and those bright, dead dolls with dust on
them.'

The street derives its title from the Earl of Coventry who,
in the seventeenth century, erected a town-house on the site
of nearby Shaver's Place. After his death it passed to a
prosperous barber who turned it into a gambling 'hell'. It

acquired its cant name either from its owner's former profession, or, more likely, from his reputation for 'shaving' his
patrons of their money.

One patron whom the barber was incapable of 'shaving',
however, was a certain Colonel Thomas Panton – perhaps
because he had a facility for cards amounting almost to
genius. One night he won a vast sum of money at the tables.
He wisely invested some of it in land – land which is covered
today by Panton Street, a little to the south of Shaver's Place.
The remainder he used to purchase an annuity of £1,500 a
year. According to *The Lives of the Gamesters*, 'After this
good fortune he had such an aversion against all manner of
games that he would never handle cards or dice again.' The
acres he purchased in this way remained the property of his
descendants until as late as 1919.

Crossing 'Panton's Land' at its eastern end is Whitcomb
Street, originally Hedge Lane, where the 'Tramp Poet',
W. H. Davies, had his lodging prior to the outbreak of the
Great War. It is something of a surprise that he ever brought
himself to live in London at all. He was a simple man who
loved the country and believed the country loved him.

> Say what you like,
> All things love me.
> Horse, Cow and Mouse,
> Bird, Moth and Bee.

A very different sort of literary fellow who lived for a time
in nearby Suffolk Street was Anthony Trollope. He did the
bulk of his work in the three hours after dawn. Allowing
himself 'no mercy', he sat down at his table at number 15
every morning at 5.30 and wrote very literally against the
clock – a pocket-watch which he set beside him to ensure that
his output never fell below the self-imposed limit of a
thousand words an hour. In this manner he completed
sixty-three books. Garrulous and contrary, aggressive and
erratic, he saw toil as the redemption and fulfilment of the

soul: the very essence of life. If callers forced him to break off he would nervously bite his handkerchief until he was free to resume. If the break became prolonged he would chew large holes in it. He kept an exact account of every penny his writing earned, and when death ruled off the ledger, in 1882, the figure stood at £66,939. 17. 6d.

With Suffolk Street we have reached the most southerly point of our exploration. We must now retrace our steps north again until we come to Leicester Square – so-called because it was once the site of the Earl of Leicester's London mansion. In the 1880s part of that mansion was redeveloped as the Empire Theatre, now the Empire Cinema. Soon after it opened, the inventor, H. Cecil Booth, came here one evening with a friend to witness a demonstration of a new dust-removing machine called the 'vacuum cleaner'. This consisted of a length of flexible tubing which, by means of compressed air, blew the dust into a plain wooden box. Booth observed that much of the dirt missed its mark and was merely redistributed around the room. It occurred to him that the answer might lie in sucking rather than blowing. A few days later: 'I tried the experiment of sucking with my mouth against the back of a plush seat in a restaurant in Victoria Street.' The experiment was such a success that he nearly choked to death.

Another invention, and one which literally was founded in Leicester Square was a gas lamp, set up at the south-east corner in 1898. The excess heat from the gas mantles was used to heat a tank of hot water; and the base of the supporting column contained a small box which, on the insertion of a halfpenny, disgorged concentrated lozenges of tea, cocoa and beef extract. The machine eventually drew so many sightseers that it became a menace and had to be dismantled.

For many years the artist, William Hogarth, lived at number 30 Leicester Square, and died there aged sixty-seven in 1764. His house was later replaced by the Sablonière Hotel where, on a cold winter's evening in 1862, Algernon Swin-

burne dined with Dante Gabriel Rossetti and Rossetti's
beautiful wife, Elizabeth. A nervous, highly-strung woman,
Elizabeth was ill at ease and by eight o'clock she and her
husband were back at home. What happened next is best
described by Hall Caine, who recorded the facts in his
autobiography:

. . . Rossetti left his wife preparing to retire for the
night, and went out again apparently to walk. When he
returned at half-past eleven o'clock, he found his rooms
full of a strong odour of laudanum; his wife was breathing
stertorously and lying unconscious on the bed. He called a
doctor, who saw . . . that the lady had taken an overdose of
her accustomed sleeping draught. Other doctors were
summoned, and every effort was made to save the patient's
life; but lingering hours without recovering consciousness
for a moment – and therefore without offering a word of
explanation – towards seven o'clock in the morning she
died . . . The blow to Rossetti was a terrible one. It was
some days before he realised fully the loss that had befallen
him; but after that his grief knew no bounds . . .

[A volume of his poems] had been inspired by his wife
. . . and with this book in his hand, on the day of her
funeral, he walked into the room where her body lay . . .
and spoke to his dead wife as though she could hear, saying
. . . she must take them to the grave . . . He placed the
little volume in the coffin by the side of his wife's face and
wrapped it round with her beautiful golden hair, and it was
buried with her in Highgate cemetery . . . Thus seven
years passed . . . and the poet began to cast backward
glances at the book he had buried . . . It was doing no good
to the dead to leave hidden in the grave the most beautiful
works he had been able to produce – was it not his duty to
the living, to himself, and perhaps even to God, to recover
and publish them?

At length the licence of the Home Secretary was
obtained . . . a fire was built one night by the side of the

grave, the coffin was raised to the surface, and the buried book was removed.

After some revision it was published under the title *Poems* in 1870. It quickly went into seven editions – one for every year it had been underground. According to Charles Augustus Howell, who was present at the exhumation, Elizabeth's hair had continued to grow; and when her body was exposed – perfectly preserved by the laudanum – her tresses overflowed the coffin. However, as no other witness could be found to corroborate this, and as Rossetti had already testified that:

> There's a Portugese person named Howell
> Who lays on his lies with a trowel,

we may safely choose to disregard the story.

Curiously enough, in 1890, Charles Augustus Howell ('the polecat Howell', said the vituperative Swinburne) was found dead in the gutter outside a Chelsea public house. His throat had been cut from ear to ear. Clenched between his teeth was a half-guinea piece. The murder was never solved.

The entire western side of Leicester Square is today taken up by Fanum House, the headquarters of the Automobile Association. As late as 1937, however, part of the site was occupied by the former home of the artist, Sir Joshua Reynolds. An old man told the banker-poet, Samuel Rogers, that one evening he encountered here a beautiful urchin sitting on Sir Joshua's steps. When he asked her why she was crying she said that Sir Joshua had given her a shilling for sitting for him, but it was a bad one and now he wouldn't change it.

At the south-east corner of the Square is Irving Street, the home of the Beefsteak Club, situated at number 9. One of its rules requires that all members talk to each other, whether they have previously met or not; and within the Club, irrespective of what their real names may be, all the waiters are known as 'Charles'. The Beefsteak is also one of the few clubs which can claim the dubious distinction of having been raided by the police – possibly because at the turn of the century the exterior had fallen into such a disgraceful state of disrepair that the powers-that-be supposed it concealed a thieves' kitchen. Only four members were present on the evening in question. When the first was asked for his name he said: 'The Lord Chancellor'. The second claimed to be the Governor of the Bank of England and the third the Archbishop of Canterbury. Assuming a long-suffering expression, the interrogating officer turned to the fourth member and said: 'And I suppose you're the Prime Minister?' 'As a matter of fact,' said Arthur Balfour, smiling broadly, 'I am'.

Adjacent to the Club, at number 10 Irving Street, is the house taken by Dickens for the model for 'The Old Curiosity Shop' – a book which, when it first appeared in serialised form in 1840, made a tremendous impact. The whole world, it seemed, waited each week with bated breath for the further adventures of Little Nell; and the news of her death was greeted by quite unprecedented displays of uproar and grief.

When Macready, returning home from the theatre, saw the print of a child lying dead by her window with strips of holly on her breast, a dead chill ran through his blood. 'I have never read printed words that gave me so much pain', he noted in his diary. 'I could not weep for some time. Sensations, sufferings have returned to me, that are terrible to awaken . . .' Daniel O'Connell, the Irish M.P., reading the book in a railway carriage, burst into tears, groaned: 'He should not have killed her', and despairingly threw the volume out of the train window. Thomas Carlyle, previously inclined to be a bit patronising about Dickens, was utterly overcome. Waiting crowds at a New York pier shouted to the incoming mail-boats: 'Is Little Nell dead?'

Opposite the eastern end of Irving Street is the Garrick theatre, part of the construction costs of which were met by the librettist, W. S. Gilbert. The project was plagued by set-backs and when a subterranean stream was discovered running close to the foundations it proved almost the last straw. Gilbert threw up his hands and suggested they abandon the scheme, recouping their losses by selling the fishing rights. In 1895 a play called *The Notorious Mrs Ebbsmith* had its première at the Garrick and during the course of its run a real-life Mrs Ebbsmith was found drowned in the Thames. A ticket-stub found on her body suggested she had been to see the play.

During the Great War, the Palace Theatre, a little to the north in Cambridge Circus, provided the world with an equally macabre coincidence. At that time the auditorium was occasionally used as a cinema. One of the films shown was D. W. Griffith's *Hearts of the World*, a war film lent a certain authenticity by the insertion of a number of genuine battle-scenes culled from contemporary newsreels. One night a woman collapsed after seeing her husband killed on screen. The tragic frames were subsequently cut.

Continuing north up the Charing Cross Road beyond Cambridge Circus, we come to New Compton Street, the stage in 1780 for a peculiar drama played out between the writer, Henry Angelo, and a fifteen-year-old girl. Angelo was returning home down the Charing Cross Road when:

. . . at the corner of New Compton Street, my feelings were powerfully excited by the figure of a young woman, meanly attired, in the attitude of dejection, leaning against the post. Pausing some time, I could not resist speaking to her and said: 'My poor girl, you seem to be very unhappy; can I be of service to you'. Several times did I address her without effect, nor would she even look at me. I was disconcerted, and with some zeal said: 'Will you be here tonight at eight?' With a deep-drawn sigh she replied: 'Yes'. I was punctual, so was she. I then begged of her to relate to me her circumstances and the misfortune that had brought her into that condition. She made no hesitation in declaring her forlorn situation with an assurance that she had not tasted food that day, the truth of which she proved by the voracious manner in which she devoured some biscuits I ordered to be placed before her. She said her christian name was Emma, but when I urged her to inform me of the particulars of her story she declined, and I could only obtain a promise to meet me again at the same hour and place the next night.

For reasons which are not quite clear, Angelo failed to keep the appointment. He continues:

It was late in life before the book of fate was opened to me, and there read that the girl, this poor, interesting figure, absorbed in deep dejection, supported by a post in Compton Street, had been destined to occupy an important place in high circles . . . The once disconsolate Emma became afterwards the renowned Lady Hamilton. The poor girl whom I had met in wretchedness and poverty was next the delight of the gay world of Naples and her accomplishments made her the admiration of all who knew her.

In fact, Angelo is being less than candid when he suggests that he had no cognisance of Lady Hamilton's fate during the intervening years. As he himself recorded elsewhere: 'Not many days after' the broken appointment he encountered young Emma walking with 'two elegantes' in Kensington Gardens, 'much improved in spirit, demeanour and dress'. Two years later he met her again, this time in Rathbone Place. 'She informed me that she lived in the Paddington Road, No 14 Oxford Street; that at present she owed her ease and affluence to "F.G." [Charles Francis Greville] and that both honour and gratitude forbade her to meet me again.'

The next turning of interest to the east out of Charing Cross Road is Flitcroft Street named in honour of 'Burlington Harry', a man who made his fortune by breaking a leg. His name was Henry Flitcroft and he was employed as a carpenter at Burlington House when he fell one day from some scaffolding. The accident drew the attention of the Earl of Burlington who afterwards became his patron.

Flitcroft Street was named after him because he designed the church of St Giles in the Fields, which stands at its far end. It is one of very few such buildings actually signed by its architect and it was completed in 1733. It replaced an earlier church which in turn had displaced an old leper hospital.

For many years it was the practice of felons to stop for a last drink of ale at the gates of St Giles on their way to execution. Not everyone availed themselves of this privilege, however, and one man, a teetotaller, who insisted on pushing on, missed thereby a reprieve which arrived two minutes after he had been hanged.

The church has several interesting interees, not least 'Unparallel'd Pendrell', who saved the life of Charles II after the battle of Worcester by concealing him in the branches of the Boscobel Oak. He was buried here in 1671. Thirty years later the vicious Countess of Shrewsbury was laid to rest nearby. As mistress of the second Duke of Buckingham, she not only connived the murder of her husband by her lover, but attended the fatal duel disguised as the Duke's page-boy. That night, wearing her dead husband's blood-stained shirt, she slept with him.

Given hindsight, perhaps the most doom-laden event in the church's history occurred in 1818 with the simultaneous christening of Byron's daughter, Allegra, and the two children of the poet Shelley. Three days later, Shelley and his brood left England for ever. Two years previously his first wife had drowned. Within six months of her christening, little Clara succumbed to the effects of the Italian climate. William, aged three-and-a-half, followed her to the grave in June 1819, a victim of the fever. In the summer of 1822

Lady Mary Wortley Montagu of Soho Square, vibrant and illuminating letter-writer. Portrait attrib. To J. B. Vanmour

Shelley himself drowned at Leghorn. The same year, Byron's daughter also died, aged five, unloved and disgracefully neglected. (Writing to a friend, Samuel Rogers remarked rather mysteriously: 'Allegra was buried at Harrow: but probably you have not heard that the body was sent over to England in *two* packages, that no one might suspect what it was.')

Allegra had not been in her grave two years when her father, the last surviving member of the christening party at St Giles – and a man who in thirty-six years of dissipated living had fallen in love with choirboys, drapers' wives, countesses, Greek urchins and his own sister – contracted marsh-fever at Missolonghi and died, anguishing whether to sue his Maker for mercy or to 'be a man to the last'.

Returning to the Charing Cross Road and passing down Sutton Row, we come to Soho Square, the home in 1734 of that marvellously vibrant and illuminating letter-writer, Lady Mary Wortley Montagu. She lived at number 10. Horace Walpole described her as 'old, foul, tawdry, painted, plastered . . .' and said her 'dress, her avarice and her impudence must amaze any one that has never heard her name. She wears a foul mob that does not cover her greasy black locks, that hang loose, never combed or curled;' and her face was plastered with 'white paint, which for cheapness she has bought so coarse, that you would not use it to wash a chimney'. Yet for all this she was a woman of considerable intellect and charm. She might have married Alexander Pope – but when he proposed to her she laughed so long and uproariously that he became overnight her most implacable enemy.

In 1836 the firm of billiard-ball manufacturers, Messrs Burroughs and Watts, came to number 19 Soho Square. It is said that more than a thousand elephants were slaughtered annually to keep them supplied with ivory.

On the eastern side of the Square is the church of St Patrick's, Soho, occupying the site of old Carlisle House, the London mansion of the Earls of that name. The Earls themselves were rather ineffectual. Their ladies, however, were not. One of them was so proud that even at death's door she could not bring herself to address her physician. In a stiff manner she turned to her maid and said: 'Pray tell the doctor he may bleed the Countess of Carlisle'. A second countess – Rosalind – was a prodigious talker and once berated for so long a man who had earned her displeasure that he fainted. When he regained consciousness she continued talking as though nothing had happened – until he fainted again.

Sometime around 1760 Carlisle House became an Assembly Room where the proprietor, the Venetian adventuress, Theresa Cornelys, held wildly extravagant parties. A regular here was the eccentric Joseph Merlin. He was then in the process of perfecting his greatest invention, the roller-skate. The evening he did so he skated through the salon at Carlisle House at high speed, at the height of a ball, playing the violin. His progress was abruptly curtailed when he crashed into a very ornate mirror – shortly afterwards described by his hostess as 'five hundred pounds worth of broken glass.' Merlin was known to Dr Johnson's friend, Mrs Thrale, who wrote to Fanny Burney that:

He told Mrs Davenant and me that he had thought of inventing a particular mill to grind old ladies young, as he was so prodigious fond of their company.

In 1771 Theresa Cornelys' 'Temple of Festivity' received a set-back which signalled the beginning of the end. During a fashionable masque a hooded figure walked through the crowded assembly in a winding-sheet, carrying a coffin. The figure's identity was never established. But the culprit may have been the great lover, Giovanni Casanova. He was an enemy of Theresa's and there is no question that he was sufficiently ruthless. He once introduced a severed hand into the bed of an enemy. On discovering it the man lost his reason.

Towards the end of the decade Theresa was arrested for debt. As if this were not bad luck enough, as she 'was stepping into the carriage to go to the Fleet prison, she struck her breast against a door, which caused her the most shocking cancer.' The actress, Becky Wells, visited her at the Fleet, 'and found her sitting up in her bed with a large crucifix exclaiming in a voice that denoted the most dreadful horror 'the devil is dragging me down', which she kept constantly repeating, and expired in the most shocking agonies.'

Leaving Soho Square by way of Carlisle Street we come to Dean Street and – at number 28 – one of the most historic houses in Soho. Now the Quo Vadis restaurant, it has been the home of Joseph Nollekens and, later, the political activist, Karl Marx. Nollekens, who was born here in 1737 was a brilliant sculptor and an even more brilliant miser. Although he left a fortune of a quarter of a million pounds 'he only ever went to his barber for a morning paper, which he afterwards carried away with a display of some nonchalance for the purpose of using it the next morning when he washed himself.' No lamps were lit in his household until well after dusk; and to save on candles the front door was always left unanswered at the first knock in case it proved to be some urchin playing a trick. The house was also starved of heat. So much so that when the Marquis of Londonderry sat for a bust he almost froze to death. On Nollekens leaving the room for a moment to fetch more clay, Londonderry, who had turned blue with cold, darted from his seat and banked up the fire. Mrs Nollekens exclaimed in a shocked tone: 'Oh! my good Lord, I don't know what Mr Nollekens will say!' Wearily, his Lordship replied: 'Never mind, my good lady – tell him to put it into my bill.' Another sitter who also had the temerity to bank up the fire was Lonsdale – a display of prodigality which cost him a thousand pounds, the sum which, until that moment, Nollekens had intended to leave him in his will.

If such a thing were possible, Mrs Nollekens was even more parsimonious than her husband. 'When she went to Oxford Street to beat the rounds, in order to discover the cheapest chop, she would walk round several times to give her dog, Cerberus, an opportunity of picking up scraps.' In proper shops, where this curious style of beachcombing was impractical, 'She requested, just at the moment she was quitting the counter, to have either a clove or a bit of cinnamon to take some unpleasant taste out of her mouth; but she was never seen to apply it to the part so affected: so that with Nollekens's nutmegs, which he pocketed from the

Joseph Nollekens, sculptor, of Dean Street, who pocketed nutmegs at Academy dinners

table at the Academy dinners, they contrived to accumulate a little stock of spices, without any expense whatever.'

Perhaps not surprisingly, when Mrs Nollekens died in August 1817 'in the seventy-fourth year of her age', there were only eleven mourners at her funeral. One of those was her husband.

A little less than half a century after Nollekens death, Karl Marx sat down in a small room on the top floor of the miser's old home and began to write *Das Kapital*. He seldom ventured abroad 'because my clothes are in pawn'. Indeed he lived most of his life in terrible poverty. He subsisted for the most part on £1 a week, money donated by his friend Engels; and when his daughter died he even had to borrow the £2 needed to purchase a coffin. In spite of this, and in spite of the cold, the incredible clutter and the relentless hoots of his children, the first volume of *Das Kapital* was published in 1867. But in the end – not withstanding his terrifying single-mindedness – life ground Marx down. He died in 1883, at the age of sixty-five, his great work incomplete. Worn out and embittered, in his last moments, when a servant asked him whether he had any advice for posterity, he roared: 'Go on, get out! Last words are for fools who haven't said enough.' He is buried in Highgate cemetery.

The John Snow public house, in nearby Broadwick Street, is named not after the English cricketer but a Soho physician who first divined that cholera was water-borne. It is easy, with hindsight, to dismiss such discoveries as elementary. But of course they were not. Nobody then understood the significance of the germ-carrying organisms known as microbes; and that one thousand bacteria, laid end to end, would do no more than cross the head of a pin, or that a hundred million could exist in a single drop of water, was completely unknown to the Victorians. As a result, in 1849, more than five hundred people succumbed to cholera in less than two weeks in the vicinity of Golden Square alone. The stench became so overpowering that even the removal wagons of Messrs Pickford had to be pressed into service to help cart away the dead.

For some part of his life – and a very varied life it was – the author of *Robinson Crusoe*, Daniel Defoe, lodged in Broadwick Street. In his early years he travelled extensively. He then fought with the Duke of Monmouth's army at Sedgemoor, found employment as a government spy, became by turns a pamphleteer, journalist and a novelist. He was pilloried, twice imprisoned for dissent, educated six children out of his own pocket and ran a civet-cat farm.

Berwick Street, which crosses Broadwick Street, is in all probability named after the Duke of Berwick. A professional soldier, he was struck dead by a cannon-ball at the seige of Philippsburg in 1734. By the strangest of coincidences, the memoirist, William Hickey, rediscovered his childhood nurse, Nanny Harris, in a first-floor room of a house in Berwick Street. It was a reunion of some significance: perhaps because as soon as she entered the service of the Hickey family, when William was about six years old:

> . . . she at once became my delight, and I was no less so hers. Every night when the servant had taken away the candle, she used to take me to her bed, there fondle and lay me upon her bosom; nor shall I forget my sensations, infant as I was, at awaking one morning and finding myself snugly stowed between her legs, with one of my hands upon the seat of Love, where I have no doubt she placed it, for she was as wanton a little baggage as ever existed, and it was some years after discovered that the Duchess of Manchester had discarded her for debauching Master Montagu (her only son) when thirteen years old, which circumstance her grace most improperly omitted to mention when recommending the girl as a confidential servant in a private family.

Our specious theorist concludes that: 'the early inter-course I had with Nanny Harris strongly influenced me through several years of my life and materially operated in fixing my attachment to women of loose and abandoned principles'.

Indeed, the attachment never abated. Not even his brother's threat to have her thrown into the Bridewell House of Correction could wean William Hickey from comely Nanny Harris a second time.

3

Fleet Street and Holborn

Holborn can look sinister at night when the massive Victorian office-blocks appear to tower above the late-walking pedestrian in a very menacing manner, so it is fitting that our first port of call should be Southampton Row, formerly the home of the macabre American writer Edgar Allan Poe. He came to number 83 in 1815, at the age of six, with his adoptive father, the wealthy tobacco merchant, John Allan. On their return to America, Poe was entered at the University of Virginia. However, as a result of his disippation and wild living he was soon asked to leave. When Mr Allan refused to pay his gambling debts, Poe ran away and joined the army. Proving as poor a soldier as formerly he had been a student, he was cashiered for 'gross neglect of duty'.

With less than a shilling in his pocket, and totally estranged from John Allan, Poe now turned to writing. In May 1836, at the age of 27, he secretly married his thirteen-year-old cousin, Virginia Clem. Two years later, his favourite black cat sitting on his shoulder, he sat down to write one of his most enduring stories, *The Narrative of Arthur Gordon Pym*, a tale of three men cast adrift in an open boat who survive by devouring the fourth member of the party, a cabin-boy named Richard Parker.

In 1847, in her twenty-fifth year, Virginia died. Thereafter Poe himself became obsessed with thoughts of death and turned for relief to laudanum and alcohol. In the summer of 1849 his life took what looked to be an upward turn. He became engaged to a respectable lady of means, forswore alcohol and even joined the Temperance Society. After giving a lecture on the evils of drink he journeyed to Baltimore to make the arrangements for his wedding. Exactly what happened next will never now be known: but about a week later he was discovered lying in the gutter, suffering from delirium tremens. Within another week he was dead.

Thirty-five years after Poe had gone to his pauper's grave, a ship called the 'Mignonette' sank in a violent storm in the Atlantic. Before she did so, four of the crew managed to put off in one of the lifeboats. After several weeks at sea three of them were rescued. When asked about the fate of the fourth, the cabin-boy, they confessed to having killed and eaten him. The cabin-boy's name was Richard Parker.

Running parallel to Southampton Row is Procter Street, constructed as recently as 1962. It commemorates a nineteenth-century lawyer and minor poet, Bryan Waller Procter. His daughter, Adelaide, likewise a poet, gained a degree of immortality with 'The Lost Chord', a modest verse which achieved widespread popularity after being set to music by Sir Arthur Sullivan.

Crossing Procter Street we come to Red Lion Square, the work of the seventeenth-century speculator Nicholas Barbone. Barbone's reputation as a jerry-builder was notorious and in 1698, while the foundations of the square were being laid, the local people came in a mob and thrashed his workmen.

Nearly forty years prior to that date, on the night of 29 January 1661, the embalmed corpses of three regicides, Oliver Cromwell, Henry Ireton and John Bradshaw had lain overnight here at the Red Lion tavern before being drawn on a sled to Tyburn where they were ritually hanged and beheaded. It has been stated that the bodies were later returned to the square and buried beneath a stone obelisk. They were not. But the area is said to have been haunted by the ghosts of the three men for many a long year. Lost in deep conversation they traversed a path now lost, vanishing at a spot close to the obelisk.

At the age of six, in 1780, Leigh Hunt came with his mother to Red Lion Square on a visit to an ancient family retainer. The old lady had a bad cold – and when she sneezed her false teeth shot out. Hunt was repelled by the sight, but was still relating the story seventy years later.

In 1854 a very different sort of man, F. D. Maurice – 'the Muscular Christian' – founded the Working Man's College at number 31 Red Lion Square. Unfortunately, his doctrinaire attitude to religion made his sermons unintelligible; and Aubrey de Vere said that listening to him preach was like 'eating pea-soup with a fork'.

Maurice's second wife was Georgiana Hare Naylor – of whom a relative, Augustus Hare, had this to say:

> I have been told that . . . Georgiana was once a very pretty lively girl. I only remember her a sickly discontented petulant woman. When she was young, she was very fond of dancing, and once, at Bonn, she undertook to dance the clock round. She performed her feat, but it ruined her health and she had to lie on her back for a year.
>
> [Georgiana found that she] liked the sympathy she excited, and henceforth *preferred* being ill. Once or twice every year she was dying, the family was summoned, every one was in tears, they knelt around her bed; it was the most delicious excitement.

According to Hare, Georgiana married Fred Maurice 'during what was supposed to be her last illness, but was so pleased with her nuptials that she recovered after the ceremony and lived for nearly half a century afterwards'.

To the north of Red Lion Square is Theobald's Road. Here, on a cold bleak morning in January 1936, the gun-carriage bearing the coffin of George V crossed a set of tramlines en route to the Lying in State in Westminster Hall. The jolting it received caused the Imperial Crown, resting on top of the coffin, to tremble violently. The Maltese cross surmounting it was dislodged and rolled into the gutter. King Edward VIII, who was walking directly behind his father's coffin, turned deathly pale and muttered: 'Christ.

What will happen next.' The incident was widely interpreted as an ill-omen.

In his last days, George V had confided to an aide: 'After I am dead, the boy will ruin himself in twelve months.' It was a prophecy which proved all too accurate. Before the end of that year the short sad reign of Edward VIII had run its course. In the December his refusal to end his relationship with the divorced Mrs Simpson led him to renounce the throne in favour of his brother.

An altogether more amusing encounter in Theobald's Road occurred when that great exquisite, Eddie Marsh, was accosted by a dubious sort of fellow who asked permission to address him as 'a man of the world'. Permission being given, he asked Eddie to buy the pot of flowers he was carrying. 'My dear man,' said Eddie, 'if you were really a man of the world you would know that the last thing you could expect of a man of the world was that he should carry about a pot of cinerarias'.

Covering in all some thirty acres, Gray's Inn, to the south of Theobald's Road, is one of the four great Inns of Court. It has numbered many famous men among its members, not least William Cecil, Lord Burghley, for forty years the mainstay of Elizabethan politics. He was admitted here in 1541 and his signature on some of the Inn's documents is still preserved. Something of a rake, he on one occasion gambled away a vast sum of money to a fellow student. Learning that his adversary slept with his head against the panel which partitioned their two rooms, he resolved to recover it. He constructed a crude but tiny megaphone which by means of a long tube he inserted through the wall to rest beneath his victim's pillow. As soon as the young man went to bed Cecil began calling upon him, in the name of the Almighty, to forsake gambling for ever or risk eternal hell-fire. The student was so shaken by the experience that he came to Cecil's door the next morning and returned every penny.

On the other side of Holborn is Staple Inn where, in 1759,

at the age of fifty, the great Dr Johnson wrote *Rasselas* in just seven days to defray the funeral expenses of his mother. The suitably eccentric-looking building occupying the south side of the quadrangle is the British Patents Office. Among the less fruitful inventions which have been lodged here over the years may be listed: a device for flushing out the Loch Ness monster by the administration of electric shocks; a walking-stick which, at the approach of rabid-looking dogs, converted into a ladder; and the blue-print for a five-mile high chimney which would enable consumptives to breathe clean air.

Fleet Street, which runs parallel to Holborn in the south, takes its name from the old River Fleet. Its course now runs entirely underground and the sewer network of which it forms a part is extensive. It has been computed that if all London's water-pipes were laid end to end they would stretch for approximately ninety thousand miles. Any system which has to cope with upwards of four hundred million gallons of liquid effluence a day has to be serviced and maintained and in consequence there is a man-hole cover for every two hundred and eighty feet of London pavement. Nonetheless, even the largest chambers remain vulnerable to 'flash' floods and the *flushers*, who clean out the channels, invariably leave a *ganger* 'up top' to watch for any change in the weather. In the event of a sudden storm he drops the man-hole cover on the pavement, the ringing tone which this sets up reverbrating through the tunnels for miles and acting as a warning to the men below to evacuate as quickly as possible. The pavement itself was first laid down in 1766 and: 'On that occasion it is said that two English paviours . . . bet that they would pave more in a day than four Scotchmen could. By three o'clock the Englishmen had got so much ahead that they went into a public house for refreshment.' Setting the fable of the Tortoise and the Hare on its head, they 'afterwards returned to their work and won the wager'.

The church of St Dunstan's-in-the-West, on the north side

The Fleet Ditch. The river now runs entirely underground

of Fleet Street, commemorates a tenth-century Archbishop
of Canterbury who was also a skilled goldsmith. He is often
depicted holding a pair of tongs because (the story goes) he
was working one day at his bench when he received a visit
from the Devil. St Dunstan found the Devil's conversation
so unpleasing that he eventually picked up a pair of forge-

tongs and pincered his nose, refusing to let go until the Devil
promised to go away and bother him no more.

For three hundred years, the road by St Dunstan's was
spanned by a high triple gateway which marked the entrance
to the City: Temple Bar. It was built in 1672 by Sir Christopher Wren and finally removed in 1878 after it had become
'an obstruction – the too narrow neck of a large decanter – a
bone in the throat of Fleet Street'. In a small room above
Temple Bar, with books and records set around every wall,
Child's Bank had its modest beginnings in the last quarter of
the seventeenth century. A pioneer of paper money, the bank
has numbered among its clients Nell Gwynne, Pepys,
Dryden, Charles II and Oliver Cromwell. Another account-
holder was the eleventh Duke of Norfolk, nicknamed the
'Dirty Duke' on account of his antipathy to soap and water.
In sixty-nine years he never once entered a bath voluntarily
and when it was no longer possible to remain at ease with him
in the same room his servants plied him with drink until he
collapsed and bathed him before he regained consciousness.
He was nonetheless the kindest of men and although his
second wife went mad he never showed her anything but
sympathy. He refused to divorce her, consoling himself
instead with a series of amours and fathering a host of
illegitimate children along the way. He supported them all,
organising quarterly pay-musters at Child's for the mothers.
These he usually attended in person, sitting behind a screen
and identifying each woman to the cashier by turn. From
time to time he was heard to mutter: 'What a dowdy! What
an old hag!'

Some time after Childs had moved to their present premises, at number one Fleet Street, Charles Dickens took it for
his model of Telson's Bank in *A Tale of Two Cities*, although
he was not very flattering, calling it:

the triumphant perfection of inconvenience. After bursting open a door of idiotic obstinacy with a weak rattle in its
throat, you fell into Telson's down two steps, and came to

your senses in a miserable little shop with two little counters, where the oldest of men made your cheque shake as if the wind rustled it, while they examined the signature by the dingiest of windows, which were always under a shower-bath of mud from Fleet Street, and which were made the dingier by their own iron bars and the heavy shadow of Temple Bar. If your business necessitated your seeing 'the House', you were put into a species of Condemned Hold at the back, where you meditated on a misspent life until the House came with its hands in its pockets, and you could hardly blink at it in the dismal twighlight.

The greatest scandal in the bank's history occurred when Mr Child's only daughter, Sarah, fell in love with the tenth Earl of Westmoreland. One evening the Earl had presented Mr Child with a 'hypothetical' case: what, he asked, should a young man do if he was refused permission to pay his addresses to a young lady? The ingenuous Mr Child replied: 'Elope with her to be sure.' The Earl took him at his word. But when the banker heard that the couple were headed for Gretna Green he called for his coach and set off in pursuit. He came in sight of them close to the Scottish border and would certainly have overtaken them had the Earl not taken the liberty of shooting the leader of the team of horses. Mr Child died of a broken heart within twelve months. He never forgave Sarah, although he did bequeath his vast fortune to her new-born daughter. The daughter became in time the redoubtable Lady Jersey and ruled London society as its undisputed queen for more than sixty years.

Fleet Street has known many famous taverns in its time and in one (The Swan) Alexander Pope is said to have tried to murder the disreputable publisher Edmund Curll by slipping powdered glass into his drink; and in another (The Great Dragon) the Common Hangman was wont to sell his 'used' ropes on execution days at sixpence an inch. Today, the streets most enduring association is with journalism.

Several of the national papers still have their offices here or hereabouts: the *Daily Express* with its splendid art-deco foyer; and the *Daily Telegraph*, the first newspaper to publish news of the relief of Mafeking.

Of the numerous little alleys which cluster around Fleet Street as if for protection, one of the most interesting is Wine Office Court. It takes its name from having once housed the office which issued licences to sell wine. It would have been a crowded bustling place because in the seventeenth century there were as many as a thousand taverns within the single square mile of the City. As Dorothy Davis has pointed out in *A History of Shopping:* 'Anyone with a little capital could turn his house into a tavern by putting an ivy bush over his door and getting a few barrels of wine from a merchant and buying a licence from the wine commissioners who were only too anxious to sell.'

Rather ironically, the Wine Office burned down in the Great Fire of 1666 – as did its near neighbour, the Cheshire Cheese, one of London's most famous taverns, rebuilt in its present form the following year. George Augustus Sala has aptly described the Cheshire Cheese as:

. . . a little lop-sided, wedged-up house, that always re-minds you, structurally, of a high-shouldered man with his hands in his pockets. It is full of holes and corners and cupboards and sharp turnings; and in ascending the stairs to the tiny smoking-room you must tread cautiously, if you would not wish to be tripped up by plates and dishes, momentarily deposited there by furious waiters. The waiters at the 'Cheese' are always furious.

The tavern has long been a haunt of literary men and although there is no real evidence to support the claim that Samuel Johnson was an habitué, the Poet Laureate, Ben Jonson, certainly was. Indeed it was here one evening that he was challenged by Joshua Sylvester to a duel of rhyming couplets. The latter began:

I, Sylvester
Kiss'd your sister.

Jonson parried with:

I, Ben Jonson,
Kiss'd your wife.

Sylvester objected that this didn't rhyme. 'No', said Jonson. 'But it's true.'

In 1903 another writer, G. K. Chesterton, spent his last ten shillings on a large meal and a bottle of wine at the Cheshire Cheese. He did so to boost his morale before canvassing a publisher for a £20 advance on a book he proposed to write. He got his money and subsequently wrote: 'What a fool a man is when he comes to the last ditch, not to spend the last farthing to satisfy the inner man before he goes out to fight a battle with wits.'

At one time the Cheshire Cheese possessed an unusually foul-mouthed parrot, an unsolicited gift to the landlord from an old sailor. He sent it in a cigar box, without disclosing that the contents were not cigars. It survived to become an integral part of the tavern's life and in 1922 was introduced to Queen Mary on her visit here. It could exactly imitate the popping sound made by a cork being withdrawn from a bottle and the glug-glug-glug of the wine being poured. The Cheshire Cheese being a favourite haunt with tourists, when it eventually succumbed to pneumonia the passing of this talented bird was noted everywhere. The *New York American* ran an article on the event headlined: 'Notorious Cheshire Cheese in Mourning as Forty-Years-Old Expert in Profanity Dies'.

By a somewhat twisting route, Wine Office Court leads into Gough Square. The handsome seventeenth-century house on the west side was formerly the home of Dr Johnson. He lived here from 1748 to 1759 and it was during this period that he compiled his famous *Dictionary*. It took eight years to complete and sold in two volumes for £4.50 the set.

Another resident of Gough Square was a well-known surgeon – who coincidentally had a tenuous association with Dr Johnson. According to *Old & New London*:

the surgeon purchased for dissection the body of a man who had been hanged at Tyburn. The servant girl, wishing to look at the corpse, stole upstairs in the doctor's absence and, to her horror, found the body sitting up on the board, wondering where it was. The girl almost threw herself down the stairs in her fright. The surgeon, on learning of the resuscitation of his subject, humanely concealed the man in the house till he could fit him out for America.

Once in America the man prospered and on his death he left his considerable fortune to the doctor in Gough Square. *Old & New London* continues: 'The sequel is still more curious. The surgeon dying some years after, his heirs were advertised for. A shoemaker at Islington eventually established a claim and inherited the money'. Unfortunately, he proved to be very mean and this was his undoing. When he refused to pay the lawyer who had helped him to the money, the lawyer said: 'I have put you into possession of this property . . . now I will spend £100 out of my own pocket to take it away again . . .' The lawyer accordingly advertised again' and a 'Mr Willcocks, a bookseller in the Strand then came forward'. After diligent enquiry it was proven that Willcocks' wife had a better claim to the money 'and the base shoe-maker returned to his last. The lucky Mr Willcocks was the good-natured bookseller who lent Johnson & Garrick when they first came up to London to seek their fortunes £5 on their joint note.'

Almost half a century after borrowing that £5, Dr Johnson breathed his last a stone's-throw from here in Bolt Court which probably takes its name from a busy fifteenth-century tavern called the Bolt-in-Tun that once stood in Fleet Street.

The name was a pun on the name of Prior Bolton whose house formerly occupied the site. It was in a window of the Bolt-in-Tun that Charles Dickens first saw a handbill advertising the Bath and Bristol coach. The proprietors were Moses Pickwick and Company.

Close to the Bolt-in-Tun, on 30 June 1784, James Boswell took his last farewell of Dr Johnson. Having dined together, the two men returned here in Sir Joshua Reynolds' coach. Johnson got down and called out 'Fare you well,' and without looking back, sprung away with a kind of pathetic briskness . . .'

A short time after the passing of 'the Great Cham', the Doctor Johnson Concert Rooms opened in Bolt Court and here 'The Vital Spark', Jenny Hill, made her music-hall début. It was not a success because some weeks later, almost at the point of starvation, she turned up at the London Pavilion clutching a theatrical agent's note of introduction to Mr Loibl. Although he read it with a face like thunder, the great impresario allowed her to audition and was sufficiently impressed to put her on the bill the same evening. The rest is music-hall history. Jenny was not called 'The Vital Spark' for nothing. Although she was very small and had not eaten for thirty-six hours, she sang and danced her heart out. The audience would hardly let her go. As she left the stage, at last, Loibl handed her the note which she had brought to him earlier in the day. It said:

My Dear Loibl: This girl is a damned nuisance. She never ceases to pester me for work and now, no doubt, she will pester you. You will kindly oblige the both of us by sending her sharply away.

Perhaps capriciously, perhaps from a sense of genuine compassion, Loibl chose the opposite course. By any standard it was a risk: he could not have known that she had any real talent. As things turned out a star was born that night.

Going north up Fetter Lane we come to Fleur de Lis

Dr Johnson holding court in a tavern. Among the assembled company are Joshua Reynolds (2nd l.), Thomas Gainsborough (4th l.), James Boswell (3rd from r.) and Joseph Nollekens (extreme r.). From a waxwork by Samuel Percy

Court, in the eighteenth century the home of the infamous Elizabeth Brownrigg, a parish mid-wife who mis-used her position to lure young women from the workhouse into her own house as maidservants. All of them were rootless. Many had no friends to enquire after them. Some were of low intelligence while others were deformed or crippled. They lived under quite appalling conditions and the slightest act of disobedience or resistance to Mrs Brownrigg's will called forth savage reprisals. The offender was suspended by her wrists from a water pipe, stripped and beaten. Although in some cases Mrs Brownrigg was forced to desist from sheer exhaustion, the attacks were usually so intense that the weak and undernourished victims quickly passed out.

Mrs Brownrigg was blessed with uncurious neighbours; and in consequence it was not until 1767 – seven years after her reign of terror had begun – that a neighbour did think to trace the source of the frequent moans and screams emanating from the house. She peered over the high wall surrounding the courtyard and saw a hideously disfigured and emaciated girl stretched upon the ground, semi-conscious. When the authorities arrived they found a second girl at the point of death. A third young woman had been whipped so ferociously that her clothes had to be removed surgically, the fabric of the cloth having been forced into the skin by the force of the lashes.

Notwithstanding that she was the mother of sixteen children, Elizabeth Brownrigg suffered on the gallows at Tyburn for what the 'Newgate Calendar' called 'murder by inches'. Her husband, a prosperous plumber, and her son, enthusiastic accomplices both, escaped with minor terms of imprisonment.

Running more or less parallel to Fetter Lane is Chancery Lane, an idiosyncratic thoroughfare which takes its name from the 'cancelli' or lattice-work screen which in former days divided the Court of Chancery from the Court of Common Pleas when the two bodies shared the Law Courts in Westminster Hall. At number 53 is the Chancery Lane Safe Deposit Company. During the Second World War the building was badly damaged in an air-raid and many of the firm's records were destroyed. As a result a number of safe-deposit boxes had to be forced open to establish the identity of the owners and this led to some intriguing discoveries. One box contained nothing but a pair of Victorian knickers, labelled: 'My life's undoing'. A second held a penny and a curl of hair. In a third was a packet of six live bullets. Written on the front, in a faded crabbed hand were the words: 'One for each of the directors.'

Carey Street, which leads west out of Chancery Lane, was

erected in about the middle of the seventeenth century and named after the Carey family who once owned a mansion on this site. The Careys were regular attenders at court and one of them, Sir Robert, was present at the deathbed of Elizabeth I. He was entrusted with the task of carrying to James I at Edinburgh the news of his accession. He accomplished it by galloping at full speed for the best part of sixty hours. As the entrance to the Bankruptcy Court is situated here, the phrase: 'to be in Carey Street' has become a synonym for insolvency.

Lincoln's Inn, which can be reached from Chancery Lane, is one of the four Inns of Court dubbed by Ben Jonson 'the noblest nurseries of Humanity and Liberty in the Kingdom'. Each is an independent body entrusted with the training and admittance of law students to the practice of advocacy. Laid out in 1618 by Inigo Jones, Lincoln's Inn Field's, to the west, covers approximately twelve acres and as such make up the most spacious of all the squares in central London. It is sometimes said to cover an area equivalent to that of the Great Pyramid, but is in fact smaller by about an acre and a half.

In 1683 Lincoln's Inn Fields was the scene of the macabre execution of William, Lord Russell who – 'infamous witnesses easily satisfying a packed jury' – was found guilty of plotting against the life of Charles II. His wife, the noble Lady Rachel, pleaded long and eloquently for her husband's reprieve but the King could not be moved. He told her: 'If I do not kill him, he will soon kill me.' Russell seems to have accepted the unjust sentence with equanimity. The pain of the axe, he said, would be momentary and less than 'the pain of drawing a tooth'. As matters turned out, death proved more agonising than his Lordship had anticipated. The headsman was the infamous Jack Ketch and according to Evelyn 'three butcherly strokes' were needed before 'The Patriot's' head was separated from his body. Ketch defended his inept performance by claiming that: 'His Lordship moved'.

By a curious coincidence another plot to murder Charles II had been fomented in Lincoln's Inn Fields thirty-four years earlier. At that date John Thurloe, Oliver Cromwell's Secretary of State, had chambers at number 13, on the north side of the square; and here one evening the two men were discussing how best to decoy the King back to England in order to assassinate him, when Cromwell suddenly became aware of a shadowy presence in the corner of the room. This proved to be Thurloe's assistant, a young man named Moreland. Cromwell drew a dagger and would certainly have despatched him had Thurloe not pointed out that he was obviously asleep. After some time spent listening to the lad's regular breathing, Cromwell sheathed up his dagger. But Moreland had not been asleep and he later divulged the plot to the King, who at the Restoration rewarded him with a knighthood.

The present number 13 is the Soane Museum, built in 1812 by Sir John Soane, the architect of the Bank of England. It is perhaps the best little-known museum in London. By a codicil of his will, the disposition of the antiquities and works of art which Sir John gathered round him in life remains exactly as it was on the day of his death.

A unique teaching collection in Lincoln's Inn Fields is the Hunterian Museum, founded by the eminent eighteenth-century surgeon, John Hunter. The 13,687 anatomical specimens of which it consists were purchased from his executors by the government of the day for £15,000. Perhaps the most interesting exhibit is the skeleton of the Irish giant, Charles Byrne, who grew to a height of 7′ 9″. Shortly before he attained his majority he developed tuberculosis. His condition was quickly rendered hopeless by an addiction to drink. There was considerable competition among local anatomists to acquire his body; but Byrne, who had a horror of ending up in a museum of this sort, made secret arrangements to be buried at sea in a lead-lined coffin. Learning of this, several of the more enterprising anatomists rushed off to hire a bathysphere. The wily Hunter merely bribed officials to fill

Charles Lamb with his sister Mary. In a house in Kingsway (now the site of Holy Trinity Church) Mary stabbed their mother to death in 1796 in a fit of insanity

the coffin with boulders and purchased the body from them for £500. Before carrying his prize home, he propped it up beside him in his coach while he called on several of his patients. He separated the twenty-two years old Irishman from his bones by boiling him in a huge vat.

Number 66 Lincoln's Inn Fields was formerly the home of 'Goody' Newcastle, perhaps the most ludicrous prime minister this country has ever known. 'A fidget, a fright and a bustle', he genuinely believed Hanover stood somewhere to the north of England; and when someone asked him what action he intended to take for the protection of Annapolis, he said: 'Annapolis! Annapolis! Oh, yes, Annapolis must be defended; to be sure Annapolis must be defended – where is Annapolis?' His particular *bête-noire* was *Long* Sir John Robinson, who was: 'a great pest to persons of high rank or in office. He was very troublesome to the late Duke of Newcastle and . . . if told that his Grace had gone out, would desire to be admitted to look at the clock, or to play with a monkey that was kept in the hall, in hopes of being sent for into the Duke.' The porter eventually grew so weary of this behaviour that: 'at his next coming . . . as soon as he had opened the gate, and without waiting for what he had to say, dismissed him in these words: "Sir, his Grace has gone out, the clock is stopped and the monkey is dead."'

Emerging from Lincoln's Inn Fields at the south-westerly corner and walking west, we come to Kingsway. It dates from 1905 and was opened by Edward VII. In fact the King was unable to remember the words of inauguration and in all probability would never have remembered them had someone not jogged his memory as he was about to go home. At the northern end of the street is the church of Holy Trinity. It occupies the site of the house in which Mary Lamb, the sister of the essayist, Charles Lamb, stabbed their mother to death in a fit of insanity in 1796.

4

Covent Garden and the Strand

Almost all the names given to geographical areas of London have a significance if we care to search for them far enough back in time and 'Strand' and 'Covent Garden' are no exception. 'Strand' is merely the old name for a water margin, in this case the strip of land which formerly bordered the Thames and which, in the sixteenth and seventeenth centuries, housed various great mansions, each with its beautiful garden sloping down to the river. Covent Garden was originally the 'convent garden' attached to Westminster Abbey. The rather foreign-sounding 'Aldwych' has its derivation in the Saxon word for an old town 'eald wic', the old town in question being the settlement given over to the Danes by Alfred after he had regained the City of London from them in a ferocious battle in 886.

In 1978, the modern-day Aldwych became caught up in warfare of a different kind. In that year, Georgi Markov, a Bulgarian exile employed by the BBC in transmitting programmes to the countries of the eastern bloc, was jabbed in the leg by a man carrying an umbrella. The tip of the umbrella contained a hypodermic needle which injected a microscopic capsule of deadly poison beneath the skin. The murder is thought to have been politically motivated and the assassin has never been identified.

On the corner with Aldwych and Catherine Street is the Strand Theatre. The longest-running comedy in the history of the English theatre, *No Sex Please – We're British*, opened here in June 1971 and to date more than two million people have seen the show. The authors claim that they dreamed it up in two hours over a Chinese meal.

Burying the dead during the Great Plague. Drawing from a
contemporary record for the year 1665

Walking a little to the west, we come to Drury Lane where
the Great Plague first took hold in 1665. Disseminated by
way of fleas indigenous to rats, it spread like wild-fire. In
some areas the mortality rate was as high as eighty-five
percent and the disease eventually claimed about one Lon-
doner in five. The raised levels of many of the church-yards
still bear silent testimony to the extent to which the corpses
had to be packed in; and when there was no more room in the
churchyards the dead were unceremoniously tumbled into
communal pits. Two of these are covered today by Liverpool
Street Station and Golden Square.

The present Theatre Royal, Drury Lane, the fourth of its
kind to stand hereabouts, was opened in 1812. It is said to
have several ghosts, the best documented being 'The Man in
Grey'. Dressed in eighteenth-century costume, he wears a
wig, a sword and a pair of riding-boots. He carries in his hand
a tricorn hat. Appearances are usually restricted to rehearsals
– although he did once manifest to an audience of a hundred
and fifty people – and he confines his activities to the upper
circle where he materialises in the end seat of row 'D'. From
there he moves to the rear aisle and vanishes through a wall in

the vicinity of the Royal Box. When approached he grows rapidly indistinct.

Sitings of 'The Man in Grey' often presage a successful run and it may be that he assists more practically. Several actors have felt a pair of unseen hands guiding them to better positions on stage; and when, as happened with Betty Jo Jones during the run of *Oklahoma!*, they subsequently decided to adopt the position of their own accord, they received a light but approving pat on the back. The identity of 'The Man in Grey' remains a mystery. But during the Victorian era, when workmen were carrying out repairs close to the spot at which he vanishes, they discovered a long-lost closet. Inside was a dusty skeleton with a dagger in its ribs.

The Duchess Theatre, situated in nearby Catherine Street, also has a history. Standing on the site of the house in which Thomas de Quincey wrote *Confessions of an Opium Eater*, it holds the unenviable record of having staged the shortest run in theatrical history, a review with so many complicated scene changes that it failed to reach its final curtain on the opening night. In January 1974 the nude review, *Oh! Calcutta* transferred here. The show has nothing to do with India and the title may be a corruption of the French phrase: '*Oh, quel cul tu as*', a rough translation of which might be 'Oh, what a lovely bum'. After seeing the show in New York the distinguished choreographer, Sir Robert Helpman, remarked: 'The trouble with nude dancing is that when the music stops everything else does not automatically stop as well.'

Parallel to Catherine Street is Wellington Street, once the home of the Victoria Club. The Club was particularly popular with bookmakers and in time became known as 'the Stock Exchange of the Turf'. The members had the reputation of being prepared to bet on anything and one man backed himself so heavily to win the Club's billiards tournament that he fainted with relief when he did so.

Passing Russell Street on our left (where in 1763, at number 8, James Boswell made the acquaintance of Dr

Johnson) we come to Bow Street. It takes its name from
'running in the shape of a bent bow' and its strongest
association is with the Bow Street Runners, the precursors of
the modern police force. They were founded by the novelist
and magistrate, Henry Fielding, who was himself once
bound over for a breach of the peace after attempting to
abduct a young girl for whom he had developed an unre-
quited passion. His work eventually devolved upon his blind
half-brother, John, who was said to be able to identify three
thousand malefactors by the sound of their voices.

The present Bow Street police station is decorated not with
the traditional blue lamp but a white one. It is said to have
been changed at the request of Queen Victoria who is
thought to have disliked the original because it evoked
painful memories of the death of her husband, Prince Albert.
He expired in the Blue Room at Windsor.

The Queen would no doubt have observed the lamp on her
visits to the Royal Opera House, which stands on the western
side of the way. The building dates from 1858 and incorporates a private box which could pass for a small dwelling. It
has its own separate entrance and formerly belonged to the
Dukes of Bedford, the ground landlords. It is equipped with
its own toilet and is warmed by its own fire. The lease is
currently held by Covent Garden Properties Ltd. and
apparently there is no restriction as to what property people
call 'user'. This means that in theory there is nothing to
prevent the lessees from turning it into a discothèque or even
an all-night café for vagrants. They have no plans for doing
so.

It was outside the Royal Opera House, in 1779, that
Martha Ray, the mistress of the card-playing Earl of Sandwich, was shot in the face at point-blank range. Her assassin
was an aspiring suitor, James Hackman, a clergyman and
ex-army officer. Poor Martha died instantly, causing a Grub
Street hack to pen the immortal lines:

A clergyman, O wicked one!
In Covent Garden shot her;
No time to cry upon her God,
Its hoped he's not forgot her.

Martha's ghost is said still to haunt the apartments she shared with the Earl of Sandwich at the Admiralty in Whitehall. The Reverend Mr Hackman – duly hanged at Tyburn – has left no imprint on time and space.

Another ghost associated with the area is the actor, William Terris, who was stabbed to death at the stage door of the Adelphi Theatre in 1897 by a colleague who was jealous of his success. George Bernard Shaw is thought to have written *The Devil's Disciple* with Terris in mind; but Terris fell asleep while the author was reading it to him. After the work had established itself in America, Terris, so to speak, woke up. But he was murdered before he had the chance of playing the part in London. His ghost chooses to haunt Covent Garden underground station which he regularly used for travel between the theatre and his house in Putney. He is most often seen in the last two months of the year, the most propitious date being 16 December, the anniversary of his death.

A one-time resident of Bow Street was the seventeenth-century dramatist, William Wycherley, who, at the age of seventy-five, and for the sole purpose of thwarting the expectations of a relative who stood to inherit some property at his death, married a girl fifty years his junior. Eleven days later he died. Asked by his wife in his last moments whether he had any words of advice for her, he said: 'My dear, it is only this: that you will never marry an old man again.'

That curious blend of fighting-man and romantic, the cavalier lyrist, Sir Richard Lovelace, lived in Long Acre. While he was engaged for the King in the Civil Wars, his sweetheart, Lucy Sacheverell, received a false report of his death and married another. The man who wrote 'four walls do not a prison make, nor iron bars a cage', became thereafter a prisoner of his own melancholy. He is said never to have raised his eyes from the ground again; and according to one source he spent the latter part of his life vegetating in his darkened basement in Long Acre where he died of starvation in 1657.

Before it removed to its present home at Nine Elms, the market of Covent Garden was served by a veritable army of fruit-importers in Long Acre. One of these was Messrs Ffyfe & Hudson. The first consignment of bananas to reach England were stored in their cellars here in 1878; and at sixpence a dozen they proved popular in spite of the conservative nature of the English.

The most senior of Covent Garden's public houses is probably the 'Lamb and Flag' which stands in nearby Rose Street, number 33. Dating from 1623, it became known as 'The Bucket of Blood' after Dryden was set upon in front of the tavern by the hired thugs of the Earl of Rochester. The Earl suspected Dryden of being behind a particularly vicious lampoon of him. He wasn't: but he received a thrashing which Rose Street has never forgotten. An account of the affair is inscribed on the wall of the 'Lamb and Flag'; and on December 16 each year, the anniversary of the attack is celebrated here – 'Dryden Night'. Precisely at eight o'clock, the hour the incident occurred, the landlord supplies his customers with mulled wine in which to drink the poet's health.

Dominating the southern end of St Martin's Lane is the Renaissance-style Coliseum, opened in 1904 with a roof garden, the world's first revolving stage and a glass train which carried royalty to their box. During the performance it was used as an ante-room. Like most good theatres, the Coliseum has its resident ghost, a young subaltern killed in action shortly before the Armistice in 1918. The figure appeared in the second row of the dress circle the same evening – the seat he had occupied on the last night of his leave. The spectre was very active between the wars but is now seen less frequently. A more modern theatrical ghost is

The Lamb and Flag pub in Rose Street. From an attack here on
Dryden, it was known as 'The Bucket of Blood'

that of Sir Charles Wyndham, the builder of the nearby
Albery Theatre. A handsome, distinguished-looking man of
upright carriage, he occasionally manifests in the lobby of the
Albery prior to a performance, mingling with the incoming
crowds.

A third theatre in St Martin's Lane is the Duke of York's.

It opened in 1892 and was heated at that date by a number of open fires, dotted at strategic intervals around the auditorium. In 1926 managerial control of the theatre passed to Violette Melnotte, a brilliant but rather callous woman who, when one of her actors attempted to take his life by putting his head in the theatre oven, wrote to her solicitor enquiring whether he could be legally compelled to refund the price of the gas.

At its northern extremity, St Martin's Lane runs into Seven Dials, formerly a 'maze of streets, courts, lanes and Irishmen'. Within a few years of being built, it became the worst kind of rookery (so called from the tendency of rooks to congregate together) and by 1751 every fourth house was a grog shop. By 1849 more than three thousand people were crammed into less than a hundred dwellings hereabouts; and when one of the houses caught fire, thirty-seven people were discovered living in a single room less than fifteen feet square. They had approximately a shilling between them.

Late one afternoon, after lunching at the Savoy, the distinguished King's Counsel, Sir Patrick Hastings, came strolling through Covent Garden in the company of the American actress, Tallulah Bankhead. He was accosted in Seven Dials by a street urchin who offered for sixpence to stand on his head. Tallulah said: 'Why, I'd do it myself for half that' – and did.

Garrick Street, to the south east of Seven Dials, is named after the great eighteenth-century actor, David Garrick. There is a club which bears his name at number 15 and it is the very essence of what a gentlemen's club should be. The atmosphere is mellow and civilised and the dining room maintains two sets of menus – one for members and one for their guests, the latter without prices. The Club has always had a predominantly theatrical following although each generation tends to think that the quality of new members is no longer what it was. This was illustrated many years ago when a crusty old aristocrat was approached by the Secretary and reminded that he had not renewed his subscription. 'And I shan't', he said. 'The place is going to the dogs.' After the Secretary had left, he turned to the actor-manager, Sir Herbert Beerbohm Tree and added: 'When I joined all the members were gentlemen.' Tree muttered: 'Then I wonder why they left.'

At the end of Garrick Street is King Street, which still possesses several houses that sport mahogany doors (a reminder of the female resident who first introduced the wood to this country); and shortly before his removal to Keswick, in 1800, the poet, Samuel Coleridge, was lodging at number 10. As yet unenslaved by opium or the philosophical introspection which were later to flaw him, and stimulated by the new-formed intimacy with Wordsworth, he proved 'a marvellous talker'. Samuel Rogers called upon him here one morning and listened to him talk 'for three hours without intermission about poetry, and so admirably that I wish every word he uttered had been written down'. Wordsworth, however was not always so uncritical. On a subsequent occasion, he and Rogers listened to Coleridge discourse for a mere two hours, Wordsworth appearing to listen with profound attention and 'every now and then nodding his head'. As the door closed behind them, however, Rogers said: 'Well for my own part, I could not make head or tail of Coleridge's oration. Pray, did you understand it?' Wordsworth stumped down the steps and muttered: 'Not one syllable.'

One literary man who refused to be intimidated by Coleridge's loquacity was the essayist, Charles Lamb. On one occasion he met the author of *The Ancient Mariner* in the street and was irresistibly drawn by the button of his lapel into a quiet corner where Coleridge embarked upon a long tirade against the artificiality of the work of his contemporaries. Noticing that Coleridge had closed his eyes (presumably the better to concentrate) Lamb quietly drew forth his pocket-knife and severed the button. If we are to believe the essayists version of events, he returned the same way an hour later to discover the Kubla Khan of the 'new language' of poetry still standing there, still with his eyes screwed up and still talking to the button.

An earlier resident of King Street was the composer, Dr Thomas Arne. He was born at number 31 in 1710. To placate his unmusical father, an upholsterer who intended him for the Bar, he practised the harpsichord one-handed – using the other to dampen the sound of the instrument with his handkerchief.

More recently, Moss Bros was founded in King Street. In 1881 Moses Moses opened a shop selling second-hand clothes and hiring out new ones. It is said that on the day it opened, he placed a sign in the window which read: *Mr and Mrs Moses having left off clothing of every description invite an early inspection.*

At the bottom of King Street is Covent Garden, laid out in the 1630s by Inigo Jones for his patron, Francis Russell, fourth Earl of Bedford. Hailed in its time as a marvel of aesthetic uniformity, it was modelled on the spacious and airy Piazza at Leghorn and set the standard for square-building for the next two hundred years.

On its northern flank, where it borders with Russell Street, one of the original houses yet survives. It was once the home of that bluff old royalist, Sir Edmund Verney. Although he had no sympathy with the despotic policies of Charles I, when the Civil Wars came his simple code of honour required that he give him his support. He said: 'I have eaten his bread and have served him near thirty years and will not now forsake him; and choose rather to lose my life (which I am sure I shall do) to preserve and defend those things which are against my conscience to preserve.'

In 1642, while carrying the King's Standard at the battle of Edgehill, Verney was surrounded by Cromwellian infantry. He was quite alone, but when the Roundhead officer called for his surrender he said: 'My life is my own, but my Standard is the King's'. He died defending it and even after death his lifeless hand continued to hold the standard in an unbreakable grip. His arm had to be severed at the wrist before the standard could be carried off; and when it was eventually recaptured by the Royalists the hand was still clinging to it. An almost super-human force was required to prise it loose. Among so many dead on the field of battle, Sir Edmund's body could not be found. The hand, however, was returned to his country seat in Buckinghamshire and buried in the family vault at Claydon House. The ring he was wearing remains there yet; and his ghost is still occasionally said to be seen near the vault, presumably looking to reclaim its lost hand.

One of Sir Edmund Verney's closest friends was the hoary old Sir Arthur Aston who fought at Edgehill alongside Sir Edmund's son, also called Edmund. Sir Arthur had a wooden leg and when this was carried away by a cannon ball some of the soldiers, not being aware that it was false, began calling for a surgeon. Being a droll sort of fellow, the young Verney set up a counter-cry for a joiner. Both Aston and the younger Verney met their end defending the Royalist cause in Ireland. Ironically, Aston was clubbed to death on Mill Mount with his (replacement) wooden leg.

Sir Edmund's old home in Covent Garden was later occupied by the portrait-painter, Sir Godfrey Kneller – a man of great sense but suspect sensibilities. As a magistrate he operated a simple code of justice and when it transpired that an employer, who had charged his manservant with theft, had introduced the money into his path with the intention of tempting him to steal it, Kneller discharged the domestic and locked up the master. The same robust common sense pervaded his attitude to painting. When told that the Heraclean painter, Zeuxis, had painted a boy holding a bunch of grapes which looked so natural that a bird had tried to peck them off the canvas, Kneller remarked: 'If the boy had been painted as well as the grapes the bird would have been afraid to meddle with them.'

At the Restoration, Sir Kenelm Digby was living 'in the last faire house westward in the north portico of Covent Garden'. An exotic flower reared in an age which nurtured and encouraged the exotic, Sir Kenelm was the son of Sir Everard Digby, executed in 1606 for his complicity in the Gunpowder Plot. Evelyn records that when the executioner held up Sir Everard's severed head and cried: 'Behold! The head of a traitor', the head replied: 'Thou liest'.

Sir Kenelm, broad as a barrel, six feet four in his hose and built according to Ben Jonson 'like some Imperial room', is best remembered for his quack remedies. One of these was the 'Powder of Sympathy', a chemical compound, largely consisting of powdered vitriol, which he claimed would cure any wound inflicted by a sword. Curiously, it was applied not to the wound but to the tip of the offending weapon. Another of his cure-alls was 'calcinated powder of toads'. However, we may doubt that any of these nostrums were much use as Stubbes called their author 'the very Pliny of our age for lying'. Aubrey said he 'was the kind of man who would have made himself respected in any part of the world had he drop't out of the clouds . . . provided he did not stay there above six weeks.'

Opening out of the east side of Bedford Street and easily overlooked, is Inigo Place leading to the 'actors' church, of St Paul's, Covent Garden. Among the notables buried here are: the court painter, Sir Peter Lely; the satirist, Samuel Butler (who left instructions that his feet should be placed touching one of the outer walls – he did not say why and he did not care which); the highwayman, Claude Duval; the wood-carver, Grinling Gibbons; Dr Thomas Arne, the composer of 'Rule Britannia'; the actress Vivien Leigh; and Tom Davies, who first introduced Boswell to Johnson. Davies had formerly been an actor but renounced the stage and opened a book-shop when a critic said he spoke 'a sentence as curs mouth a bone.' Boswell thought him a man of 'good understanding'; but Dr Johnson considered him too thin-skinned: 'What a man is he who is to be driven from the stage by a line?' he asked. 'Another line would have driven him from his shop.'

In 1951 the theatrical impresario C. B. Cochrane, known to everyone as 'Cockie', was buried in the church after dying in tragic circumstances in his suite at the Hyde Park Hotel. Leaving his wife asleep, he rose early with the intention of taking a bath to ease the pain of an arthritic hip. As he leaned forward to run more hot water his hip 'locked' and he was unable to turn it off. His screams eventually aroused his wife, but sadly the burns he suffered proved fatal.

Rather unromantically, Maiden Lane, which junctions with Bedford Street in the east, takes its name not from some local maiden but the 'midden' or dung-heaps which formerly abounded in this area. The painter, J. M. W. Turner, was born on the site of what is now number 21; and the metaphysical poet, Andrew Marvell, lodged at number 9 in 1677.

St Paul's Church, Inigo Place, where many a celebrity lies buried

His father, Andrew Marvell senior, had expired thirty-six years earlier under rather strange circumstances. He had no sooner embarked on a ferry and uttered a cheery: 'Ho, for heaven!' than the boat sank.

Exchange Court, a turning to the right out of Maiden Lane going west, recalls the New Exchange, a bazaar which stood on this site from 1609 to 1737. It was here, in 1653, that a Portugese gentleman stabbed to death a Frenchman in the belief that he was his old enemy, M. Gerard. He was duly sentenced to death. It was only on mounting the scaffold that he discovered his mistake. He saw M. Gerard standing in front of him, waiting to die in turn for his involvement in a plot to overthrow the Lord Protector.

At the point where it crosses Bedford Street, Maiden Lane becomes Chandos Place. It is named after the third Baron Chandos whose only claim to fame is that his daughter married the Earl of Bedford who owned this land. His descendant, the second Duke of Chandos, came by his wife in a much less orthodox manner. Staying at a country inn, he was disturbed by the commotion of a servant auctioning off his wife in the courtyard below. The Duke hurried down to watch the fun. The girl's beauty so impressed him, and her quiet dignity and resignation contrasted so favourably with the husband's coarseness and brutality, that he bought her and married her himself.

He was succeeded in the title by the son of this union, the third Duke. Being something of a dynast, when *his* son was born, around the year 1778, the third Duke arranged a very showy christening. The heavy embroidered christening robe cost £700; and the guest-list encompassed every person of rank in the Kingdom, including George III and Queen Charlotte. But at the height of the ceremony, when the nurse approached the font and parted the robe, the infant was found to have suffocated under the blaze and heat of the chandeliers. The Duke died of the shock. His wife shut herself up in their house and lived the rest of her life as a recluse.

William IV Street, which leads down to the Strand, commemorates the third son of George III and the last of the Hanoverians. A bluff, good-hearted eccentric, he was known as 'the Sailor King' and ruled England six days short of seven years. Like the ancient Nasamonians, he insisted on dying in a sitting position, expiring in the Blue Room at Windsor, a room in which George IV and Prince Albert also breathed their last.

The Strand today is a long commercial thoroughfare crowded with tourists and shoppers. A haven among the bustle, at number 92, is the Coal Hole public house, a one-time haunt of the poet, Dylan Thomas. It is rumoured that one evening he received a severe fright here at the hands of the Black Magician, Aleister Crowley. Dylan was doodling on a piece of paper at one end of the bar when he suddenly noticed the 'Great Beast' studying him intently across the room. Crowley, too, was equipped with pencil and pad and a few minutes later, on his way out, slipped a sheet of paper on to the poet's table, face down. It was the best part of an hour before 'the Rimbaud of Cwmdonkin Drive' could summon the courage to turn it over. When he did he discovered an exact replica of his own doodle.

The most impressive building at the eastern end of the Strand is Somerset House, named after Protector Somerset, Regent to the boy-king Edward VI, who built a palace on this site in 1547. Inigo Jones died at Somerset House in 1652; and here on 3 September 1658, the anniversary of two of his greatest battles, Oliver Cromwell also expired. At the height of the worst storm in living memory, with the sound of the 'rocking winds' in his ears, he muttered: 'My desire is to make what haste I may to be gone.' At the moment he died, his supporters were crowning him in effigy in the next room.

Until quite recently, Somerset House served as the central registry for births, deaths and marriages. Indeed, at least one marriage came close to being contracted here. According to Ford Madox Ford, the philosopher Herbert Spencer somehow acquired a key to the door leading to the roof and regularly walked there with George Eliot (Mary Ann Evans). On one of these jaunts he proposed to her. He seems to have quite hit on the manner – going down on one knee and clasping her hand – but he forgot to remove his hat and for this, or some other reason, she refused him.

Dominating everything around them from their position on the north side of the way are the Law Courts, a mock twelfth-century Gothic pile which took sixteen years to build and was opened in 1882. Fashioned from eighty thousand tons of stone and thirty-five million bricks, there are thirty law-courts, more than a thousand rooms and a frontage stretching nearly two hundred yards. The exterior clock once killed a man. About a quarter of a century ago, as the Keeper was leaning in to wind it, his tie became entangled in the mechanism, strangling him. *Old & New London* records that some 'thirty close, foul and filthy courts, lanes and alleys were demolished to accommodate the building and that the removal of these slum dwellings left 4,000 people homeless.'

Returning westwards, past Aldwych and still on the north side of the Strand, we come to Burleigh Street which takes its name from the mansion of William Cecil, Lord Burghley, Elizabeth I's great Chancellor. The Queen seems to have been genuinely fond of Burghley and visited him here several times. On one occasion she arrived wearing a high and very elaborate head-dress. The door lintel was low. The servant blanched but was forced to ask whether her Majesty would *stoop*. Elizabeth said she would never stoop for the King of Spain, 'but I will stoop for your master.' When Burghley regretted that the gout in his legs had prevented him from coming to the door to welcome her, she waved the apology away: 'My Lord,' she said, 'we do not make use of you for the badness of your legs, but for the goodness of your head.'

A little further west is Southampton Street where phosphorous was first manufactured in this country. The librettist, William Schwenk Gilbert, was born at number 17 in November 1836 – and was shortly afterwards kidnapped. His parents got him back on paying a ransom of £25, a figure

which, even allowing for a hundred and fifty years of inflation, appears to have been insultingly low. In 1871 Gilbert
began an association with Sir Arthur Sullivan which was to
produce fourteen major light operas in eighteen years. In
1889 they fell out over the cost of a carpet for the Savoy
theatre and the rift was never properly healed.

Gilbert lived the last fifteen years of his life at Harrow. He
occasionally ventured abroad however and it was during one
of these trips – to America – that he was asked by a lady
whether he liked Bach, which she pronounced 'Baitch'. He
said he did. The lady next asked whether 'Baitch' was still
composing. 'No', said Sir William. 'Decomposing'. He enjoyed the life of a country squire, but not all of its recreations.
'Deerstalking would be a very fine sport,' he said, 'if only the
deer had guns'. In 1911, at the age of seventy-four, he met his
death in his own lake, gallantly rescuing a lady from drowning. To the Edwardians, who tended to equate extraversion
with prodigality, it came as something of a shock to learn that
he had left an estate of £118,000, more than twice that of the
more sober Sir Arthur Sullivan.

Almost opposite Southampton Street is Savoy Court the
only street in England where traffic is required by law to
drive on the right-hand side of the road. It does so because, if
approached from the left, the construction of the court in
front of the Savoy Hotel would prevent the larger limousines
from turning round.

Taking its name from the palace of Count Peter of Savoy
which stood on this site from 1246 until 1381, the Savoy
Hotel opened in 1899 – and the first gold sovereign received
on that morning is still preserved in the manager's office. At
that date the price of a double room was twelve shillings.
Over the years the hotel has accommodated many distinguished guests and more than a few eccentric ones. In 1925
George Galli, the silent film-star, left the hotel and disappeared for thirty years. He was eventually discovered in a
small town in France, working as a priest. Mae West claimed
to have been visited in her room by her dead mother; and

Claude Monet painted the Thames from his window. Madame Fahmy caused a sensation by shooting her husband to death here; and Luisa Tetrazzini, the massive Italian soprano, embarrassed the staff by cracking the pedestal of her toilet. She had two grand pianos installed in her suite: one tuned for humid days, the other for dry ones. Louis Armstrong played his trumpet in bed; and Signor Marconi, the pioneer of wireless telegraphy would eat nothing which had not been minutely chopped up by the waiters.

For several years, the Savoy was the permanent home of the American comedienne, Elaine Stritch. When a newspaper columnist asked her how she could afford the prices, she said: 'I can't. After dark they make me scrub the fifth and sixth floors.'

5

The Mall, the Parks and the Palace

It is hard to believe that as late as 1825 Hyde Park Corner was semi-rural. At that date the only effective traffic-control was a turnpike-gate flanked by two lodges. Now, with more than a hundred and fifty vehicles negotiating it every minute, it is one of the most dangerous locations in London. The constant lines of traffic which converge on it from the five approach roads travel at considerably less than the 5.87 miles an hour averaged by the rest of central London's traffic.

Surveying this busy scene from a position hard by Apsley House is Sir Edgar Boehm's statue of the Duke of Wellington. The Duke is shown astride 'Copenhagen', the charger he rode at Waterloo. 'Copenhagen' lived to the great age of twenty-eight and after his death the Duke had one of his hooves fashioned into an ink-well. It is impossible to view the pair without being reminded of the words of Marya Mannes: 'People on horses look better than they are. People in cars look worse than they are.'

Before it was moved to its present position, the Wellington statue stood on the site now occupied by the Triumphal Arch, a rather over-refined structure surmounted by Adrian Jones' preposterous tableau of 'War Being Restrained by Peace'. One of the uprights of the Arch contains a three-storey police station and the other acts as a ventilation shaft to dispel the exhaust fumes which would otherwise build up in the underpasses running to and from Piccadilly.

Until recently, on the west side of Hyde Park Corner was St George's Hospital, designed in 1828 by William Wilkins, the architect of the National Gallery. A hospital has stood here since 1733 and one of the original benefactors was

Queen Caroline, the wife of George II. She was a popular woman and when she died, in 1737, packs of playing-cards were for a time sold minus the queens as a sign of the deep loss which was felt at her passing. On her deathbed she urged the King to remarry. His answer has become immortal: 'No', he replied, 'I will take mistresses.'

Sir Henry Irving's somewhat brittle marriage was shattered one night at Hyde Park Corner. The year was 1871 and the actor and his wife were travelling home from a party given to celebrate the triumphant first night of *The Bells*, the melodrama which served to establish him as a major star. At Hyde Park Corner, Henry ventured to break the icy silence which had reigned since the couple had left the theatre by making some modest comment on the event. His wife, who was afraid that she was losing her husband to fame, said in a withering voice: 'Are you going on making a fool of yourself like this all your life?' Without a word, Irving signalled the driver to stop and got down. Although he continued to support his family, and always remained very fond of his children, he walked away without a backward glance and never lived with them again.

Leading out of Hyde Park Corner to the east is Constitution Hill. Charles II frequently took his morning stroll here although there is no real proof that the name derives from these 'constitutionals.' One day, Charles encountered his brother – 'the not very lovable Duke of York, afterwards the completely unlovable James II' – on the Hill. Charles was attended only by the Duke of Leeds and 'my Lord Cromarty.' James 'had been hunting on Hounslow Heath and was returning in his coach escorted by a party of the Guards . . . The Duke . . . immediately got out . . . and said he was greatly surprised to find his Majesty in that place with such a small attendance, and that he thought his Majesty exposed himself to some danger.

'No kind of danger, James', said Charles, 'for I am sure no man in England will take away my life to make you king.'

Since those words were spoken, there have been more attempts to take away royal life on Constitution Hill than anywhere else in England. On 10 June 1840 that 'amiable fieldmouse', Queen Victoria, was fired upon here by a lunatic named Edward Oxford as she drove in an open phaeton with the Prince Consort; and further efforts to eliminate her were made on the Hill in 1842 and 1849. Edward VIII had a similar brush with an attacker in July 1936. He was returning on horseback to Buckingham Palace from reviewing troops in Hyde Park, when a man suddenly appeared brandishing a revolver. A policeman attempted to disarm him, and the assailant threw the weapon at the King. The Duke of York – soon to become king himself – seeing only the flash of sunlight on metal and thinking that the missile was a bomb, very gallantly spurred his horse forward in an attempt to shield his brother. The attacker's name was McMahon and he was sent to prison for twelve months. The sentence would certainly have been longer had the court not accepted that he had committed the offence merely in order to draw attention to certain grievances of his own and not with any serious intent to injure the King.

On 29 June 1850, close to the wicket-gate which formerly led into the park, the founder of the police force, Sir Robert Peel, was thrown from his horse, suffering injuries from which he died three days later.

Grosvenor Place, which runs parallel to the western wall of Buckingham Palace was in the 1860s the home of Algernon Swinburne. He lived at number 18. He was then in his early twenties and having been predisposed to masochism by the beatings he had received at Eton was a regular caller at a 'correctional' establishment run by two rouged and flaxen-haired ladies at number 7 Circus Road, St John's Wood. Sixty years on, Sir Osbert Sitwell met the poet:

who owned to eighty-six years, and a fine impressive machine he looked, as he told me how much he had enjoyed his long life. 'If a man – or a schoolboy for that matter –' he continued, 'does not get on well, it's his own fault. I well remember, when I first went to Eton, the head-boy called us together, and pointing to a little fellow with a mass of curly red hair, said: 'if you ever see that boy, kick him – and if you are too far off to kick him, throw a stone . . .' He was a fellow named Swinburne,' he added. 'He used to write poetry for a time, I believe, but I don't know what became of him.'

Soon after his removal from Lincoln's Inn Fields, Lord Chancellor Erskine settled in Lower Grosvenor Place, then known as 'Arabella Row'. A brilliant advocate, but self-confident to the point of smugness, he brushed aside evidence which was not to his liking and he had a tendency to address juries as 'my dear little twelvers'. His best friends were two leeches which he nicknamed 'Clive' and 'Howe'; and he said that on the Day of Judgement, when all things would be revealed, he would be pleased to learn why his shoes always pinched.

Passing down Buckingham Gate, we come to Bird Cage Walk which commemorates the collection of exotic birds which once hung in their cages here, an adjunct to the royal menagerie in St James's Park. The Walk was also the site of the royal cockpit where birds wearing two-inch spurs fought each other to the death. James Boswell found this 'sport' so enthralling that he once watched it for five hours.

At the Buckingham Palace end of Bird Cage Walk is the Wellington Barracks. Although the figure has not been observed for many years, several guardsmen have sworn on oath to seeing a headless female traverse the parade-ground here during the small hours. At a certain point she slowly disappears into the earth, as though descending a flight of steps. Sentries have also been disturbed by the sound of a sash-window being pushed up, followed by a plaintive voice calling for a light. Any soldier brave enough to call back simply heard the demand endlessly repeated, until it eventually faded away. The manifestation is thought to be the restless spirit of a woman who was murdered and decapitated in the barracks by her soldier husband. Her torso was thrown into the waters of St James's Park. Her head was never recovered.

Forming the northern boundary of St James's Park is The Mall, a processional route taking its name from a croquet-like game called pell-mell which was played here at the Restoration. At its south-western end, immediately in front of Buckingham Palace and almost blocking it from view, is Sir Thomas Brock's humourless memorial to Queen Victoria. A close examination of the central figure of the enthroned Queen – thirteen feet high and carved from a single block of

The ball game from which The Mall took its name

marble – reveals that she is wearing her wedding-band on the 'wrong' hand. This was the German fashion and Victoria adopted it in deference to her husband, Albert, who was a Prince of Saxe-Coburg-Gotha. After her marriage, the infatuated young Queen developed a partiality for all things German, including the habit of soaking her cake in her coffee.

Queen Victoria came to the throne of England in 1837; and by the turn of the century the vast majority of her subjects could remember no one else. When she died, at Osborne House, on the Isle of Wight, in 1901, the nation experienced an extraordinary sense of loss. One of Lord Northcliffe's most reliable reporters was despatched to cover the story. When no copy was received, a second reporter was sent in search of an explanation. He discovered his colleague sitting at a table in his hotel bedroom, staring tearfully at a sheet of paper on which were written seven words. On the floor were twenty or thirty other sheets of paper, each bearing the same seven words: 'Never since the death of Jesus Christ . . .'

Buckingham Palace, the stolid Palladian building to the west of the Victoria Memorial, is the official London residence of the Queen. It stands on the site of a much earlier house (1666) once owned by John Sheffield, Earl of Mulgrave, whose haughty manner earned him the title of 'Lord Allpride'. Queen Anne, however, was kindly disposed towards the Earl – perhaps on account of the mild flirtation she had enjoyed with him when she was a plain and relatively insignificant princess of fifteen – and in 1703 she created him Duke of Buckingham.

'Lord Allpride' at once began work on a new house to match his improved station. Unfortunately, due to his reluctance to pay his bills, progress on it was slow. The architect was kept permanently short of funds and was only able to extract a promise of payment by tricking his Grace on to the roof and threatening to throw the pair of them into the courtyard.

When the Duke died, Buckingham House passed to his

widow, an illegitimate daughter of James II, who was described by Walpole as 'more mad with pride than any
mercer's wife in Bedlam'. After listening to a sermon on the
subject of sin, she said: 'It is monstrous to be told that you
have a heart as sinful as the common wretches that crawl the
earth'. When she lay on her deathbed she made her ladies
promise that none would sit down in her presence until the
surgeon pronounced life extinct.

In 1762 John Sheffield's former home was purchased by
George III and later renamed Buckingham Palace. It thus
became the first and last royal residence to be called after a
subject. It is viewed today by some eight million visitors a
year and is surpassed as a tourist attraction only by the Tower
of London.

In March 1974 the Queen's daughter, Princess Anne, and
her husband, Captain Mark Phillips, were returning down
The Mall to Buckingham Palace from a function in the City
when the royal car was overtaken by a Ford Escort saloon
which forced it to stop. The driver approached the chauffeur
as though to ask for directions. The police-inspector sitting
beside the chauffeur, sensing something was wrong, made a
cautious attempt to get out. As he did so the man produced a
gun and shot him in the chest. Despite his wound, the
inspector was able to draw his own weapon and fire back.
The bullet missed. When he attempted to fire again he found
the gun had jammed.

The attacker ran to the rear door of the limousine and
attempted to drag the Princess from the car by her arm. A
tug-of-war developed with Captain Phillips's hanging on to
his wife's other arm. The inspector, attempting to help
Captain Phillips, was shot again, in the stomach and the
chest. The chauffeur was also shot. At this point a young
police constable and a journalist who had witnessed the
shootings from a passing taxi, arrived on the scene. They too
endeavoured to tackle the gunman and they too were shot.

Fortunately, the sound of gunfire had alerted a number of
other police officers in the vicinity and the attacker was

eventually overpowered. A twenty-five-year-old labourer
with a long history of mental disorder, he was found to be
carrying a ransom note, addressed to the Queen, demanding
three million pounds for the Princess's safe return. He was
eventually ordered to be detained indefinitely under the
Mental Health Act. All the wounded made good recoveries.

Happily, not all encounters in The Mall have been of such
a desperate character. The kind old Duke of Montagu one
day met here a very sorry-looking fellow, down-at-heel and
half-starved. He told his Grace that he had left his family in
Yorkshire and walked to London in the hope of finding
work. The Duke saw that he was honest and told him to come
and dine with him on the following Sunday. When he arrived
his host greeted him very pleasantly and mentioned in an
off-hand sort of way that some other guests had already come
and were waiting in the drawing-room. The 'other guests'
proved to be the man's family, whom Montagu had brought
to London at his own expense. In the midst of a tearful
reunion, the Duke produced another surprise – a legal
document by which he undertook to pay his new friend a
yearly allowance of £200 for the rest of his life.

To the south-east of The Mall is St James's Park, formerly
marsh and swampland. It was enclosed in 1536 by the
land-grabbing Henry VIII who added it as a deer park to his
new Palace of Whitehall. At the Restoration, Charles II had
the area landscaped and to emphasis that it was private
property, the gates were locked each night at 10 p.m.
However, as at least six thousand people had keys, this was
really more of a symbolic gesture than a serious attempt to
exclude.

There was once a tradition that one could not be arrested in
St James's Park, unless the crime was very grave; but in 1677
Richard Harris was committed to Bedlam for throwing an
orange at the King; and six months later, Deborah Lyddal –
'who doth frequently intrude herself into St James's Park,
where she hath committed severall disorders' – suffered the
same fate for offering to throw a stone at the Queen.

On a sharp winter's morning in 1649 a man already under arrest, Charles I, walked through the park to his execution in Whitehall, pausing only to point out to his guards a tree planted by his brother, the long-dead Prince Henry. Three years later, Lord General Cromwell had here 'some private discourse' with Bulstrode Whitelocke, then a Commissioner of the Great Seal. Cromwell said: 'What if a Man should take upon himself to be a King?' Whitelocke replied: 'I think that remedy would be worse than the disease.'

At the eastern end of the park's central lake is Duck Island, the governorship of which was formerly a sinecure office in the gift of the monarch. Charles II invested it in the French writer and wit, Charles Saint-Evremond, a great lover of champagne, 'a great epicure and as great a sloven.' Pope recounts that in the latter part of his life, Saint-Evremond, who lived to be ninety-three: 'used to be always feeding his ducks; or, the fowls that he kept in his chamber. He had a great variety of them; and other sorts of animals all over his house. He used always to say that 'when we grow old, and our own spirits decay, it re-animates one to have a number of living creatures about one, and to be much with them''.'

A later governor of Duck Island was the appropriately-named Stephen Duck, who in March 1756 committed suicide – by drowning. A Wiltshire farm labourer who achieved some fame as a versifier, he became librarian to Queen Caroline and was known as 'The Thresher Poet'.

The bridge which spans the lake affords at its centre one of the finest possible views of London. Away to the east the various spires and domes, silhouetted against the cupolas of the War Office, produce a strangely Muscovite effect. The first bridge was erected by John Nash in 1814. It was replaced in 1857 by a second structure and it was either near or on this that G. K. Chesterton proposed to his future wife. The present bridge dates from 1957.

One man frequently to be seen in the park was Benjamin Disraeli, who came here to recuperate from the cut and thrust of parliamentary debate. One day he was sitting on a canvas stool, looking out over the lake, when he was spotted by the artist, James McNeill Whistler. A sensitive man, Whistler had no wish to intrude: but he greatly desired to paint the old man's portrait. Hesitatingly he approached and introduced himself. Disraeli gave no sign of having heard him. Out of nervousness, Whistler began to gabble: inarticulately expressing admiration, proffering clumsy compliments and generally fawning in a quite uncharacteristic manner. At last he could think of nothing more to say. After a moment's silence, and without lifting his eyes from the prospect before him, Disraeli said in a sepulchral voice: 'Go away, little man, go away.'

Until The Mall was cut, and the physical separation made a new name advisable, Green Park, to the west, was an integral part of St James's Park. If its character today is somewhat shapeless and anonymous this is probably because its fifty acres have never been formally laid out. It also suffered lasting damage at the hands of the Kentish forces of Sir Thomas Wyatt which camped here in 1554 after marching on London in opposition to Queen Mary's proposal to take a Catholic husband. Having ruined the park by digging it up for fortifications, he next ruined himself by declaring for Lady Jane Grey: a rash tactic which ultimately cost the lady her head as well.

On the subject of the macabre, there is a gnarled old tree close to one of the paths which is avoided even by the birds. It exudes an air of brooding malevolence and the park-keepers say that at certain times of year disembodied voices and muted laughter can be heard emanating from the trunk.

In 1820 the life of the Duke of Wellington was inadvertently saved by Lord Fitzroy Somerset in the Green Park. Unknown to him, while he was strolling home to Apsley House from his desk at the Ordnance Office, his footsteps were being dogged by one of the Cato Street conspirators who was waiting for a chance to stab him in the back. Happily, the appearance of Somerset persuaded the man to

Algernon Charles Swinburne, poet and master of invective, who often took a stroll in Green Park

retire and before another attempt could be made the plot was uncovered and the conspirators arrested.

It was the second time that Somerset had come between Wellington and almost certain death. At Waterloo the two men had been riding so close together that the ball which shattered Lord Fitzroy's arm might, had it missed him, have killed his companion. The arm had to be amputated. As it was being taken from the surgeon's tent, Fitzroy shouted: Hallo! don't carry away that arm until I've taken off my ring.' The ring in question was his wedding-band, the gift of his wife, the Duke of Wellington's niece.

Green Park also has an association with Swinburne, who sometimes came here with Edmund Gosse. On one occasion the two men fell to discussing Emerson, who had severely criticised Swinburne's *Poems and Ballads*. The poet's two letters of remonstrance having gone unanswered, Gosse – knowing the little man's tendency to invective – said: 'I hope you said nothing rash?' Swinburne said he had not. He had been the very soul of reasonableness. 'I merely wrote: "You are a wrinkled and toothless baboon who, first hoisting into notoriety on the shoulders of Carlyle, now spits and splutters from a filthier platform of your own finding and founding."'

6

Parliament Square to Trafalgar Square

In former days, Parliament Square was known as Thorney Island, a swamp-infested area not fully developed until the building of Westminster Bridge in the middle of the eighteenth century. It was laid out in its present form by Sir Charles Barry in the 1840s as a pendant to his new Houses of Parliament which stands to the east.

In the central garden plot are statues to a number of politicians, the most recent being Ivor Robert-Jones' figure of Sir Winston Churchill, leaning in bull-dog-like aggression towards the House of Commons. Another politician on the lean is General Smuts, by Epstein. The figure appears almost to be skating and viewed from the ground the features seem distorted. This is because Epstein executed the work at eye-level, never imagining that it would be displayed on a pedestal.

Jan Smuts was a highly proficient exponent of guerrilla warfare and during the Boer War is said to have had an unusual encounter with Churchill, who had been sent out to South Africa as the war-correspondent of a London newspaper. Captured in an ambush, he was taken before Smuts for adjudication. As he was not in uniform, there was some talk of shooting him as a spy. Against the advice of his superior, Smuts vetoed the proposal. Had he not, the only statue in the Square today might well be Hitler's.

Nearby, and looking across the square is Thomas Woolner's excellent bronze statue of Viscount Palmerston, a wilful but highly competent Foreign Secretary and Prime Minister. The figure has been called: 'The Best-Dressed Statue in London,' and Mr Desmond Macarthy has said it ought to be

'The Best Dressed Statue in London': Lord Palmerston
in Parliament Square

'an object of pilgrimage to all tailors in England'.

On the western side of the Square is a statue to Abraham
Lincoln, unveiled in 1920 by a man with the unlikely name of

Elihu Root. The gift of the American people, it is a copy of a
statue in Lincoln Park, Chicago. (Osbert Sitwell felt we
might suitably revenge ourselves on the American people by
sending some surplus-to-requirements statue of Queen Victoria for erection in Lincoln Park.) On Good Friday 1865,
Lincoln was assassinated by a disaffected actor, John Wilkes
Booth. He had fully intended staying home on the day in
question but his wife insisting on going to the theatre, he
said: 'All right, Mary, I'll go, but if I don't go down in history
as the Martyr President I miss my guess.'

Crossing to the southern side of Parliament Square we
come to the ancient church of St Margaret's, Westminster,
dedicated to St Margaret of Antioch, a virgin-martyr who
suffered many extravagant ordeals – including being swallowed alive by the Devil disguised as a dragon – before being
ultimately beheaded. The churchyard which surrounds it,
covered now by bland and anonymous paving-stones, was a
menacing and noisome place, especially after dark. Theo-
dore Hook often used to pass through it at that hour and
claimed regularly to have encountered a ghost lingering in
the porch. Disbelieving him, one of his friends dressed up in
a sheet and hid in the porch to scare him. When Hook came
by he stared for a moment and said: 'So, there are two of you
tonight, are there?' and walked on.

Taking the path which runs due west from St Margaret's,
we come to the great west door of Westminster Abbey. A
little in front of it is a large column, a memorial to the boys
of Westminster School who gave their lives in the Indian
Mutiny and the Crimean War. It stands on the site of the old
Gate House prison which existed here for three hundred
years. Sir Walter Raleigh spent his last night on earth here;
and thirty years later Sir Richard Lovelace composed in the
Gate House 'To Althea From Prison', a poem which contains
the lines:

> Stone walls do not a prison make,
> Nor iron bars a cage;

> Minds innocent and quiet take,
> That for an hermitage.

Although there has been a church on the site of Westminster Abbey since 616, the present structure has suffered a great deal of reform. It is essentially Early English in style and is said to have several ghosts. One of these occasionally materialises near the Grave of the Unknown Warrior. Capless, his khaki uniform stained with mud, he stands in an attitude of prayer, head bowed, hands clasped in front of him. He pays no attention to the crowds but with unseeing eyes walks a short distance, hands outstretched in supplication, before suddenly vanishing.

An older ghost, but one not seen since 1934, is Father Benedictus, a fourteenth-century monk brutally slain by thieves who robbed the King's Treasury here in 1303. They showed no mercy and received none themselves. After they had been flayed alive, their skins were nailed to a door as a warning to others. Minute particles of skin may still be seen beneath the studs of the door.

The robed figure of Father Benedictus, tall and lean, hook-nosed and thin-mouthed, usually manifested between 5 and 6 p.m. On a few occasions he remained visible for as long as thirty minutes. He is said to have held short conversations but mostly chose to wander about, staring very contemptuously at the tourists. Predictably pale, he walked a little above the ground – at the level on which the floor existed before the contemptible tourists wore it down – and most people had no idea that the self-possessed gentleman with the sad brown eyes was anything but flesh and blood until he made a spectacular exit through the masonry.

The Abbey has come to take a surprisingly liberal attitude to suicide and in 1822 Viscount Castlereagh was interred here after cutting his throat with his pocket-knife. The eccentric historical painter, Benjamin Robert Haydon, was convinced that the mental disorder which led to this was induced by eating 'hot buttered toast, to a healthy stomach indigestible, to a diseased one ruin. His servant the last morning brought it to him ignorantly; Lord Castlereagh ate heartily of it; his brain filled with more blood, he became insane, and cut the cartoid artery.'

A more likely cause was a nervous disorder aggravated by overwork. A quarter of a century later Haydon also cut his throat, although there is no record of his having eaten hot-buttered toast on the morning in question.

Proceeding up the short flight of steps at the eastern end of the Abbey we come to the Chapel of Henry VII. Beneath it is a crypt containing, among others, the last remains of Frederick, Prince of Wales, the father of George III. Perhaps unjustly, he was detested by his relations and when his mother wished that she could like him better, his youngest sister retorted: 'Pray, mama, do not throw away your wishes on what cannot happen, but wish that he may die and that we may all go about with smiling faces and glad hearts – and of course crêpe and hoods.' In 1751 Frederick duly obliged. He was killed by a tennis-ball which burst an abscess. When the news was carried to court, his father, George II, hardly troubled to look up from his game of cards and his epitaph was left to the wits:

> Here lies poor Fred
> Who was alive and is dead.
> There's no more to be said.

Another of George II's children interred here is Princess Amelia. The day prior to the funeral, an old historian, observing that the vault had been opened for an hour or so to dispel some of the mustiness, obtained permission to go down and make a copy of an inscription on one of the coffins. Delighted at this stroke of good fortune, he lost all account of time and when he decided to return to the land of the living he found that the vault had been closed. He was forced to spend the night staring at shelf upon shelf of royal coffins and was extricated the next morning half-dead with shock.

Retracing our steps, we come to the bridge leading to the Chapel of Edward the Confessor. The rather plain-looking tomb which rests on it belongs to Henry V. The wooden effigy was once surmounted by a head of silver, but this was stolen, probably at the Reformation. The present head dates from 1971 and is made of plastic.

The embalmed remains of Henry's wife, Queen Katharine of Valois, were originally interred in the Lady Chapel. When that was demolished her open coffin was unceremoniously dumped by the tomb of her husband and forgotten. Here it

David Garrick, in the role of Richard III, as depicted by Hogarth. He is buried in Poet's Corner, Westminster Abbey

remained for close to three hundred years, the bones 'firmly united and thinly closed with flesh, like scrapings of tanned leather', attracting a great number of morbid sightseers. One of these was Samuel Pepys, who noted in his diary: 'and here we did see, by particular favor, the body of Queen Katharine of Valois; and I had the upper part of her body in my hands, and I did kiss her mouth, reflecting upon it that I did kiss a queen, and that this was my birthday, thirty-six years old, that I did kiss a queen.'

South-east of the spot where this little drama would have been played out is the Lady Margaret Chapel and the ostentatious tomb of Mary, Queen of Scots. The vault beneath contains numerous coffins, jumbled one on top of the other in what has been called 'a chaos of royal mortality'. All Queen Anne's seventeen children lie here, including the only one to live beyond infancy, William, Duke of Gloucester, who expired in 1700 at the age of eleven from 'excessive dancing on his birthday'.

In Poets' Corner the statue of Shakespeare, looking like a 'sentimental dandy', stands close to a cluster of important graves, the first being that of David Garrick who on the morning of his interment, in January 1779, was carried to his last resting place by six Peers of the Realm. It has been said that as the van of his funeral procession began filing into the Abbey the tail was still forming up in the hallway of his house in the Adelphi.

One of the mourners at Garrick's funeral was Dr Johnson. Five years later he was laid to rest beside him. Towards the end of his life, the great sage had been 'disturbed with terror at the prospect of the grave' and he left a curious exhortation that 'if my executors think it proper to mark the spot of my interment by a stone, let it be so placed as to protect my body from injury'.

On the western side of the transept is the grave of Sir William Davenant, the poet and playwright who lost his nose to the pox. A sometime manager of the Theatre Royal, Drury Lane, he spent his childhood at a tavern run by his parents on the London to Stratford road; and as the inn was sometimes patronised by Shakespeare, was fond of telling people that he was the product of an illicit union between the Bard and his mother. In 1638, after a far from friendly contest with Tom May, Davenant was appointed Poet Laureate. During the Civil Wars, this and other disappointments led May to enlist with the Parliamentary forces. He survived the conflict only to die a year later from having 'tied his nightcap too close under his fat chin, which choked him when he turned on the other side.' His Puritan masters interred him here, but on Charles II's return he was unceremoniously evicted. Eighteen years later, the man who had deprived him of the Laureateship also usurped his grave.

In 1928 the ashes of Thomas Hardy were buried at Davenant's feet. The novelist had wanted a humble interment at Stinsford, his birthplace and the village depicted in his books as 'Mellstock'; but those who order these things decreed that he should to go the Abbey. Only his heart was buried at Stinsford – and perhaps not even that. There is a story that on the morning of the ceremony his sister absent-mindedly left the open casket on the kitchen table and that the contents were consumed by Hardy's cat.

Almost the last object to note in the Abbey is the monument to the poet and dramatist, William Congreve, erected shortly after his death in 1729. It was paid for by his close friend, Henrietta, Duchess of Marlborough. On his death, Congreve left Henrietta seven thousand pounds with which to buy a diamond necklace; while she, for her part, commissioned two small figures of the playwright. The first was an automaton with which she held long 'conversations'; and the second, made of ivory, was a faithful replica of the man, even down to the blisters on his feet. These Henrietta ordered her physicians to bathe, as in life they had bathed the real ones.

In front of Congreve's monument lies the actress, Nan Oldfield. She died the year after Congreve, aged forty-seven. Because she left orders that she was to be interred in her best clothes, the name 'Nancy' has since become a derogatory epithet applied to any over-dressed person. Her funeral was presided over by Dr Parker who remarked, a shade ambiguously, that he had officiated 'very willingly and with much satisfaction'.

In the Abbey cloisters is a monument to the first female novelist, 'Incomparable Atrea', Aphra Behn, whose first career was as a government spy working in the Low Countries. It is said that it was she who appraised Charles II of the Dutch plan to sail up the Thames and sack London. Unfortunately, this idea struck the King as so preposterous that he was still chortling when the enemy's top-masts hove in sight.

The monumental figure of Daniel Pulteney, at the southeast corner of the cloisters, is said on moonlit nights to turn a page of his stone book as the clock strikes twelve; and nearby, in the Little Cloister – an enclosed square with a fountain at the centre – is a memorial to Thomas Smith, who died in 1664. The quaint inscription records that 'through the spotted veil of the small pox' he 'render'd a pure and unspotted soul to God'.

On the eastern side of Parliament Square is the New Palace of Westminster, better known as the Houses of Parliament. The edifice is nine hundred feet long and incorporates nine hundred statues, including those of every monarch from William the Conqueror to Queen Victoria. It took twelve years to build and was completed in 1852. It has two miles of corridors, approximately a thousand rooms and a hundred staircases. One of the architects associated with its building was Augustus Welby Pugin who died insane in the year it was completed.

In St Stephen's Hall, beyond the Porch, is a statue to Lord Falkland, minus one of its stone spurs. It was broken off in 1908 by a suffragette. She bound herself to his Lordship with chains and had to be removed by force. The Palace is no stranger to violence and the two red lines which in the Commons divide the government benches from those of the main party of opposition are a reminder of this. They were drawn, at a width slightly in excess of two extended sword-lengths, for the purpose of containing quarrels. They did not always succeed. In 1809 Lord Castlereagh (of the hot buttered toast) fought a duel with George Canning over government policy; and the Duke of Wellington fought another with the Earl of Winchilsea. Lord Erskine also felt it necessary to prosecute his case by force of arms; and in 1798 William Pitt the Younger fought a duel with the Whig politician, George Tierney. As Pitt was extremely thin and his opponent extremely stout, some humorist suggested that Pitt's outline should be chalked on Tierney's front and that any perforations outside that area should be deemed not to count.

At the north-west corner of the Palace is the Albert Tower, housing 'Big Ben'. It has been endlessly copied and there is even a replica atop a monastery in Peru. The four dials stand two hundred feet above ground level and a double-decker bus could be driven with ease through any one of them. The minute-spaces are a foot square, the numerals two feet high. The hands are fastened to the centre of the dials by gilt roses the size of small dining-tables.

The mechanism which drives the clock is smaller than might be expected. It was made by Dent's of Pall Mall who, for many years, sent an employee to the House twice a week to wind it. The driving mechanism took twenty minutes to prime; but the spring operating the chimes, five hours.

The clock keeps excellent time, losing less than a tenth of a second a day. It has never been more than four seconds slow and at one time adjustments were made by adding to or subtracting from a small stock of coins lodged in a tray affixed to the pendulum. Apart from a recent overhaul, it has only stopped twice – once when an MP who was explaining the function of the mechanism to a party of visitors inadvertently allowed his umbrella to become entangled in it. The hour bell, 'Big Ben' – a name frequently misapplied to the tower itself – is usually said to have been named in honour of Sir Benjamin Hall, the then Commissioner of Works. It may, in fact, commemorate the popular Victorian prize-fighter,

Ben Caunt, who at the age of forty-two fought a contest lasting sixty rounds which ended in a draw.

About 1867, London's first traffic-lights were installed at the north-east corner of New Palace Yard. Fifty years ahead of their time, they were powered by gas and operated by a policeman. On 2 January 1869 they exploded, seriously injuring the officer on duty.

On the south side of New Palace Yard is Westminster Hall, dating in part from 1099. Its outstanding feature is a superb hammer-beam roof, completed three hundred years later from six hundred and sixty tons of Sussex oak. There is a long-standing misconception that the wood was imported from Ireland, in consequence of which, said Fuller, 'no English spider *webbeth or breedeth to this day*'. Many of the beams have necessarily been replaced. That many remain was illustrated in 1923 when carpenters carrying out repairs to the rafters came across several tennis balls dating from the time of Henry VIII.

As plain 'Charles Stuart', Charles I was arraigned for treason in Westminster Hall in 1649. It was a nervous business, not least because he refused to plead, arguing that it was a contradiction in terms to accuse a king of treason. For this, and other reasons, many of his sympathisers chose to absent themselves. When Lord Fairfax's name was called, his wife cried out: 'He hath too much wit to be here.' She continued at regular intervals to heckle the court from the gallery and the President, John Bradshaw, eventually instructed the troopers lining the walls that if she spoke again they were to shoot her where she sat. There was no question that he meant it. When Lady Anna de Lisle called the judges 'traitors and rebels' she was dragged into the centre of the Hall where her dress was roughly pulled down and her shoulder and forehead branded with a hot iron. Bradshaw eventually grew so agitated at these persistent outbursts that he took to coming to court in a bullet-proof hat.

Although, after Charles's execution, his greatest enemy was installed as Lord Protector in Westminster Hall, the king would have been the first to appreciate that 'nothing mortal endures and there is nothing sweet which does not end in bitterness'. Soon after Charles II sat down to his coronation banquet in the Hall, Cromwell's embalmed body was roughly disinterred from its resting place in Westminster Abbey and his head was placed on a spike above the Hall on the twelfth anniversary of Charles I's funeral. It remained there for almost a quarter of a century. Blowing down in 1685, it was appropriated by one of the sentries and is now in the possession of the Protector's Suffolk descendants who keep it in a box almost as ancient as the head itself.

In recent times it has been the custom for monarchs to lie in state in Westminster Hall. In three days in May 1910 more than half a million people came to pay homage here to Edward VII; and during four days in January 1936, 809,182 mourners filed past the bier of his son, George V. (The record attendance for a lying-in-state, however is claimed by Moscow which estimates that in 1953 more than five million people descended on the Kremlin to view the body of Joseph Stalin. A mathematician has pointed out, however, that this would only have been possible in the time alleged if the mourners had been marshalled into two columns each passing the catafalque at a speed of twenty-two miles an hour.)

Old Palace Yard, now an anonymous parking lot to the south of Westminster Hall, was formerly the courtyard of the old Palace of Westminster. Here King Canute is thought to have lived and here in January 1066 died Edward the Confessor. Some five hundred years later, Guy Fawkes suffered for his complicity in the Gunpowder Plot; and in 1618 Sir Walter Raleigh also went to his death here, running his finger along the blade of the axe and pronouncing it 'a sharp and fair medicine to cure all my diseases'. He refused a blindfold saying, 'think you I fear the shadow of the axe when I fear not the axe itself?' When an over-zealous official complained that he was facing the wrong way, he said: 'What matter how the head lie so that the heart be right?' His torso was buried in St Margaret's, Westminster, close to the altar. His head was preserved by his widow in a red velvet bag which she never let out of her sight until her own death, thirty years later, at the age of eighty-two.

Parliament Street, to the north, forms the southerly section of a wide thoroughfare linking Parliament and Trafalgar Squares. In the centre of the road, opposite Richmond Terrace Mews, and marking the boundary with Whitehall, is Sir Edwin Lutyens' Cenotaph, a memorial to the dead of two world wars. The name derives from the Greek and means a hollow tomb. Although it appears very angular, it boasts not a single straight line, being composed of a series of almost imperceptible curves which, if carried high and low enough, would meet nearly a thousand feet away from their starting points. At one time it was traditional for men passing the Cenotaph to remove their hats. Today, most people hardly spare it a glance. It seems that in the words of Ralph Waldo Emerson: 'Every hero becomes a bore at last.'

Whitehall, which extends north from the Cenotaph, takes its name from the old Palace of Whitehall, once the London residence of the kings of England. On the western side of the way is Horseguards, the finest remaining example of Palladian architecture in central London. In 1901 the arch which stands at its centre was the subject of a curious precognitive dream. The office of the Master of the Horse was invested at that date in the Duke of Portland who was busy arranging the coronation procession of Edward VII. He dreamed one night that as the coronation coach passed through the arch at Horseguards the crown surmounting it became firmly wedged against the roof. The dream was so vivid that the Duke decided to measure both arch and coach. In doing so he discovered that at some time during the sixty-four years which had elapsed since the previous coronation the road beneath the arch had been raised; and but for his dream, the coach would have come to grief exactly as predicted.

Historically, the most important building in Whitehall is the Banqueting House, designed by Inigo Jones for just 8s 4d (41½p.) a day. In all probability, Charles I was executed on a scaffold situated somewhere beneath the second front-facing window of the Banqueting House in 1649; but the exact site is a matter of dispute. As Benjamin Disraeli once said: 'Never ask who wrote *The Letters of Junius*, or on which side of Whitehall Charles I was beheaded. For if you do you will be certain to be considered a bore.'

At number 37 Whitehall is the Old Shades public house. The distinctive red triangle above its door is the emblem of the brewing company, Bass Charrington, and the first symbol ever to be registered as a trade-mark. When these were first introduced, in 1875, one of the company clerks sat up all night on the steps of the Registry to ensure being first in line in the morning.

Close to the Old Shades stands a statue to Spencer Compton, eighth Duke of Devonshire, known to his friends as 'Harty-Tarty'. Blessed according to Mr Gladstone with 'an infinite capacity for taking pains', 'Harty-Tarty' was an able rather than an outstanding politician. His gravest fault was a blind adherence to Dr Johnson's famous precept of seldom thinking 'with more earnestness of anything than he did of his dinner'. He so hated foreign food that in Paris, half way through an elaborate banquet, spying a joint of roast beef approaching the table, he shouted: 'Hurrah! Something to eat at last.' The incident was indelibly imprinted upon his memory and he was able to recall it without difficulty twenty years later.

Of all Whitehall's tributaries, the most famous is Downing Street, for two hundred years the official residence of the Prime Minister. Embodying the very finest traditions of honest English statescraft, it commemorates a man who was neither honest nor English. Sir George Downing was an Irish-born place-seeker, the son of a lawyer, who was taken to America at the age of fifteen, where he became only the second man to graduate from Harvard University. In 1643 he returned to England and enlisted under the Parliamentary banner. At the cessation of hostilities, Cromwell appointed him Ambassador to the Hague where he wormed his way into the good graces of the exiled Charles II with such skill that when the monarchy was restored he not only retained his office but was granted a barony.

Sir George was greatly disliked by his colleagues, however, who saw in him the epitome of the corrupt and ambitious courtier. In America his name became synonymous with treachery, the phrase 'a regular George Downing', having passed into the language as a term to describe any person suspected of double-dealing. Samuel Pepys worked for Downing for a time but found him so 'perfidious a rogue' and 'so stingy a fellow I care not to see him; I quite cleared myself of his office and did give him liberty to take anybody in'.

Conceived as England's memorial to her greatest sailor, Trafalgar Square, at the far end of Whitehall, was constructed between 1829 and 1841. Its centrepiece is Nelson's Column, one hundred and sixty-seven feet tall. The statue of Lord Nelson, which extends the height by a further seventeen feet, weighs sixteen tons and is the work of Edward Hodges Baily who in 1844 designed the Ascot Gold Cup. Twelve days before the statue was erected, fourteen stonemasons dined on top of the column in a 'topping-out' ceremony – a bean-feast traditionally given by employers to their workmen at the conclusion of any large-scale project.

At its corners, the Column is watched over by four bronze lions, sometimes known as 'the postman's friend'. The Post Office regularly receives crank letters addressed to 'Lord Nelson, Trafalgar Square', but as its staff are not required to risk life and limb in the course of their deliveries, these are usually returned, marked: 'Unable to deliver. Four large lions guarding.'

The statue of Sir Henry Havelock, at the south-east angle of the Square, is unique in that it was the first to be executed entirely from photographs. The sculptor was William Behnes, the son of a Hanoverian piano-maker. In 1861, the year he completed it, he was made bankrupt and lost everything. Three years later, he died, having been found 'one night literally in the gutter with threepence in his pocket, somewhere close to the Middlesex Hospital'.

The site of the statue was formerly occupied by the Golden Cross, a busy and bustling coaching-inn frequently mentioned by Dickens. David Copperfield stayed here in a room which 'smelt like a hackney carriage and was shut up like a family vault'; and it was from here that the Pickwick Club set out on its journeyings. Here, also, Mr Jingle related the tragical incident of the coach hurling out through the arch:

'Terrible place – dangerous work – other day – five children – mother – tall lady – eating sandwiches – forgot the arch – crash – knock – children look round – mother's head off – sandwich in her hand – no mouth to put it in – head of a family off – shocking, shocking!'

To the right of the Havelock statue is a hollow granite pillar, one of the curiosities of London and a truly vintage piece of 'secret' history. A door has now been installed but at one time the only clue to its purpose was a number of fissures, rather like castle arrow-slits, set into its sides. Sometime in the late nineteenth century it was set up as a secret observation post and used by the police to monitor the marches and demonstrations which have always congregated here. Just sufficiently large to hold one policeman, it had a hand-cranked telephone bracketed to the wall for summoning reinforcements from nearby Scotland Yard if matters looked like getting out of hand (see the frontispiece).

At the foot of the north parapet can be found the Board of Trade's Imperial Standards of Length, a series of bronze strips embedded in granite. The manner in which measurement derived is uncertain, although in the Middle Ages an inch was said to be the breadth of the average thumb. Henry I decreed that a yard was the exact distance from the tip of his nose to the tip of his outstretched index finger.

On the grassy knoll which laps the eastern wing of the National Gallery is Grinling Gibbons' bronze statue of James II. Perhaps because all the other statues hereabouts have their backs to him, he gives the impression of being still in disgrace.

James succeeded to the throne in 1685, on the death of his brother, Charles II. He at once renewed the persecution of the Covenanters and introduced highly unpopular – and illegal – taxes. In July of that same year he crushed the rebellion of the Duke of Monmouth with unparalleled ferocity. All these things, together with his determination to re-establish Catholicism as the predominant religion, led in 1688 to his deposition by his son-in-law and daughter, William and Mary. When it was clear that all was lost, James slipped quietly away to France. A few days later his usurping daughter arrived at the Palace of Whitehall and was seen to run from room to room, callously bouncing up and down with unconcealed glee on each of the beds in turn.

In France, James was sympathetically received by the Catholic Louis XIV and granted a pension. Apart from one maladroit attempt to regain his throne, he remained there for the rest of his life, dying at St Germain in September 1701. His embalmed body was left for ninety-two years in the custody of the English Benedictines at Paris. The monks kept it in the hearse in which it had arrived against the day when the political and religious climate would allow it to be returned to England and interred in Westminster Abbey. That day never came. At the French Revolution the peasants broke up the hearse and requisitioned the lead coffin for bullets. A witness of these events was an English prisoner by the name of Fitz-Simon:

The body lay exposed a whole day. It was swaddled like a mummy, bound tight with garters. The corpse was beautiful and perfect; the hair and nails were very fine. I moved and bent every finger: I never saw so fine a set of teeth in my life. A young lady, a fellow prisoner, wished much to have a tooth; I tried to get one out for her, but could not, they were so firmly fixed. The feet also were very beautiful. The face and cheeks were just as if he were alive. I rolled his eyes, and the eye-balls were perfectly firm under my fingers. Money was given to the sans-culottes for showing the body. They said he was a good sans-culotte and that they were going to put him in a hole in the churchyard.

Although Robespierre did issue some such instruction, James was not finally buried until a hundred and twelve years after his death. In 1813 he was interred at St Germain by order of the Prince Regent, afterwards George IV.

Strangely, of all the statues in Trafalgar Square the one to George IV stands closer to James' than any other. It is a poor work, sculpted after the Roman fashion neither with stirrups nor a saddle. But then George was himself something of a poor work. He was known to his comtemporaries as 'The First Gentleman of Europe', a title which Mackworth Praed felt he debased:

> A noble nasty course he ran,
> Suberbly filthy and fastidious,
> He was the world's first gentleman
> And made that appellation hideous.

Throughout his reign, George subsisted in a permanent state of guilt. Thwarted by excessive appetites and an unstable character from living up to his own ideals of kingship, he proved an undutiful son, a faithless husband and an uncaring father. He drowned his inadequacies in drink, the after-affects of which he attempted to counteract by massive blood-letting, often opening the vein himself. Sustained by the love of a good and sensible woman, things might have been different – but to Caroline of Brunswick, the bride selected for him by his father, he took an immediate and obdurate dislike. He encouraged his courtiers to humiliate her; and the marriage service, at which Caroline wore a beaver hat and too much make-up, was conducted with 'the Prince looking like death'. At one point he made as though to

Lady Jersey (2nd l.) dancing the first quadrille at Almack's. Lady Jersey was mistress to George IV whose statue stands in Trafalgar Square

flee. He was only prevented from doing so by his father, George III, who left his pew and put a restraining hand upon his shoulder. At the wedding-breakfast, his mistress, Lady Jersey, sprinkled Epsom salts on the bride's food while George looked on, sniggering behind his hand.

Although the couple soon separated, Lady Jersey never ceased from tormenting her young rival and abused her behind her back in the most malicious fashion. To her face she professed friendship, cleverly reducing her to an object of ridicule by persuading her to dress in a ludicrous manner on the grounds that it would revive the interest of her indifferent husband.

Much given to sudden outbursts of emotion, George regularly wept on the shoulders of his advisers and once even dared to kiss the cheek of the Duke of Wellington. On receiving the news of his accession, he retired to pray and is said to have repeated the Lord's Prayer one hundred and ten times.

At the north-eastern corner of Trafalgar Square is the church of St Martin's-in-the-Fields (1726). The most influential and attractive work of the Scottish architect, James

Gibbs, it has been widely copied and Westminster Council yearly pays a sum to the parish for the repair and upkeep of the steps, worn away by the people who come to admire it.

The great Elizabethan philosopher, Sir Francis Bacon, was baptised in the church which formerly stood on this site. One morning 65 years later, he was driving in Highgate, pondering the problem of how to preserve flesh after death, when, in Pond Square, he spotted a chicken. Climbing from his carriage he rang the bird's neck and stuffed the carcass with snow. The experiment was a success: but as a result of it Bacon contracted a fatal chill and died the following month. It might be expected that if any one shade were to linger in Pond Square it would be his: but the chicken it is that haunts. Large and white, featherless and friendless, it has been seen on numerous occasions either perched in the branches of the trees or running around in circles, frenziedly beating its wings and clucking. In recent years the sightings have grown both less common and distinct – and it may be that after three centuries the poor fowl's sense of outrage has at last begun to abate.

Among the host of eminent people who have found a place in the church or the churchyard of St Martin's may be mentioned: Rose, Charles II's gardener, who is usually credited with having introduced the pineapple into England; the furniture-maker, Thomas Chippendale; Nell Gwynne; and George Farquhar, author of *The Beaux Stratagem* – a play which would certainly have made his fortune had he written it anywhere but on his deathbed.

Before we leave the Square we should spare a thought for the pigeons which congregate here in their thousands. Although they are not by nature adventurous creatures and most of them live and die within a mile of their birthplace, they have adapted to city life very well. A few have even learned to utilise the underground, using their mysterious talent for navigation to find their way down even to the deepest and least accessible tunnels. They ride the trains taking as much notice of the people as the people take of each other. They seldom travel more than one stop, but why they should choose to ride at all is a mystery: they are certainly not lazy birds. The Duke of Wellington once owned a carrier-pigeon which flew five thousand miles – and dropped dead from exhaustion just one mile from home.

[7]

St James's

Although its inhabitants would probably deny it, the area of St James's remains a timeless bastion of male chauvinism. Within a short compass here one can acquire mellow cigars, fine wines, monogrammed silk shirts, hand-made shoes, beautifully-cut suits, ludicrously expensive guns and rare works of art.

The epitome of this grand old style of living was the fourth Duke of Queensberry, known to his intimates as 'Old Q'. He was enormously rich and once built a house in Arlington Street – the westernmost boundary of St James's – for the sole purpose of ogling a lady who lived opposite. He loved women and recharged his libido by eating hot-buttered muffins while soaking in a bath of almond-scented asses' milk – and by inhaling the breath of dairy maids.

The dukedom might never have come to 'Old Q' had one of his relatives not forfeited the title by reason of insanity. According to Augustus Hare the relative was exceptionally violent and had to be kept under permanent lock and key. One day, in 1707, the door was left ajar and he escaped. A hasty search of the house and grounds producing no trace of him, all but one of the servants were sent off to scour the streets of Edinburgh. The one left behind decided to repair to the kitchen for a glass of beer. There he found his 'master' sitting quietly in front of the range, spit-roasting the pot-boy.

Bennett Street, which joins Arlington Street on its eastern side, commemorates Henry Bennett, Earl of Arlington. In 1706 the co-founder of *The Spectator*, Sir Richard Steele, was living here. He was lucky in love – meeting his second wife at the funeral of his first – but hopeless with money. Dr

Johnson once dined with him in Bennett Street and was surprised at the number of liveried servants hovering around the table. When he asked his host how he could possibly afford to maintain such a train of domestics, Steele said 'that they were bailiffs who had introduced themselves with an execution'. Reasoning that he 'could not send them away' he had 'thought it convenient to embellish them with liveries that they might do him credit while they stayed'. The other guests found this so amusing that they dug into their pockets and paid Steele's debt on the spot.

Ryder Street, a turning to the east out of St James's Street, commemorates Captain Richard Ryder, a royal master-carpenter, who was involved in the street's initial construction in 1674. At number 9 is the Eccentric Club, chiefly remarkable for a bar clock which works in reverse, a cunning device which has caused many a new member to miss his train. Notices stating that 'Ties Will Be Worn At All Times' have a tendency to be left leaning against oil-paintings of voluptuous nudes.

Just further south-west is St James's Place, a quiet little back-water memorable for having once been the home of William Huskisson, the politician. He lived at number 28. Osbert Sitwell described Huskisson as: 'unequalled in nonentity . . . a nonentity to which Providence added, as a decoration, a ruthless flower of the grotesque . . . since it killed him in the presence of his mortal enemy, the Duke of Wellington'. Intent on making up his quarrel with the Duke, Huskisson was run down by Stephenson's 'Rocket' while rushing across the line at the opening of the Liverpool and Manchester Railway in 1830. Ironically, he had always been a champion of the railways and a prime mover of the Enabling Act which had helped to further their increase. His career was studded with calamity and he was probably accident-prone. During his honeymoon a horse fell on him.

At the southern end of St James's Street is St James's Palace. It stands on the site of a twelfth-century hospital

founded for the upkeep – and of course detention – of
fourteen 'leprous maidens'. They lie buried in one of the
inner courtyards where their graves, marked by small
crosses, can still be seen. In the second quarter of the
sixteenth century, Henry VIII coerced the landlords, Eton
College, into exchanging the hospital for land of a lesser
value in Suffolk. He replaced the old building with a
magnificent palace for himself and Anne Boleyn.

An unusually grisly spectre said to haunt the Palace is the
ghost of a man called Sellis, the valet of Ernest Augustus,
Duke of Cumberland, who maintained apartments here. A
bucolic man, violent and short of temper, the Duke was the
fifth son of George III. In 1810 he is said to have involved
himself in an affair with Sellis' daughter. When she discovered that she was pregnant, the girl killed herself. Shortly
afterwards, as he was passing through one of the darkened
State Apartments on his way to bed, the Duke was struck
down from behind. Within the hour, Sellis was discovered
on his cot with his throat cut. The affair became the talk of
the court. One faction believed Sellis was a blackmailer who
was killed to prevent his master's exposure – the incident
then being made to look like a quarrel ending in suicide. In
all probability the attack was authentic and motivated by
revenge. The Duke was struck so ferociously that the blow
exposed a part of his brain and it is unlikely that he would
have inflicted such a wound upon himself, even for the
purposes of credibility. Overcome by fear of the consequences, Sellis then ran to his own room and took his life. His
ghost is said to manifest in the room in which he died, the
head, which was almost severed from the body, lolling
against the headboard at a grotesque angle.

Another violent episode in the Palace's history took place
outside the Gate House, on the evening of Tuesday 6 December 1670, when, as the clock struck six, the infamous Colonel
Blood attempted to kidnap the Duke of Ormond. Ormond
had dispossessed his rival of certain Irish estates, compound-
ing the offence by acting harshly towards some of Blood's

kin. With the Colonel at its head, a gang of mounted cut-throats manhandled the Duke from his carriage and roped him to the largest man available. They then galloped off in the direction of Tyburn, where they proposed to hang him. Fortunately, his servants were able to raise the alarm in time and the Duke was saved. Nine years later he died and was succeeded by his grandson, a very stoical man, who lived to be eighty-one. In 1746, realising that his last hour had come, the second Duke turned to the gentleman next to him, a stranger, and said: 'Excuse me, sir, if I make some grimaces in your presence, but my physician tells me that I am at the point of death.' With equal civility the stranger replied; 'Do not, I beg you, sir, put yourself under any constraint on my account.'

Number 3 St James's Street is occupied by Berry Brothers and Rudd, one of the oldest wine-merchants in London. The firm was founded here in 1696. Inside the shop is an old set of scales, a reminder of the days when condiments were sold here. In three hundred years they have weighed about thirty thousand customers, including Lord Byron, Beau Brummell and 'Fighting' Fitzgerald. On the day that Fitzgerald came here one of his acquaintances popped his head in at the door and remarked: 'I smell the blood of an Irishman.' Fitzgerald leapt out of the scales, drew his sword and cut off the man's nose, remarking: 'I'll be damned if you'll ever smell another.'

A familiar figure around St James's, 'Fighting' Fitzgerald was a psychopath who drank copious draughts of his own blood in the belief that it would prolong his life by a thousand years. In his youth he kidnapped his brother and once imprisoned his father in a cave with a wild bear. At least some of his madness may have been inherited, because his uncle, the Bishop of Derry, appears to have had no wits at all. On a visit to Italy he insisted on peering into an erupting volcano, sustaining injuries which killed him. His body was brought home for burial in a small ship. In order to conceal from a superstitious crew that he had a corpse on board, the captain packed the Bishop in a crate which he labelled 'Antique Statue'.

The fine eighteenth-century shop at number 6 St James's Street houses Lock's, the hatters, who in 1850 gave the world the bowler hat, named after the employee who designed it. It was commissioned by a hunting man named Coke who wanted a practical sort of hat which would not come off when he jumped fences. When Mr Bowler handed it to him, he placed it on the floor and jumped on it. Apparently satisfied with the result, he jammed it on his head and left the shop without uttering a word. Another of Lock's stocks-in-trade was the top hat, first introduced into London in 1797 by a man named James Heatherington. It caused such a consternation that Heatherington was arrested and fined £50 for going about in a manner 'calculated to frighten timid people'. Class-distinction being what it is, only parvenus still call it a top hat. The middle-classes refer to it as a 'silk hat'; a gentleman asks for a 'topper'.

Once 'the Common Rendezvous of infamous Sharpers and noble Cullies', White's, at numbers 37–38 St James's Street, is the oldest of all London clubs. It was founded in 1693, removing to its present site forty years later. It was then a notorious gambling 'hell' and it was said that the members would rather have left a passer-by who had collapsed in front of their windows to his fate than risk voiding the bets they had laid on his recovery. One member, Lord Alvanley, bet three thousand pounds on two drops of rain running down a window – and was enraged when the bet was nullified by their merger. Another staked himself to remain under water for twelve hours. (He lost.) Lord Mountford hazarded twenty guineas with Sir John Bland that 'Beau' Nash would outlive Colley Cibber and would certainly have won had not both he and Sir John committed suicide before the matter could be resolved. Perhaps the strangest of all the Club's bets, however, concerned an enthusiastic golfer named Milbanke who challenged any member to drive a golf-ball from a designated spot in the City to the steps of the Club in less than

White's of St James's Street, once notorious for its gambling as seen here in a scene from Hogarth's *Rake's Progress*

two thousand strokes. The challenge was accepted and the 'round' completed one thousand eight hundred and thirteen strokes under 'par'. Yet another curious bet involved flighting a saucer in through one of the windows of the Devonshire Club, then situated on the opposite side of the road.

All this, of course, was as nothing to the real gaming that went on at White's. Lord Masham once lost three thousand pounds at hazard here in three hours; and in 1755 another member lost £32,000 at the tables in one evening. Play invariably continued until very late and when a new member remarked on the lights having been kept burning all night, an old-campaigner replied: 'They have not been out, I should think, since the reign of Charles II'. The Club is a strong bastion of the Tory party and when the socialist politician, Aneurin Bevan – who had previously classified all Tories as 'Lower than vermin' – dined here in 1950 he had his bottom kicked. The culprit later resigned.

At the spot where St James's Street junctions with Piccadilly, Hoby's, the royal bootmakers, once had their shop. Mr Hoby was 'a pompous fellow with a considerable vein of sarcastic humour'. When a young Guards ensign by the name of Horace Churchill complained 'that his boots were so ill-made that he should never employ Hoby for the future', the proprietor, 'putting on a pathetic cast of countenance called to his shopman, "John, close the shutters. It is all over with us. Ensign Churchill withdraws his custom . . ."' Gronow says that 'Hoby was tolerated as a sort of privileged person and his impertinence was not only overlooked, but was considered as rather a good joke.' He believed that he was at least partly responsible for the success of the Duke of Wellington and used often to say: 'My boots and prayers bring his Lordship out of all his difficulties.'

In 1827 a fish merchant from Temple Bar, William Crockford, came to St James's Street and founded yet another club. The gambling at Crockford's was almost as deep as at White's, and by the time its owner died, in 1844, he was a millionaire. Unfortunately, his departure proved very inconvenient in certain quarters and on the day of his death his corpse had to be propped up for several hours in a chair positioned before a first-floor window of the Club in order to maintain confidence in one of his horses which would have been withdrawn from an important race if his death had become known prior to 'the off'.

At number 60 St James's Street is Brooks's Club, long composed of 'the first men for rank and talent in England'. The food, however, has sometimes left a little to be desired; and Sir Edwin Lutyens was so non-plussed by the fare that on one occasion he had to ask the waiter what he was eating. 'Piece of cod,' he was told. 'Indeed', said the architect, 'which passeth all understanding'. The composer, Sir Edward Elgar, often used to telephone his Worcestershire home from Brooks's just to hear the sound of his barking dog.

A short distance from Brooks's are the offices of Chubb and Sons, locksmiths. The company was founded in 1817 by a Portsea ironmonger, Jeremiah Chubb, who in that year

William Crockford, 'Keeper of Hell Gaming House', St James's Street, a portrait by Thomas Rowlandson

devised a burglar-proof lock. He was so confident that it could not be picked that he arranged for it to be given to a London burglar lying in one of the prison-hulks off Portsmouth. The convict was provided with all the necessary tools and promised £100 and a free pardon if he could open it. After nearly three months he had to confess himself beaten.

To the west of St James's Street is Stable Yard, once the location of Harrington House, the home of the Stanhopes. Gronow records that the Stanhopes were much given to the 'sempiternal occupation of tea-drinking'. It seems to have been less an occupation than an obsession. When General Lincoln Stanhope 'made his reappearance at Harrington House . . . after an absence of several years in India . . . and found the family as he had left them at his departure, drinking tea in the long gallery . . . his father's only speech of welcome to him was, "Hallo, Linky, my dear boy, delighted to see you. Have a cup of tea?"'

Lord Petersham, the great dandy who gave his name to a type of silk ribbon and overcoat, popularised the wearing of cossack trousers and owned a different snuff-box for every day of the year, lived at Harrington House. Gronow records that; 'I heard him, on the occasion of a delightful old light-blue Sevres box he was using being admired, say, in his lisping way – "Yes, it is a nice summer box, but would not do for winter wear."' He was greatly devoted to the colour brown which was apparently 'caused by his having been desperately in love with a very beautiful widow of that name. In addition to his other eccentricities he never ventured out of doors until 6 p.m.'

Set into the garden wall of Marlborough House, a little to the east of Stable Yard in Marlborough Road, is the National Memorial to Queen Alexandra, perhaps the finest work of its kind in London. It was executed by Sir Alfred Gilbert who also designed the statue known as 'Eros' in Piccadilly. Queen Alexandra was the wife of Edward VII and despite her husband's many faults they remained happily married for forty-seven years. If Alexandra had a fault it was her notorious unpunctuality. It was a source of constant distress and embarrassment to Edward and he might easily have said, as Sir William Eden once did: 'I have been married twenty-five years and I have spent five of them waiting on the doorstep for my wife.' The negotiations for her marriage to Edward were conducted with a protracted cryptic stealth typical of British statesmanship at that time; and this almost psychotic furtiveness greatly irritated Alexandra. It was subsequently to irritate her brother, who remained entirely unaware that the British were lobbying to obtain the throne of Greece for him until he chanced to read of it in a newspaper containing his sardine sandwiches.

In the opening years of the nineteenth century, Pall Mall, at the top of Marlborough Road, became the first London Street to be lit by gas – although at first even the great Sir Humphry Davy ridiculed the idea. 'It would be as easy to bring down a bit of the moon to light London,' said he, 'as to hope to do so by gas'. Laymen too were cautious and for a while no one dared touch the lamp-posts for fear of being burned.

For the last sixteen years of her life Nell Gwynne was a resident of Pall Mall. Her house stood on the site of what is now number 79 and she was often to be seen leaning over her garden wall, chatting with her royal lover, Charles II, as he strolled with his dogs in the park. Nell had at least one child by Charles, a boy, who in all probability was conceived in Pall Mall in a fabulous bed of solid silver which cost a thousand pounds and stood in the centre of a room lined entirely with mirrors. After the birth of her son, Nell came close to estranging the King by her attempts to secure a title for him. Normally very indulgent, on this Charles would not give way. In frustration, Nell is said to have grasped the child by his ankles, dangled him out of the window and threatened to let him drop. Charles passed a weary hand across his brow and said: 'So be it. Pray, spare the Earl of Burford.'

Next door to Nell Gwynne's former home is Pall Mall's oldest building, Schomberg House, parts of which date back

Nell Gwynne, mistress of Charles II, whose home at 79 Pall Mall contained a solid silver bed. Portrait by Sir Peter Lely

to 1698. About 1765 the house was divided into three by the first of its many strange inhabitants, John Astley. Being poor, Astley seldom moved very far from home but one day, receiving an invitation to a fashionable dinner which he could not decline, he made himself as presentable as possible and set out. Unfortunately, the room in which the meal was served proved impossibly hot and all but Astley removed their coats. The other gentlemen were at first too polite to notice this oversight. But as the room grew warmer and Astley's discomfort more acute, they began to chaff him. At this the artist gave in and laughingly removed his jacket – to reveal an old and tattered waistcoat held together at the back by a vivid canvas gusset which had formerly hung in his studio as 'A Country Scene with Waterfall'. Happily, he later married money and never wanted for waistcoats again.

Having quarrelled with Thicknesse, his patron, Thomas Gainsborough came to live in one of the sections of Schomberg House in 1774. He was then forty-seven years old and entering upon the last and greatest phase of his career. His superb portrait of Sarah Siddons (1785) was painted at Schomberg House, although by all accounts it caused him considerable difficulty. When Reynolds had painted Mrs Siddons he had signed his work with a flourish, saying: 'Madam, my name will go down to posterity on the hem of your garment.' The irascible Gainsborough could only grate: 'Madam, is there no end to your nose?'

In the year that Gainsborough was at work on that portrait, the third section of Schomberg House was leased to the notorious 'Doctor' Graham who kept body and soul together by charging barren couples a hundred pounds a night for the privilege of sleeping in his 'Magnetic Celestial Bed'. This 'Wonderful Aid to Fertility' consisted of a thirteen-hundred-weight slab of magnetic iron overlaid by a mattress stuffed with the hair of stallions. It was surmounted by a heavy canopy supported by forty glass pillars. Each pillar was adorned by a gilded nymph, music emanating from the mouth. A real-life nymph briefly employed by 'Doctor' Graham at Schomberg House was the fifteen-year-old Emily Hart. Part of her job entailed impersonating the 'Goddess of Health' and flitting through the various apartments in diaphanous robes. Emma, as she was known, later married Sir William Hamilton and in time became the mistress of Lord Nelson.

Sarah Siddons, painted by Thomas Gainsborough at his studio in
Schomberg House, Pall Mall

The Travellers' Club, at the spiritual heart of Pall Mall,
has a rule that members must have travelled at least five
hundred miles from London in a straight line; a rule now
rendered meaningless by modern air travel. It also has a
tradition of blackballing candidates and Thackeray, Cecil
Rhodes, Sir Edwin Landseer and Lord Randolph Churchill
were all treated in this way on first applying. In spite of this,
the quality of membership often left a great deal to be

desired. One man reported the Committee to the Inland Revenue for failing to affix postage-stamps to its receipts; and another blew his brains out in the billiard-room. When this calamity was reported to the Steward, he said: 'I'll take damn good care to see the fellow never gets into any other club I have anything to do with.' Soon after his accession, a portrait of Edward VIII was hung in a corridor of the Travellers'. On the morning of the day he announced his decision to abdicate, it was found lying face-down on the floor. The porter who discovered it had been on duty throughout the night and insisted that it could not have been placed there by any human agency.

Members of the Athenaeum – the club which stands on the corner with Waterloo Place – are elected for their intellectual achievements, which may explain why the telephone cubicle was at one time said to be covered with more graffitti than any other in London. The series of vast marble caverns which comprise the public rooms are greatly admired but uncomfortable, cold and sterile. Although he was not a member, F. E. Smith was in the habit of popping into the Athenaeum to use the lavatory. One day he was taken aside by a porter who informed him that the Athenaeum was a private club and that in theory he was trespassing. 'I see,' said F.E., feigning surprise, 'it's a club *as well*, is it?'

Carlton Gardens, which leads out of Pall Mall to the south was once the 'residence' of the newspaper tycoon, Lord Northcliffe. In August 1922 he died in a wooden shack on top of number 1, a house then owned by the Duke of Devonshire. At the time of his death he was fifty-seven, but looked seventy. His illness had been officially reported as a 'disordered appendix', but in fact he was mad. Just before he died, his mind befuddled by drugs, he staggered from his bed and telephoned the editor of one of his newspapers. 'There is a story going the rounds', said he, 'that I am off my head. I hope we are covering it.'

Carlton Gardens has been the home of several well-known men, some of them weighty, some of them, like Sir Alfred

Bossom, little more than the tinder which serves to ignite the spark of other men's wit. When Sir Alfred was first introduced to the House of Commons, Churchill was heard to rumble: 'Bossom? Bossom? What manner of name is that? It is neither one thing nor the other.'

For a quarter of a century, number 11 Carlton House Terrace, which extends eastwards from Carlton Gardens, was the home of the Liberal statesman, W. E. Gladstone. His wife was a rather squirrel-like woman who cultivated squirrel-like instincts. Lady Augusta Fane remembers that: 'At a supper party the hostess was somewhat astonished at the hurried exit Mrs Gladstone had made. Only afterwards was it discovered that she had stuffed several ham sandwiches into the ample bosom of her dress, and that they had contained a great deal of mustard.' Mr Gladstone also disliked waste. It was his custom to fill his stone hot-water bottle with tea. As he slept on average only four hours a night it was usually still hot enough to drink in the morning.

A little to the north of Carlton House Terrace is Waterloo Place. Number 12b was once the home of Sir William Eden Bart. (the father of the Conservative prime minister, Sir Anthony Eden), who firmly believed that he was the plaything of unseen forces whose sole purpose was to render him ridiculous. One exceptionally rainy morning he came downstairs to breakfast and paused to tap the barometer in the hall. It was forecasting sunshine. When it refused to change its mind Sir William gathered it in his arms, walked to the front door and flung it down the steps, muttering: 'Go and see for yourself, you damned fool.'

Walking northwards from Waterloo Place and taking the first turning on the left we come to St James's Square, originally called 'the Piazza'. The equestrian statue of William III which stands in the enclosed garden at the centre is very fine. The curious mound incorporated into the plinth is the famous mole-hill over which Sorrell stumbled in 1702 giving the King a fall from which he died. The Jacobites were always very grateful to the mole for this and used to drink a toast each year, on the anniversary of William's death, to 'the gentleman in black velvet'.

In nearby King Street are the premises of the fine-art auctioneers, Messrs Christie's. Ambrose Bierce once defined an auctioneer as 'A Man who proclaims with a Hammer that he has picked a Pocket with his Tongue.' Yet undoubtedly the smoothest-tongued resident of King Street was the swindler, Horatio Bottomley. During the First World War he had a flat on the site of what is now St James's House. In a long career his pseudo-patriotic enterprises and bogus companies netted Bottomley more than a million pounds. He possessed an almost hypnotic degree of persuasiveness and at least one choleric gentleman, calling here to horse-whip him, stayed to invest even larger sums in his schemes, some of which, such as the 'Nil Desperandum Mine Company', should not have fooled a child. 'H.B.' was not entirely heartless, however, and could usually be depended upon to help a fellow rogue. When he heard that the sleeping-car attendant on a train he sometimes used had been sent to prison, he detailed someone to send his wife some money. It transpired that the man had been jailed for bigamy. 'What a hero!' chortled 'H.B.' 'In that case better send both his wives some money.' In 1922 Bottomley's frauds caught up with him and he was himself sent to prison, for seven years. One morning he was working on a mailbag outside his cell in Wormwood Scrubs when the Governor passed on his rounds. He was accompanied by a man who had known the swindler in balmier days. The man nodded and said: 'Morning, Bottomley. Sewing I see.' 'No', replied 'H.B.', 'Reaping.'

Jermyn Street, which is linked to King Street by Bury Street, was once the residence of the truant Mr Howe. In 1706, having announced his intention of going on a trip to Holland, he disappeared for seventeen years. In fact he only moved as far as Westminster and on Sundays walked to St James's church to look on his wife unobserved. When she moved away from Jermyn Street he contrived to get himself invited to the house opposite her new residence in order to watch her entertaining. Without ever giving any explanation for his absence he returned to the bosom of his family in 1723 and left it no more.

From 1675 to 1681 the great Duke of Marlborough lived in a house on the site now occupied by the royal shirt-makers, Turnbull and Asser; and it was during this period that he married the beautiful Sarah Jennings. Sarah was a wilful and quarrelsome woman who alienated everybody with whom she came in contact. She blacked out the portrait of a relative and wrote underneath: 'Her heart is blacker'; and when her grandson, Jack Spencer, reached marriageable age she furnished him with a list of prospective brides. His choice fell on Lady Ann Carteret. As soon as the couple returned from their honeymoon, Sarah read them a lecture on the subject of respect. 'Well, now', said she, 'I am the root and you are only the branches and therefore you must always pay me a great deal of deference.' Jack retorted: 'That is all very well – but I think the branches would flourish a great deal better if the root was under ground.'

As might be expected, the Haymarket, at the eastern end of Jermyn Street, takes its name from a market for hay and cattle which operated here from about the year of the Great Plague. At the southern end of the street is the Haymarket Theatre, built by John Nash in 1820. The fine portico is seen to best advantage from the perspective of Charles II Street. It was beneath this portico that the librettist, W. S. Gilbert, was approached one night by a red-faced gentleman who, mistaking him for a porter, said: 'Call me a cab.' 'Very well', said Gilbert, 'you're a four-wheeler.' 'What the devil do you mean, sir?' spluttered the gentleman. 'Well,' said Gilbert, wrapping his cloak about him and climbing into his own carriage, 'you asked me to call you a cab. But I could never call you hansom.'

Many famous men have been associated with the theatre on this and the adjoining site. One manager, Charles Macklin, lived to be almost a hundred (a feat which he attributed to his habit of strip-washing in brandy); while his successor, Samuel Foote, kept upon his desk a bust of the great David Garrick. He told visitors that he would not normally have allowed the avaricious actor to stand 'so near my gold; – but you will observe he has no hands.' The best-loved of all the theatre's actor-managers, however, was Sir Herbert Beer-bohm Tree. Walking down the Haymarket one morning, he was stopped by Oscar Wilde who praised the red-silk lining of Tree's top-hat. Sir Herbert said: 'As you admire it so much I see I must give it you.' Wilde was overcome – until Tree ripped the lining from the hat, deposited it in the startled playwright's hands, and hurried on his way.

In 1897 Tree took the enormous profits realised by his production of *Trilby* and built Her Majesty's theatre, on the other side of the street. He topped it with a huge copper dome and beneath this established his private apartments. Here he gave regular dinner parties, known as 'Sir Herbert Tree's At Domes'. The guest of honour at one of these was the volatile tenor, Giovanni Grasso. At the conclusion of the festivities, Grasso insisted on embracing each of his fellow diners at least three times. Tree was bidding his guests farewell outside the theatre when, without a word, the little Sicilian disappeared inside again. In a confidential aside, Tree said: 'He has forgotten to kiss the fireman'.

Sir Herbert had few interests outside his work, but his desire to save seconds often led him to squander hours. There is a story that one afternoon – before he was estranged from his family and took up permanent residence in the dome – he left Her Majesty's with his nose buried in his correspondence, climbed into a cab and muttered: 'Take me home.' When the driver said: 'Where's that, guv?' Sir Herbert looked up briefly and snapped: 'Do you really suppose that I would give my address to the likes of you?' (He had in fact rather assumed that the man would recognise him – and everyone knew where Sir Herbert lived.) At his destination, and still reading, Tree climbed out and rang the front door bell. When the maid appeared, he murmured: 'Come in', turned on his heel, climbed again into the cab and said: 'Take me to the theatre.'

Occupying the lion's share of the Haymarket frontage of St Alban's House is the American fast-food restaurant, McDonalds. The company was founded in Chicago in 1955. Since then it has retailed more than twenty billion hamburgers. It believes in a thorough training programme for its employees and the Haymarket branch can boast several B.H.'s: Bachelors of Hamburgerology.

During the Victorian era the Haymarket was a notorious centre of prostitution, vast numbers of females thronging the streets, many of them little more than children. Prices were low because supply far exceeded demand. There were at least ten thousand freelance members of the 'linen-lifting tribe' walking the streets; and in 1845 some four thousand brothels operated in central London alone, then a much smaller area than it is today.

Working to a very different tariff, the grand courtesans of the Stuart era used to drive in their carriages down the Haymarket; and in 1681 Nell Gwynne's coach was attacked here by an angry mob which mistook her for the King's French mistress, the universally-detested Louise de Kéroualle. Good-humoured as ever, Nell struck her pretty head out of the window and cried: 'Do not stone me, good people – I am the *Protestant* whore.'

8

The Thames, the Temple
and the Victoria Embankment

Sometimes called 'the spine of London', the river Thames has played a great part in the capital's history. In 1603 the body of Queen Elizabeth was borne up the Thames from Richmond for burial in Westminster Abbey. And convicts began their long journey to Botany Bay from here. (The parapet beyond Chelsea still bears the sheen imparted by their bottoms as they sat in chains waiting to be loaded aboard the transport ships.) In 1805 Lord Nelson's remains were brought up the Thames from Greenwich; and prior to his burial at Bladon in Oxfordshire Sir Winston Churchill was carried by way of the river to his funeral service in St Paul's.

Although 'Old Q' thought the Thames a bit of a bore – 'What is there to make so much fuss of,' said he, 'I am quite weary of it; there it goes, flow, flow, flow, always the same' – its waters are constantly changing. It is a tidal river with more than seven hundred ebbings and flowings each year. Indeed, dynasties topple and kings come and go, but the Thames, it seems, goes on for ever. James II was reminded of this early in his reign when he requested a loan from the City Aldermen. Being refused it, he threatened to remove the court from London to Windsor. The Lord Mayor replied: 'Your Majesty hath power to do what you please, and your City of London will obey accordingly; but she humbly desires that when Your Majesty shall remove your Court, you would please to leave the Thames behind you.'

During this period, the river was still teeming with life. In the fifteenth century two whales had been sighted in the Pool of London; and in the year of James II's deposition (1688) another managed to swim up as far as Greenwich where, said John Evelyn, it expired 'after a horrid groan'. The winters were so cold that the waters often froze over. Eagles' talons froze to the backs of their prey; and an out-of-town barber, up on a spree, who fell in to the river drunk, was found next morning not drowned, but bobbing along upright, stiff as a board, having frozen to death.

We begin our journey at Westminster Bridge, today one of the major routes into London from the south. It was erected in 1863. Strangely, the opening ceremony took place at a quarter to four on the morning of the 24 May, the precise hour of Queen Victoria's birth. A twenty-five gun salute was fired, the number of years of her reign.

The old bridge, which stood on, this site from 1750, had several literary associations. In 1781 the poet, George Crabbe, came close to throwing himself off it; Boswell boasted of having made love on it; and Wordsworth was so inspired by the view from it that he wrote 'Upon Westminster Bridge', a sonnet which begins with the line 'Earth hath not anything to show more fair.' Timbs records that old Westminster Bridge was built of 'about 42 percent of magnesian limestone' – and that a Dr Ryan, realising that carbonate of magnesia is a compound of purgative medicines, once pointed out that in the unlikely event of it being 'covered with water and sulphuric acid, it would be converted into Epsom Salts'.

At the western end of Westminster Bridge is a statue to Boadicea, a first century warrior-queen of the Iceni tribe. She and her daughters appear frozen in perpetual flight from the ladies' toilet behind them. After the death of her husband, King Brasutagus, their little East-Anglian kingdom was overrun by the Romans. Boadicea's two daughters were brutally raped. The Queen was spared this indignity. Unlike her rather romanticised statue, she was a fat, harsh-featured matron with a raucous voice and a bush of wild knee-length hair.

On her release from captivity, Boadicea rallied her forces

and sacked Colchester, London and St Albans, leaving in her wake seventy thousand Roman dead. The Governor of Britain, Suetonius Paulinus, eventually crushed the rebellion by playing upon her essential stupidity and ignorance of military tactics. When the two armies met, the Iceni were overwhelmingly defeated, their dead outnumbering those of the Romans by two hundred to one. Boadicea and her daughters promptly swallowed poison. She lies buried somewhere under Platform 10 at Kings Cross station.

To the east of Westminster Bridge is the Victoria Embankment, a curving four-lane highway which follows the northern bank of the Thames for a mile and a quarter from Westminster Pier to Blackfriars Bridge. It cost one and a quarter million pounds and was built on forty acres of marshland reclaimed from the river. In all, the work took six years and the avenue was officially opened by Queen Victoria in 1870. Her rather drab widows'-weeds provided a distinct contrast to the finery of some of the other dignitaries; and when the wife of the Archbishop of Canterbury swept up in her liveried carriage, one of the bystanders shouted: ''Ullo! 'Ere comes the Queen's cook!'

Opposite Westminster Pier, on the south side of the river and resting on a concrete 'raft' five feet thick, is County Hall, a large Renaissance-style building housing the administrative offices of the Greater London Council. It has four miles of corridors and nine hundred rooms. The Clerks' Department, with nine miles of steel shelving, is a bureaucrat's dream. The site itself is known as 'Pedlar's Acre', supposedly after an old pedlar who was sheltering one day from a storm in the lea of the nearby church of St Mary's, Lambeth, when he was joined by a priest who persuaded him to walk in and join the congregation. The pedlar later prospered and invested his money in land. On his death he left 'Pedlar's Acre' to the church in recognition of the unexpected kindness and fellowship he had met with there.

Walking east, we come to Hungerford Bridge. A little beyond it is a curious stone obelisk known as 'Cleopatra's

Needle', fashioned about 1454 B.C. and indisputably the oldest monument in London. Although it was presented in 1819 to George IV as a Coronation gift by the Egyptian Viceroy, it did not arrive in England until George had been dead for forty-seven years. The delay was largely due to a series of international disputes. When these were resolved, in 1876, a buoyant cylinder was constructed to contain the obelisk; but in the Bay of Biscay, the little craft entrusted with the task of towing it to England ran in to a dreadful storm and six of the crew perished before its load could be cut adrift. It was eventually recovered and erected here in 1878. At that date two earthenware jars were sealed into the base. They contained among other things a case of cigars, various coins, a portrait of Queen Victoria, Bradshaw's railway-guide, an Arabic translation of the Book of Genesis, and the photographs of six of the most beautiful women in England.

The area immediately surrounding the Needle is said to be haunted. Late at night a shadowy figure is sometimes seen standing on the parapet. After a period of indecision it casts itself off, but vanishes before it can hit the water below.

On the far side of the river at this point is the arts-complex known as the South Bank. Constructed after the Festival of Britain in 1951, it was recently voted by a panel of eminent architects 'the worst development in London'. In the same style, a little to the east, is the National Theatre, sometimes known as 'The Tomb of the Unknown Actor'.

Connecting the Victoria Embankment to Trafalgar Square is Northumberland Avenue. It stands on the site formerly occupied by Northumberland House, the last of several great mansions which once graced the foreshore of the Strand. The first Duke of Northumberland was Hugh Smithson, a proud man whom Dr Johnson thought 'fit only to succeed himself'. He had the misfortune to marry a fat, bearded and impressionable lady who died of an overdose of auto-suggestion in the very year that her husband was created a duke. Being told one day by a fortune-teller that she would die exactly sixty years from the hour of her birth, the Duchess so allowed the prediction to play upon her mind that on the appointed day she bid all her friends farewell and retired to bed. That evening, hearing the clock strike six, she muttered: 'Then I have still two hours to live'. She died, exactly as predicted, on the stroke of eight o'clock. Hugh Smithson survived her by ten years. One of his illegitimate off-spring, James Smithson, later made a life for himself in the United States, where he founded the Smithsonian Institute.

In 1874 Northumberland House was demolished and its three million bricks and four hundred tons of lead were sold at auction for less than six thousand pounds. The Glass Drawing Room was re-assembled in the Victoria and Albert Museum, where it may still be seen. The fireplaces, the cornices and the doors were all packed into crates and

The glass drawing-room from Northumberland House which stood on the site of Northumberland Avenue

removed to the family's other London home, Syon House, Isleworth, where they lay forgotten for seventy-four years.

Running west out of Northumberland Avenue is Great Scotland Yard, so called from the London palace of the Scottish kings which once occupied the site. In the summer of 1829 the Metropolitan Police established their first home in Whitehall Place and as their premises abutted on to Scotland Yard the name became in time indelibly associated with the building.

The character of that original police force, which consisted of six hundred men, left a great deal to be desired. On the first day of duty six constables had to be discharged for drunkenness. During the last century both the army and the fire brigade had premises in Great Scotland Yard; and the former used to bribe the police and firemen to stage mock battles in front of the Army Enlistment Office. The young men who came to watch were then persuaded to step inside and join up.

At the southern end of Northumberland Street, which connects Northumberland Avenue to the Strand, is the Sherlock Holmes public house. The building was formerly the Northumberland Hotel and it was here that Sir Henry Baskerville put up when he came to London to consult the great detective in Conan Doyle's story *The Hound of the Baskervilles*. Although it tends to become very crowded, the pub is well worth a visit. There is an interesting collection of Holmesian curiosa in the bar: and diners in the first-floor restaurant can gaze through a glass partition at an ingenious, if fusty, reconstruction of Holmes' sitting-room at 221b Baker Street.

Although the case is now long forgotten, in the summer of 1861 number 16 Northumberland Street was the scene of a crime which would certainly have intrigued Holmes. The first act in the drama was played out at Hungerford Bridge where, as he stepped ashore from a steamer, a Major Murray was accosted by a complete stranger, a lawyer named Roberts. Roberts excused the intrusion by claiming to have some important business to discuss. The subject he raised seemed plausible and, as he insisted that the matter was urgent, Major Murray accompanied him to his chambers on the first floor of number 16. Although everything was covered with a thick layer of dust, the rooms were beautifully, even lavishly, furnished.

As Major Murray waited with an air of polite enquiry, Roberts produced a revolver and shot him. The Major collapsed on the floor, wounded in the neck. Roberts, noticing that he was still breathing, stepped over and shot him again, in the head. Satisfied that he was now dead, he turned away. As he did so, the Major somehow stumbled to his feet and hit him with a poker. A dreadful struggle ensued which, inspite of his wounds, the Major eventually won.

Staggering to the window, he threw up the sash and called

The Hound of the Baskervilles in the Sherlock Holmes pub, Northumberland Avenue

for help. When there was no response he jumped twenty feet into an area-way, all but impaling himself on a set of railings. The alarm was raised and both men were taken to hospital. Roberts died there shortly afterwards. Before he did so he told a curious story. Apart from his legal practice (he said) he also carried on a small trade as a money-lender. Murray had approached him for a loan. On being turned down he had flown into a rage, attacked him and then attempted to take his own life.

The truth was even more melodramatic. Outwardly the epitome of Victorian respectability, a good father and a gentle husband, Murray had for some years been keeping a mistress, a girl named Anne. Having got herself into financial difficulties, Anne approached a money-lender who lent her £15. The money-lender, of course, was Roberts. He developed an uncontrollable passion for Anne who, unable to meet the repayments, was forced into a clandestine affair with him. When Roberts learned of the existence of his rival he became insanely jealous and resolved to kill him.

Some months after his terrifying ordeal, Major Murray was tried for murder. The jury returned a verdict of 'justifiable homicide'. He eventually recovered from his appalling injuries and lived to be nearly ninety.

Craven Street, which runs parallel to Northumberland Street, is named after the first Earl Craven, soldier and banker to Charles I. With the exception, perhaps, of the third Earl – who was such a valued customer of the tobacconists, Carreras, that they named the 'Craven A' brand of cigarettes after him – none of his descendants achieved anything much of note. The street would certainly have been well known to Dickens, however, because it was a grotesque door-knocker here which suggested the idea for confronting Scrooge with the spectre of Old Marley's face in a door-knocker in *A Christmas Carol*. When the story achieved widespread popularity, the householder, realising its worth, had it removed to a bank vault. Sadly, it has since disappeared.

On the eastern side of Charing Cross Station is Villiers Street, named after George Villiers, Duke of Buckingham, whose mansion once stood on this site. When it was sold and demolished in 1672 a special clause was inserted into the agreement requiring that each of the streets which replaced it should in some way perpetuate his name and title. George Court, Villiers Street, Duke Street and Buckingham Street were the result. The proviso was so scrupulously observed that at one time there was even an 'Of Alley'.

From 1889 to 1891, Rudyard Kipling had his first London home at number 43 Villiers Street, now Kipling House. Here he wrote his first full-length novel *The Light That Failed* – dubbed by the critics *The Book That Failed*. In 1890, at the time of its publication, he was twenty-five years old; and having spent almost all of those years in India his sojourn in Villiers Street was bleak and friendless. A fierce little man with a fondness for black Indian cheroots, he occupied his time, when not writing, in pacing his fifth-floor apartment clad only in a dressing-gown of Japanese silk. In his autobiography he recalled: 'Once I faced the reflection of my own face in the jet-black mirror of the window-panes for five days. When the fog thinned, I looked out and saw a man standing opposite the pub where the barmaid lived; on a sudden his breast turned dull red like a robin's and he crumpled, having cut his throat.'

Kipling would have been used to solitude; his childhood had been miserably lonely. Years later he recalled it in *Baa-Baa Black Sheep*, the tale of a brother and sister farmed out to foster parents. At one point the boy is rendered so miserable that he attempts to kill himself by sucking his lead-painted soldiers.

Turning left down John Adam Street and taking the first turning on the right, we come to Buckingham Street. Occupied in part by the British Olympic Association, number 12 is a very old house indeed. The diarist, Samuel Pepys, lodged here for nine years as a guest of his servant, the trusty Will Hewer; and it was probably a happy time for him, because in

1953 the tenant encountered his ghost in the hall. As she descended the stairs she noticed him standing near the front door, more or less recognisably himself, smiling, but somewhat blurred at the edges. As is the way with these things, she had passed into the street before the full implication of what she had seen could register. By the time she recovered herself – and the hall – the apparition had vanished.

Samuel Pepys is said never to have taken a bath in his life; and another resident of Villiers Street with an equal antipathy to soap and water was Sir Humphry Davy, who occupied the basement of number 14. Obsessed by his work, he seldom ventured out or even wasted time changing shirts, preferring to slip a clean one over the old. When the number reached five he stripped off and began again. In 1829 he died – some said of 'eating too freely of pike'. By a curious circumstance, his old home was recently taken over by The Consumers' Association and *The Good Food Guide*.

To the north of John Adam Street is Durham House Street, a modest little cul-de-sac recalling the eleventh-century residence of the Bishops of Durham. In 1540 Henry VIII held a banquet at Durham House to celebrate his short-lived marriage to 'The Flanders Mare', Anne of Cleves; and thirteen years later Lady Jane Grey was married here to Lord Guildford Dudley. From 1584 until the accession of James I nineteen years later, the mansion was leased to Sir Walter Raleigh. According to tradition, it was while he was living here that a servant saw him smoking a pipe and drenched him with a jug of ale, thinking him on fire. Wrong on this occasion, the servant was right in principle because Durham House did eventually burn down.

A little to the south is Robert Street, once the home of George Bernard Shaw. He lived opposite J. M. Barrie, author of *Peter Pan*, and habitually threw biscuits or cherry-stones at his study window when he wished to attract his attention.

On 20 January 1779 'the most versatile actor in the history

of the British stage', David Garrick, died at his house in nearby Adelphi Terrace. At that date he had been married for thirty years to the Viennese dancer, Eva Marie Violetti. Mrs Garrick lived on at Adelphi Terrace for a further forty-three years, 'a little bowed-down old woman, who went about leaning on a gold-headed cane, dressed in deep mourning, and always talking of her dear Davy.' She died in 1822, in her ninety-ninth year, scolding a maid who had thoughtlessly handed her a cup of tea. 'Put it down, hussy!' she said. 'Do you think I cannot help myself?' Her coffin was draped with her wedding sheets 'which', a servant told a visitor who came to the house to pay his last respects, 'both Mr and Mrs Garrick wished to have died in.' She was laid to rest beside her husband in Westminster Abbey.

Savoy Place, to the south of Adelphi Terrace, was at one time unique for possessing the only green-painted telephone kiosk in London. At that date all the others were painted red. In 1928, when the licence was first granted, the ground landlords, the Institute of Electrical Engineers, insisted that it should be painted to match the green railings in front of their own premises. The railings were melted down for armaments during the Second World War and now only the kiosk survives.

North east of Savoy Place is the Savoy Chapel, a rather grimy stone box situated on the western side of Savoy Street. A private chapel, with the smallest parish in London, it owes allegiance only to the ground landlord. In 1753 when the Marriages Act put an end to the dubious marriages which had formerly been celebrated in the Fleet Prison, the Chaplain, John Wilkinson, invoked the tradition of the Savoy's independence to carry on the trade here. He was so successful that in the space of a year he married over fifteen hundred couples and earned himself almost £2,000. When the authorities decide to prosecute and sent the Watch to arrest him, he dashed from the Chapel, discarding his surplice in flight. He was eventually condemned to fourteen years' transportation, but died of the gout before the sentence could be implemented. Most of the 'marriages' at which he officiated were later ruled invalid.

One of the first people to be buried in the Savoy Chapel was the poet, George Wither, a fanatical Puritan who, at the outbreak of the Civil War, sold everything he owned to raise a troop of horse for Parliament. Captured near Farnham Castle by the Royalists, he was sentenced to be hanged and would certainly have done so had not another soldier-poet, Sir John Denham, interceded with the King, saying: 'So long as Wither lives I will not be accounted the worst poet in England.'

One of several tombstones which until quite recently were stacked against the railings of the Chapel commemorated a former parishioner named Jane Eyre. By a curious coincidence she died in 1847, the year in which Charlotte Brontë produced her novel of that name.

A little beyond the eastern boundary of Somerset house we come to the Temple, a name used to describe both the Inner and the Middle Temple, two of the great Inns of Court. The site was originally occupied by the Knights Templar, an order of military crusaders whose members wore white tunics and were expected to attend divine service at least three times a day. Talking was severely frowned upon and all but the direst need had to be made known by means of sign-language. No inmate was permitted to be alone for any length of time and in order that each might act as a watch-dog to the other, they usually slept in pairs.

At the beginning of the fourteenth century, when it was rumoured that the Templars' Christian beliefs had been replaced by those of Islam and that the members worshipped cats and spat on the crucifix, the order was disbanded. A few years later their home was taken over by the lawyers, who have retained it ever since. It remains private property and could in theory be closed to the public at any time.

Today, the entrance to the Temple lies by way of Middle Temple Lane. It is a rather sinister thoroughfare, especially at dusk, when from time to time the shade of a long-dead barrister is seen striding towards the Strand Gate, a bundle of papers under his arm and his gown flying out behind him. The figure may be the ghost of James Saward, known to his cronies in the underworld as 'Jim the Penman'. Saward was something of a criminal genius, who, finding that his income from the law was insufficient to pay for his extravagances, turned to forgery. In a fifteen-year career this, together with his activities as a receiver of stolen goods, netted him more than a million pounds. He might have survived into respectable old age had he not at some point met an American criminal named Edward Agar. Together they planned an audacious train robbery. Unfortunately, one of their accomplices confessed. Saward was unmasked and sentenced to transportation for life.

For a time the poet, William Cowper, lived off Middle Temple Lane, in the now demolished Fig Tree Court; and here he attempted to take his life. According to *Old and New London*: 'An approaching appointment to the clerkship of the Journals of the House of Lords overwhelmed him with nervous fears. Dreading to appear in public he resolved to destroy himself. He purchased laudanum then threw it away. He picked up his portmanteau to go to France and enter a monastery. He went down to the Euston House Quay to throw himself into the river. He tried to stab himself.' When all this failed he attempted to commit suicide in Fig Tree Court by suspending himself with a garter from the back of his lodging door. The garter broke.

An equally troubled soul who lodged in the Temple for a while was Richard Porson. He was immensely strong and once carried a girl about his chambers in his teeth. Unfortunately, he had a fatal weakness for drink. One evening he persuaded a friend to search his wife's apartment, saying: 'I am quite certain that Mrs Hoppner keeps some nice bottle for her private drinking in her bedroom.' Very much to the husband's surprise, a bottle was unearthed which Porson drank, pronouncing it to be excellent gin. The wife coming to hear of this, put her hands to her face and said: 'Gin? My

God, it was spirits for the lamp.' On another occasion, as
Porson was sitting up with a sick friend, a servant put his
head round the door looking for a bottle of embrocation.
Porson said: 'I drank it an hour ago.' In spite of these epic
drinking bouts, Porson seems never to have lost his wits.
When an enemy rebuked him by saying: 'Dr Porson, my
opinon of you is most contemptible,' he replied: 'Sir, I never
knew an opinion of yours that was not contemptible.'

In 1874, the year he met Florence Ricardo, Charles Bravo
was living at number 1 Essex Court, Temple. Mrs Ricardo
was then a widow, Mr Ricardo having died three years
previously of what was officially described as delirium tremens. Her husband was no sooner buried than Florence
formed an attachment to Dr Gully, the physician who had
treated him in his last illness. Being relatively well-off she
also employed an Anglo-Indian woman by the name of Cox as
her companion.

By the time Florence met Charles Bravo her attachment to
Dr Gully had begun to cool. Charles, who may possibly have
been a fortune-hunter, was nevertheless a very personable
young man and shortly before Christmas 1875 he and Florence were married. The relationship thereafter quickly deteriorated; and five months later, after three days of intense
agony, Charles died of antimony poisoning. The police
evinced a considerable interest in the affair. There were
rumours of suicide; but as just about everybody connected
with the case had reason for wishing Charles Bravo dead,
there were darker allegations too. Dr Gully was portrayed as
the spurned and jealous lover. He also had access to poison.
Mrs Cox, it transpired, had disliked Bravo intensely and had
lived in daily fear that he would discharge her. Florence, for
her part, was already suspected of having poisoned one
husband and the premature demise of a second, under
equally doubtful circumstances, was viewed with the
greatest suspicion. Despite a protracted enquiry, however,
the mystery was never solved. Three years later, Florence
herself died, of drink.

Sarah Malcolm who strangled her employer in the Temple in 1732, drawn by Hogarth two days before she was hanged

An equally curious murder in the Temple occurred in 1732 when a twenty-two-year-old charwoman named Sarah Malcolm strangled her employer and her employer's companion in Tanfield Court. So that there should be no witnesses to the crime, she then cut the throat of the maidservant, Annie Price. The motive appears to have been robbery because after Sarah's arrest £53 in banknotes was found concealed in her hair. She seems to have been an exceptionally pretty young woman and the case aroused considerable interest. Two days before she was hanged in Fleet Street, William Hogarth went to the Fleet to take her likeness; and her skeleton afterwards became a popular exhibit at the Botanical Gardens in Cambridge.

Both Oliver Goldsmith and Dr Johnson lived for a time in Brick Court, to the west of Middle Temple Lane, the former dying there in 1774 from a surfeit of James's Powders, a preparation which his physician had expressly forbidden him to take. At the last, when asked whether his conscience was clear, he replied: 'No, it is not.'

Goldsmith lies buried to the side of Temple Church, built in 'the round', it is said, to commemorate Christ's sepulchre. It is one of only four such churches in England. Of the various tombs here perhaps the most interesting is the one to Lord Robert de Ros, often mistaken for a Knight Templar. In fact, as *Old and New London* has pointed out: 'as he has no beard and wears flowing hair, contrary to the rules of the Order', he could only have been at best an 'Associate of the Temple'. He was probably too worldly even for that. He was fined £800 by Richard I for allowing an important French prisoner to escape from his custody; and he was one of the twenty-five barons who coerced King John into signing Magna Carta.

During the occupation of the Knights Templar the church served not only as a place of worship: it was also the place where those who offended against the strict code of the Order were punished. The restrictions were tedious and almost without number.

If any officer absented himself at meals, anyone sitting in his place was compelled to pay his fee and assume his office. Any offender, if he escaped into the oratory could claim sanctuary, and was pardoned if he returned into the hall humbly and as a servitor, carrying a roll on the point of his knife. No one was allowed to sing after the cheese was served.

More serious offences merited flogging – and worse – and the church is known to have possessed a penitential cell in which at least one person died. As it measured less than five feet by three and allowed the incumbent neither to stand nor to lie down, it was nicknamed the 'little ease'. One man – charged with desertion – survived it only to be sentenced on his release to go without food for four days each week for a year. The little food which he received on the other three days was dog-meat which he was required to share with the Temple hounds.

An old brick house which until 1828 stood in Inner Temple Terrace, to the south of the church, at one time possessed a sun-dial with the strange inscription: 'Begone about your Business'. According to tradition, it came about as the result of an absurd blunder. When the dial-makers sent a rather stupid lad down to the Temple to enquire what motto should be inscribed on it, he mistook a reprimand for loitering for his official instructions.

King's Bench Walk, to the east of Inner Temple Terrace, has known many famous residents. Goldsmith lived at number 3 and Sir Harold Nicolson, diplomat and biographer of George V, at number 4. The author of *King Solomon's Mines*, Rider Haggard, occupied number 13 for a time and wrote here a strange tale of a woman who had her last will and testament tattooed on her body.

A more sinister resident was Montagu John Druitt, a middle-aged gentleman not called to the Bar until 1885. Prior to that date he had practised as a doctor. He was a strange, wild-eyed man with an intense aura of cruelty and sexuality. In 1888 he filled his pockets with stones and took his own life by jumping into the Thames from the parapet of Chiswick Bridge. The police, who had been following his movements for some time, were so convinced that he was Jack the Ripper that they shortly afterwards closed their file on the case.

In the middle of the eighteenth-century William Murray, first Earl of Mansfield, lived at number 5 King's Bench Walk, retaining as one of his clients Sarah, the termagent Duchess of Marlborough. Being very quarrelsome, Sarah was always engaged in litigation of one form or another and was forever popping into his chambers to discuss progress. One night she called without an appointment, only to find his Lordship had gone out. She refused to leave her name, but the servant afterwards said that he knew it to be the Duchess of Marlborough from her fearful swearing. Mansfield eventually grew so tired of this harassment that he returned her retainer of a thousand guineas, deducting only five guineas for out-of-pocket expenses.

Passing out of the Temple by way of Tudor Street, and taking the turning into Dorset Rise, we come to Salisbury Square where, for the best part of thirty-five years the printer and novelist, Samuel Richardson, the author of several 'large still books', had his printing works. He used to creep down to the printing shop early in the mornings to hide coins among the piles of type in order to encourage the setters to work harder.

To the north of Salisbury Square is Ludgate Circus, formerly the site of one of the gates into Roman London. Until it was sold in 1760 for £148, there was a small prison over Lud Gate and to this a number of romantic tales attach. The prisoners were allowed the privilege of soliciting gifts and favours from the people passing beneath their cells; and one young man, named Stephen Forster, caught the eye of a pretty young widow. For £20 she purchased his release and married him. In time he not only triumphed over his past but rose to become Lord Mayor of London.

After the death of Edward IV, his mistress, Jane Shore, was immured for a time in Lud Gate by Richard III. She was also required to do penance for her immorality at St Paul's Cross. In the charming, quaint language of the period, Holinshed recorded the event:

> In hir penance she went, in countenance and pase demure, so womanlie, that albeit she were out of all araie, save hir kertle, while the wondering of the people cast a comlie rud in her cheeks (of which she before had most misse), that hir great shame wan hir much praise among those that

Lud Gate stood on the site of Ludgate Circus. In 1760 it was sold
for £148

were more amorous of hir bodie, than curious of hir
soule.

In the fullness of time, Jane triumphed over her adversar-
ies. With the death of Richard on Bosworth Field, she was set
free. She lived on for forty-eight years more, dying in 1533,
aged eighty.

London's first official post-box was erected on what is now
the north side of Ludgate Circus in 1855; and for many years
there was a central bench here with the curious inscription:

'Rest but do not loiter.' The present Circus was laid out between 1864 and 1875. At that date the King Lud public house, on the north-eastern corner, was noted for its gargantuan portions of Welsh rarebit. On the twenty-fifth anniversary of the present Queen's coronation, beer and spirits were sold here at 1953 prices. There was only one disadvantage: they had to be paid for in pre-decimal currency.

Some time in October 1891 a dapper, rather cross-eyed little American named Neill Cream met a young prostitute called Elizabeth Masters in Ludgate Circus. The couple spent part of the evening together and arranged to meet a few days later. Cream failed to keep the appointment – which may have been very lucky for Elizabeth. Although she was not aware of it, Cream had only recently been released from an American penitentiary after serving a life sentence for second degree murder. A few days after his encounter with Elizabeth, he met another doxy, Matilda Clover, whom he persuaded to swallow a capsule of nux vomica, passing it off as a harmless pick-me-up. She died in agony and Cream went on to poison several more young women before he was finally arrested. In November 1892 he went to the gallows in Newgate Prison. As the trap-door opened beneath him, he shouted, ambiguously: 'I am Jack the . . .' When his body was cut down, one of the warders was heard to mutter:

> Bacon's not the only thing
> That's cured
> By hanging from a string.

9

The Tower of London

On first catching sight of it today – with its modern walk-ways, its newly scrubbed walls and efficient plate-glass 'admission points' – the Tower of London gives the appear-ance of being little more than a harmless dollar-catchment. Yet over the years it has been the repository of perhaps more human misery, suffering and torture than any other building in the world. Before we examine it in detail, however, we must first look at the area immediately surrounding it, notably Tower Hill. It has a history almost as macabre as the Tower itself.

For several hundred years – from 1388 to 1747 – Tower Hill was a major venue for executions. During this period at least seventy-five traitors perished here and the site on which they met their deaths is marked today by a memorial plaque in nearby Trinity Square. It specifically commemorates Lord Balmerino and the Earl of Kilmarnock, two Jacobite nobles beheaded for their part in the Scottish rebellion of 1745. The executioner on that occasion was a man named John Thrift, himself a murderer, who had been pardoned on condition that he take up killing people for the government. Prior to the arrival of his victims he suffered an acute attack of nerves; and on mounting the scaffold and spying the block he fainted and had to be revived with a glass of wine. When Lord Kilmarnock was brought up he burst into tears. After a further glass of wine – and some soothing words from Kilmarnock – he grasped the axe; but a moment later threw it down again in a torrent of tears. He then fell on his knees before his Lordship and begged his pardon. A further period elapsed before he could be persuaded to retrieve the axe, but having done so he severed Kilmarnock's head with one neat blow.

Lord Balmerino's end was more prolonged. Five blows had to be struck before the head was completely severed; and after the first, Balmerino is said to have screwed his head round on the block and bestowed upon Thrift 'the most hideous smile'. The public never forgave this inept performance, and when he died, a few years later, Thrift's body was conducted to the grave in the churchyard of St Paul's, Covent Garden, by a jeering drunken mob which stoned the coffin and pelted the mourners with rotten vegetables and putrefying cats.

In 1685 the dramatist, Thomas Otway, died on Tower Hill – though not from the axe. His greatest work, *Venice Preserved*, having made him no money at all, he was reduced to begging here for a living. One day, the story goes, he accosted a man who not only recognised him but was so stricken by his plight that he gave him a guinea. Close to starvation, Otway ran pell-mell to the nearest coffee-house, ordered a gargantian meal . . . and choked to death on it. An alternative version suggests that he was killed by drinking a glass of water, having overheated himself in giving chase to a man whom he had seen commit a murder on Tower Hill. The victim is said to have been Otway's best friend.

If Tower Hill was then a haunt of criminals it later became a focus for the numerous quack doctors of London. Going under such names as the Rupture Master, the Infallible Greek or the Prophetical Merlin they imposed their nostrums and secret arcanums on an endlessly gullible public. They claimed to be able to cure the Leprosie, the Canker, the Cholic, the Spleen, the Ague or the Flowing of the Gall merely by delving into their bags for such wonderful panaceas as the Guilded Pill, the Universal Potion or the Tincture of Mars. There was one 'impudent mountebank' who even claimed to have a pill for curing earthquakes. Each of these 'Masters of the Art of Physick' was always very careful to add 'A Caveat to the Unwary' against trusting themselves to less patently honest practitioners; and they usually buttressed their sales-patter with testimonies from the famous. All too often – as in the case of 'the Emperor of Turkey's brother' – the residences of these eminent men were usually as remote as their cures miraculous.

Over the years, street entertainers of various sorts have found a home on Tower Hill and at one time there was an ex-sailor here who used to sing his songs wearing 'a model of the brig Nelson upon his hat'. The most colourful modern-day busker is undoubtedly the Highland Piper, Ailean Nicholson, for twenty-five years a pipe-major with the Seaforth Highlanders. In 1979 he was arrested for obstructing the highway here; but on being hauled before the magistrates he produced a Royal Charter signed by George III, designating Tower Hill a 'free area'. He was nonetheless found guilty and fined £10. Perhaps as a result of these kinds of overheads he usually asks a small fee of people wishing to photograph him. Those who refuse find that the time it takes to focus their cameras is usually just sufficient for Ailean to duck behind a tall traffic sign.

In all probability, Byward Street to the west of Tower Hill takes its name from the two-word password – or 'bi-word' – which was formerly needed to gain admission to the Tower. In 1649 a ship's-chandler had his premises here and one evening blew himself to pieces while rather foolishly attempting to package twenty-seven barrels of gunpowder by the light of a naked candle. The explosion destroyed several adjoining houses and caused considerable loss of life. That at least one person made a miraculous escape, however, we know from the account of the incident left us by Samuel Pepys. He recorded in his diary:

Next morning there was found on the upper leads of Barking Church, a young child lying in a cradle, as newly laid in bed, neither the child nor the cradle having the least sign of any fire or other hurt. It was never known whose child it was, so that one of the parish kept it as a memorial;

for in the year 1666 I saw the child, grown to be then a proper maiden, and came to the man that had her all that time, where he was drinking at a tavern with some other company then present. And he told us she was the child that was so found in the cradle upon the church leads as aforesaid.

The church mentioned by Pepys exists to this day. Now known as All Hallows by the Tower, it stands a little to the south of Byward Street. Although there has been a church on this site since the seventh century, the medieval building was sadly decimated by the Blitz. It has two American associations: John Quincy Adams, the second president of the United States, was married here; and in 1644 William Penn, the founder of Pennsylvania, was christened at the font. A year later, after his execution on Tower Hill for endeavouring to 'overthrow the Protestant religion', William Laud, Archbishop of Canterbury, was briefly interred near the altar. (His body was later removed to St John's College, Oxford, where his ghost is said still to manifest – usually in the library where it plays a game of football with its own head.)

By tradition the altar of All Hallows bears no cross; the reason being that it would mask the features of Christ in the painting of 'The Last Supper' situated immediately behind it. The tomb of Alderman Coke and the exquisite memorial to the Great War dead are of particular interest; while the organ loft was formerly haunted by the ghost of a white Persian cat. It belonged to a Miss Rist who was organist here from 1840 to 1880. She was a great animal lover and during the winter months used to spread sand on Tower Hill to give the horses a better purchase on the snow and ice. When her cat died she asked permission to bury it in the church. Although this was withheld it is thought she may have buried her pet here clandestinely. In any event, its ghost was twice seen by Reginald Hall when he visited the church – although his visits were separated by an interval of thirteen years.

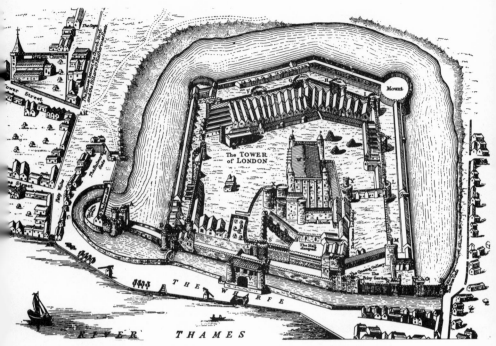

A plan of the Tower of London, from a survey made in 1597 by
W. Haiward and J. Gascoyne
A. Middle Tower. B. Tower at the Gate. C. Bell Tower. D.
Beauchamp Tower. E. Devilin Tower. F. Flint Tower. G. Bowyer
Tower. H. Brick Tower. I. Martin Tower. K. Constable Tower.
L. Broad Arrow Tower. M. Salt Tower. N. Well Tower. O. Tower
leading to Iron Gate. P. Tower above Iron Gate. Q. Cradle Tower.
R. Lantern Tower. S. Hall Tower. T. Bloody Tower. V. St
Thomas's Tower. W. Caesar's, or White Tower. X. Cole Harbour.
Y. Wardrobe Tower. AB. House at Water Gate, called the Ram's
Head. AH. End of Tower Street.

Sadly, the old organ loft was destroyed during the Blitz and
the little Persian cat has been seen no more.

Turning our attention at last to the Tower, we must first
consider its various roles – as a fortress, as a palace and as a
state prison. Covering some eighteen acres, it was originally
constructed (on a much smaller scale) by William the

Conqueror to guard the approaches to London by river. With the exception of Elizabeth I, who intensely disliked it, it remained the residence of every English monarch until 1625 and the expiration of James I from 'a surfeit of ripe fruit'.

During those years – and for some considerable period thereafter – a host of eminent people were held prisoner within its walls, many of them destined never again to leave. In 1399 Richard II was forced to abdicate in the Tower after adopting French manners and principles abhorrent to his English nobles; and Henry VI, another weak king, was murdered in the Wakefield Tower in 1471. Fourteen years later the 'two little Princes', Edward V and his brother, the Duke of York, were 'smother'd with pillows' in the Bloody Tower, next door. In the dungeons beneath, Guy Fawkes was hideously tortured for his part in the Gunpowder Plot; and in the same dungeons the infamous Judge Jeffreys died in 1689.

As a result of her identification with the Protestant religion, even great Bess was held captive within the Tower for a time. While still a princess, she was arrested on the orders of her Catholic half-sister, Queen Mary. On first coming in she was so terrified of the Tower's awesome reputation that she squatted down on the cobbles and refused to move. She was eventually persuaded to do so only by the repeated assurances of the Constable that she should not be harmed – and by the sudden onset of a thunderstorm. Two months later Mary relented and Elizabeth was removed to the far less sinister Palace of Woodstock under 'house arrest'.

Elizabeth's great courtier, Sir Walter Raleigh, spent almost a quarter of his life in the Tower; and even Samuel Pepys, that mildest of men, was briefly incarcerated here on a trumped up charge of complicity in the Popish Plot.

Perhaps the most unfortunate of all the Tower's prisoners, however, was Arthur Plantagenet, Viscount Lisle. A bastard son of Edward IV, he was shut up here on suspicion of treason. His father eventually ordered his release; but on hearing the news Arthur was so overcome that he dropped down dead of shock.

An altogether more resilient internee was Sir Henry Wyatt, a prisoner of Richard III. He survived in a dark and dank cellar for two years with the aid of one of the Tower cats. They kept each other warm at night; and through the day the cat took to bringing him the pigeons she caught. In 1485, when Richard was overthrown, Wyatt was released. He survived for fifty-two years more but never forgot the cat and commissioned a portrait of her, showing her passing her latest trophy through the bars of his cell. Sadly, his grandson, Sir Thomas Wyatt, proved less of a survivor. After fomenting a rash plot to raise the country against Queen Mary he was thrown into the Tower and beheaded.

Fittingly, the first man to be mewed up in the Tower was Ranulph Flambard, its builder. Bishop of Durham and justiciar of England under William Rufus, he was charged with simony. Aided by a rope smuggled to him in a cask of wine, he used his intimate knowledge of the Tower's geography to scale the wall at its lowest point and flee to Normandy – although he nearly jeapordised the plan by insisting on taking his bishop's crozier with him.

The most daring escape in the Tower's history, however, was effected by William Maxwell, Earl of Nithsdale, who in 1715 rebelled in favour of the 'Old Pretender'. Captured at Preston, he was removed to London, tried for high treason and sentenced to death. The night before he was due to die he was visited by his wife, Winifred. In the darkness of his cell he put on the female clothes which she had brought him and, in the hope of passing as her maid walked with her to the main gate, holding a handkerchief to his face to hide his flaming red beard. As their journey routed them past the scaffold on which he was scheduled to lose his head a few hours later, it is hardly surprising that by the time they reached the outer wall he was in a state of such obvious distress that the guard had to hold open the door in order for him to pass out. His two fellow-conspirators were executed the following morning.

It might have been expected that anyone who had made a fool of the authorities in this manner would have been remorselessly hunted down: but the Hanoverians always retained a sporting sense of fair-play. When advised of Nithsdale's escape, George I merely remarked: 'It was the best thing a man in his position could have done.' Nithsdale fled to Rome with his wife and lived there for the remaining thirty years of his life.

Another of the Jacobites incarcerated within the Tower after the rebellion of 1715 was Sir William Wyndham, an exceptionally superstitious man. Having twice been warned by soothsayers to beware 'of a white horse', he took great care to see that he never mounted such an animal. But on being carried into the Tower he happened to glance up at the Hanoverian coat-of-arms above the gate. At its centre was a white horse. On his release, thinking the prophecy 'spent', Sir William bought himself a magnificent white charger. It promptly threw him and kicked him in the head. One of his descendants was Captain Henry Wyndham, who distinguished himself at the battle of Waterloo by helping to shut the gates of the beleagured buildings at Hougemont. His niece, who was susceptible to draughts, remarked that it was 'the first time in history that a Wyndham ever shut a door'.

Walking north from the Outer Ward we come to Tower Green, described by Macaulay as 'the saddest spot on earth'. So many people of royal or noble blood have died on this site that there is a tradition which says no grass will ever grow here again. Anne Boleyn, the second wife of Henry VIII, accused of adultery with her own brother, came to Tower Green to die on May 19 1536 – according to one source 'laughing and weeping by turns'. In fact, as she was careful to tuck her gown around her feet before kneeling in front of the block, she seems to have exhibited a remarkable composure. In order to delay matters she had requested that she be despatched by a skilled swordsman. As there were none then in England a special envoy had to be sent to France to fetch one. So that there should be no last minute unseemliness, he concealed his sword in the straw surrounding the block, removed his shoes, and crept up on Anne unawares. Her body was thrown into an old arrow chest and given the simplest of burials. Henry went into mourning for her for just twenty-four hours.

Eighteen years later another Queen of England, the seventeen-year-old Lady Jane Grey, also lost her life here, having been pressurised by her ambitious father-in-law into accepting a crown which was rightly Mary's. She reigned for just nine days. 'Bloody' Mary might on this occasion have been prevailed upon to be merciful; but the rebellion of Sir Thomas Wyatt sealed Jane's fate. On February 12 1554, unable to prevent her small and frail body from being convulsed by violent shivers of fear, she walked to the scaffold to die. Turning to the executioner she said: 'Will you take it off before I lay me down?' When the blindfold was applied she stumbled around the scaffold, groping for the block and tearfully murmuring: 'Where is it? Where is it?'

In 1970 the ghost of Lady Jane Grey manifested to a lady tourist in the White Tower. With her long hair, characteristic black dress and white cap, she was clearly recognisable. A circular gold pendant rested on her breast. When the tourist attempted to approach, the apparition suddenly vanished, inducing in the lady an understandable shortness of breath.

An altogether less submissive victim was Margaret Pole, Countess of Salisbury, the mother of Reginald Pole, Archbishop of Canterbury. When the King first raised the question of his divorce from Katharine of Aragon, he found Reginald inclined to comply. Later, he changed his mind and after expressing strong disapproval fled abroad. As the son had passed out of his reach, the spiteful Henry condemned his mother to death in his place. Her execution was perhaps the most bungled in history. Although she was well over eighty, she put up a fierce resistance and the first three blows missed her entirely. On the anniversary of her death her screaming phantom is said still to re-enact her last moments here, running round and round the scaffold until overtaken

Lady Jane Grey beheaded on Tower Green, in 1554, aged 17.

by the executioner who throws her down and brutally hacks off her head.

The last execution within the Tower took place on 14 August 1941. The victim was a rather pathetic German spy named Josef Jakobs. Dropped by parachute to act as an *agent provocateur*, he was carrying only a sliver of frankfurter with which to sustain himself and broke an ankle on impact. Unable even to hobble, he was arrested almost as soon as he landed. As a result of his injury he was afforded the 'privilege' of remaining seated when shot.

Given that so much suffering has been endured within its walls, it is only fitting that the Tower should be haunted. The shades of Anne Boleyn, of the two 'little princes' and Sir Walter Raleigh are perhaps the best attested; and it is said that on moonlit nights the central keep and the execution site on Tower Green are sometimes overshadowed by the silhouette of an enormous axe. The Chapel of St Peter ad Vincula – to the north of Tower Green and after Westminster Abbey one of the most important burial-grounds in England – also has its ghosts. On certain nights of the year the windows of the Chapel are said suddenly to blaze with light; and one man who summoned the courage to peer in claimed to have seen a gorgeously arrayed procession wending its way down the aisle, led by Anne Boleyn.

The imposing central keep of the Tower was completed in 1100. Known as the White Tower, from the white Caen stone of Normandy with which it was built, it stands ninety feet high. In parts, the walls are fifteen feet thick. The interior is now given over to a display of arms and weaponry. Among the exhibits which are now, or were once, on display here can be counted Henry VIII's heavy armour cod-piece – into which superstitious women used to stick pins in the hope that it would make them fertile; and the Puckles machine-gun, designed to fire round bullets at Christians and square ones at Turks.

North of the keep is the Jewel House, containing the Royal Regalia or Crown Jewels. The centrepiece of the collection is

Henry VIII's armour cod-piece, a fertility aid for the superstitious. Now housed in the Armoury, The Tower of London

St Edward's Crown, weighing over 5 lbs and studded with
more than three thousand diamonds. Made in 1661 for the
coronation of Charles II, it incorporates a large uncut stone –
the Black Prince's Ruby – worn by Henry V in the thick of
the fray at Agincourt. A second superb gem is the Star of
Africa, set in the Royal Sceptre. The largest cut diamond in
the world (530 carats) it is one of several stones fashioned
from the 3000 carat Cullinan Diamond which was discovered
lying on the floor of a South African mine in 1905. When it
was decided to transport it to England there were very real
fears that someone would try to steal it. To prevent this, a
cheap imitation was brought home amidst a blaze of publicity
whilst the real diamond was sent by post.

Passing out of the Tower and crossing the moat we come to the restaurant, formerly the site of the Royal Menagerie. Founded in the thirteenth century, its first inmates were three leopards given to Henry III. The collection was soon afterwards supplemented by a huge Norwegian bear which became a famous London sight, sitting on Tower Wharf at the end of a long chain and pawing salmon out of the river. In later years the lions became the chief attraction here and it was commonly believed by foolish folk that one of them was always named after the monarch of the day. When he died, the story goes, the lion expired in sympathy. Another misconception concerned the fictitious ceremony of 'The Washing of the Lions', an event scheduled each year for April 1. At one time, anyone prepared to feed their unwanted pets to the lions were admitted to the Menagerie free of charge.

During the Second World War the Tower was hit by bombs no less than fifteen times. Twenty-three people were killed – as well as two of the ravens, birds associated with the Tower since time immemorial. This must have been a great worry to the authorities because there is a long-standing tradition which insists that if the ravens ever disappear from the Tower, England will fall. If nobody seriously believes this, they are nonetheless scrupulously well cared for. Their keeper receives an allowance to cover the cost of their food; and one of his duties is to see that their wings are clipped. It is widely believed that certain misfortune awaits anyone who kills a raven; and they are said to possess the power to revenge themselves on those who harm them. Between the wars a guardsman stationed here kicked one of them. He later walked in his sleep and fell into the moat, breaking both legs. During the same period a visiting Nazi officer was being shown round the Tower by the Constable when they encountered one of the ravens on Tower Green. The German remarked on its disreputable appearance and apparent ill-temper, adding: 'For our own emblem, we Nazis prefer the eagle.' The raven waddled over and promptly bit him on the ankle.

The Constable of the Tower is usually a high-ranking army officer. He is supported in his duties by the Yeoman Warders, sometimes called 'Beefeaters'. About forty in number, they derive their odd title from the French word 'Boufitier', meaning 'Keeper of the King's Buffet'. No man may become a Yeoman Warder unless he has served at least twenty-one years in the armed services and – having reached the rank of NCO – been discharged with an exemplary conduct. In spite of this, the waiting-list grows longer every year. Although the practice has long since ceased, they were at one time allowed to sell their jobs, but not to bequeath them. As a result, they still toast each other with the words: 'May you never die a Yeoman Warder.'

Leaving the Tower behind and walking east, we come to Royal Mint Street, for many years the home of the Royal Mint where coins of the realm were struck. When the Mint was still situated within the Tower one of its Masters was the English scientist, Sir Isaac Newton, the formulator of the

A Victorian engraving of the Royal Mint

Law of Gravity. Despite being a brilliant mathematician, his
basic arithmetic was so inadequate that he used to get one of
his own clerks to help him cast up his sums. In the seventeenth century workers at the Mint were supplied with 'cups'
fashioned from the skulls of condemned criminals spiked on
London Bridge. They believed that ale consumed in this way
provided a cure for the respiratory complaints caused by
working in a metal-foundry. The word 'sterling', which is
used to describe English money, in all probability derived
from 'easterling' a name given to the money-makers when
they worked here, in the eastern part of the City.

South-east of Royal Mint Street loom the great towers of
Tower Bridge, opened in 1894 at a cost of £80,000. Its Gothic
mien stems from the architect's desire that it should blend
with its near neighbour, the Tower. The two sections of the
central span, each weighing approximately a thousand tons,
can be elevated in approximately ninety seconds. They have
been raised in all some 350,000 times without mishap or
breakdown. Before the present hydraulic mechanism was
installed the bascules were lifted by a team of trace horses and
their old stables on the bridge survived almost until the
outbreak of the Second World War. In its hey-day the bridge
kept eighty men fully employed, including a permanent
watch of fourteen men which was changed three times a day.
Now, although approximately twelve thousand vehicles
cross it each twenty-four hours, the central span is almost
never raised, commercial shipping having largely deserted
the Pool of London.

In December 1935 a number 78 bus, finding itself at the
point of no return as the bridge began to open, accelerated
and jumped the three foot gap to the other side. The driver
was given a medal and awarded £10 out of public funds.

The pigeons which have always favoured the underside of
the central span for nest-building are clever birds. They
design their nests in such a way that in spite of the raising and
lowering of the bascules their young remain secure even at
the terminal angle of eighty degrees.

10

Passionate Bloomsbury

Almost the first thing which strikes anyone setting out to walk through Bloomsbury is that here is an area fallen on hard times. It takes its name from Blemund's bury – a bury meaning a manor-house – which stood here in Saxon days. It was laid out as a fashionable residential area in the eighteenth and nineteenth centuries. When, in the fullness of time, the fashionable world moved westwards to Belgravia and Chelsea, Bloomsbury was taken over by men of business – merchants and professional men. When they in turn defected to the balmy stockbroker-belts of Essex and Surrey the artists and writers moved in. Because of the intensity of their life-style, the area became known as 'Passionate' Bloomsbury. Few of its houses are privately occupied any longer. Many have been converted into small hotels catering for the millions of tourists who descend on London every year.

The western boundary of Bloomsbury is formed today by Tottenham Court Road. At the point where it junctions with Oxford Street stands the Dominion cinema, built in 1929. It occupies the site of Henry Meux's Horse Shoe Brewery. (A name which lingers on in the public house next door.) In 1768 Henry Meux constructed here an enormous vat to contain three thousand gallons of beer. Half a century later it collapsed with an immense roar. The pressure of the ale tumbling from the cask caused other vats to collapse and ten thousand gallons of beer consigned eight people to 'a portery grave'.

Walking north up Tottenham Court Road we come to Percy Street and a corner-site formerly occupied by Jay's, the jewellers, the scene in 1947 of a particularly nasty murder.

One bleak morning, soon after it had opened for business, the shop was robbed by three armed men. As they came tumbling out of the door, shouting and brandishing their revolvers, a passing motor-cyclist named Alec de Antiquis, a father of six, attempted to block their path. One of the gang shot him in the head. As a crowd gathered round the dying man his murderers made good their escape. After several weeks of intense police activity the culprits were arrested and convicted. Two of them were sentenced to death. By a strange coincidence, one of them, a twenty-three-year-old named Charlie Jenkins, was the second member of his family to be convicted of murder within the space of three years. In 1944 his brother, Tom, had acted as a getaway driver for a team of crooks who robbed a jewellery shop in the City. When a passer-by tried to stop them by jumping on to the running-board of their car, he was violently repelled. As he fell, his jacket caught on the door-handle and he was dragged along beside the car for upwards of a mile, sustaining appalling injuries from which he later died.

A second turning out of Tottenham Court Road is Torrington Place, for many years the home of 'Wee' Georgie Wood, the 'pocket-sized Coward'. He died here in Gordon Mansions in February 1979 aged eighty-three. A brilliant raconteur who stood just 4' 9" in his socks, he was put on the stage at the age of five by his ambitious mother. Originally billed as 'The Boy Phenomenon', he dropped the name after one theatre advertised him as 'The Boy Euphonium'.

A star in the north of England before he was ten, Georgie was a tireless worker for charity and a very funny comedian: but his lack of inches was a source of constant grief to him. He nearly married once, but the girl's mother begged him to end the relationship, saying: 'Let's face it, Georgie, you're a midget.'

Although he became rich and famous, George never forgot the remark and could never recount the story without bursting into tears. His misery was often acute and he more than once contemplated suicide. In 1940, during an air-raid, he slipped out of the Coventry theatre where he was appearing and deliberately went for a stroll among the bombs. Everything around him was flattened: George escaped with nothing more serious than a piece of grit in his eye.

With age and experience, George mellowed. He even learned to treat his shortness with a degree of humour. When a very tiny woman was spotted struggling across the lobby of the Savage Club with a shopping basket laden with groceries, the Yorkshire actor, Edward Chapman, growled: ''Oo's that?' Somebody said: 'Georgie Wood's housekeeper.' Chapman said: 'But where's George?' His companion replied: 'In the shopping basket.' The next day the man received a call from the little comedian, who said: 'I understand you made a remark about me in the club yesterday.' The man said: 'Yes, George. I did. Who told you?' Wood said: 'Nobody told me. I heard you from the shopping basket.'

Running parallel to Tottenham Court Road is Gower Street, named after Gertrude Leveson Gower, the wife of the fourth Duke of Bedford, the ground-landlord. Something of an autocrat, the fourth Duke of Bedford was described by 'Junius' as the possessor of a name 'glorious till it was yours'. His marriage was probably not a happy one: he was no great admirer of women. On one occasion, at Woburn Abbey, after he had supervised the putting up of the portraits of all the Dukes, an assistant suggested that they might now make a start on the Duchessess. The Duke was shocked. 'Hang the Duchesses?' he said. 'But they are not even of the blood.'

In the nineteenth century Gower Street was christened 'Godless' Gower Street when University College, at its northern end, decided to omit religious instruction from its curriculum. Ironically, the College had been brought into being, in 1826, in order that non-sectarian students might receive an education free from religious discrimination.

One of its founders was the Utilitarian philosopher, Jeremy Bentham. He firmly believed that the finest memorial to man is man preserved (the 'auto-icon') and he survives

The auto-icon of Jeremy Bentham, who believed that the finest
memorial to man is man preserved. At University College, Gower
Street

to this day as its finest exponent. His skeleton, padded and clothed, can be seen in the cloister near to the entrance, in an air-tight case of glass and mahogany. The head still exists but is presumably too gruesome, despite being embalmed, to put on public display. The head surmounting the skeleton is made of wax.

In spite of the opinions he held in life, it may be that Bentham has since changed his views on 'auto-icons'. Sharp rappings are sometimes heard on the glass, thought to be demands for a decent burial; and his ghost is said sometimes to chase after members of the staff, waving the philosopher's favourite walking-stick, 'dapple', above its head in a very bellicose manner.

Another Bloomsbury ghost is Lizzie Church, sometimes seen around the wards of University College Hospital, on the other side of the way. At the turn of the century, while training at the hospital, she inadvertently administered a fatal overdose of morphine to a patient, her own sweetheart. She usually manifests at the bedside of someone about to receive a morphine injection.

At one time, Jeremy Bentham's skeleton used to be placed in the boardroom for meetings of the Governors of University College Hospital, but this practice may now have ceased. He was recorded in the minutes as being 'present, but not voting'.

Four days before Christmas 1846, the first public operation using a general anaesthetic was performed at University College Hospital by the great Scottish surgeon, Robert Liston. The patient's name was Frederick Churchill and with the aid of chloroform his leg was painlessly amputated in less than thirty seconds. Liston's speed with a scalpel was legendary: but it cannot truthfully be said that he was always very deft. On a subsequent occasion, when called upon to perform a similar operation, he not only removed the limb but swung in such a wide arc that he amputated the patient's left testicle and two of the assisting surgeon's fingers.

Before the area was finally developed, the land around

Gower Street was open fields. In one of them, on St John the Baptist's Day in 1694 the chronicler John Aubrey: 'saw at midnight twenty-three young women . . . looking for a coal, beneath the root of a plantain, to put under their heads that night and they should dream who would be their husbands.'

The meadow in question later became known as the 'Field of Forty Footsteps', from a duel fought here with pistols over a woman with whom two men were both hopelessly in love. As the woman looked on, they each took twenty steps, turned and fired, killing one another instantly. It is said that as a result of their tragic encounter, the grass crushed

'The Field of Forty Footsteps' (1830), site of a famous duel. This meadow ended in Upper Montagu Street near the back of Gower Street

beneath their feet withered, died and could never be persuaded to grow again.

East of Gower Street is Gordon Square. The Bloomsbury Group met in Clive Bell's house here, between the wars, and another of its members, Duncan Grant, lived at number 37. The American writer, Gertrude Stein, whose own work was often obscure and meaninglessly repetitious, was contemptuously dismissive of the Bloomsbury Group. She called it 'The Young Men's Christian Association – with Christ left out, of course.'

After her separation from the artist, G. F. Watts, the beautiful Ellen Terry lived for a time in nearby Taviton Street. She married her querulous and bucolic husband when she was just seventeen. Watts was forty-six. The first time he kissed her, Ellen rushed home to her mother and announced that she was pregnant. Prior to the marriage, Watts had lived with his mother, 'the most determined celebrity hunter in London'; and after the divorce he moved from country-house to country-house, basking in the adoration of a series of middle-aged hostesses who could never do enough for him. Ronald Pearsall described him as 'the prime parasite of the century', adding: 'his hostess, Mrs Prinsep, said that "he came to stay three days, he stayed thirty years".' Artistically, Watts was competent, but rather morbid. His capacity for taking pains, however, is not in doubt. Of one sketch he said: 'I drew that so carefully – so carefully – I drew it with my shoes off.'

In November 1851 Charles Dickens came to live in Tavistock Square, to the east of Taviton Street, settling for this purpose on Tavistock House, which he described as 'decidedly cheap – most commodious – and might be made very handsome'. He took it for forty-five years, paying a premium of £1,450, and here he wrote *Bleak House*. The property was later sold to Georgina Weldon who so disliked it that she published with her own money a leaflet entitled: 'The Ghastly Consequences of Living in Charles Dickens' House.'

Another novelist who lived in Tavistock Square was Virginia Woolf who, until the house was destroyed in the Blitz, lived at number 52. When her husband, Leonard, came down to survey the smoking ruins of their former home he found it: 'a curious and ironic sight, for on the vast conical heap of dust and bricks precisely and meticulously perched upright upon the summit was a wicker chair which had been forgotten in one of the upper rooms. Nothing beside remained except a broken mantelpiece against the bare wall of the next-door house and above it intact one of Duncan Grant's decorations.'

Walking down Woburn Place we come to Russell Square, the spiritual heart of Bloomsbury. It was laid out in the first quarter of the nineteenth century by James Burton for the landowner, the fifth Duke of Bedford. The Duke – with some enchanting baroque children at his feet – is commemorated today by a statue on the south side of the gardens. The plough on which he leans and the ears of corn which he is holding in his left hand, record his long association with agriculture. Attractive though it may be, the statue is in some respects misleading. In real life the Duke was a rather disreputable man. In order to win a wager he once procured a man to eat a live cat. Like most of the noble cullies of the period he aspired to be a fashionable dresser – but without much success. On one occasion he was stopped in the street by Beau Brummell who stared at him in great pain and said: 'Bedford, do you call this thing a coat?'

His ancestor, the third Duke of Bedford, was an equally odd sort. Lady Mary Wortley Montagu remarked that he arrived at the age of sixteen 'without a competent knowledge either of practical or speculative anatomy, and literally thinking fine ladies composed of lillies and roses'. On his wedding night he was so shocked to learn what was expected of him that he decided 'to let his estate go to his brother, rather than go through the filthy drudgery of getting an heir to it'.

The author of 'Elegy in a Country Churchyard', Thomas Gray, for a time occupied a house on the site of what is now the Imperial Hotel; and the painter, Sir Thomas Lawrence, lived at number 65 Russell Square for almost a quarter of a century. When he was painting here the portrait of General Platoff, mounted Cossacks stood sentinel outside his door 'with their long spears grounded'.

To the west of the square is Keppel Street where, in March 1851, 'after a terrible operation,' Charles Dickens' father died 'O so quietly'. Dickens was so overcome that he walked around the streets all night. Another literary association is with the novelist, Anthony Trollope, who was born at number 6 Keppel Street in 1815. At the age of nineteen he entered the Post Office and as an Inspector of Posts travelled upwards of three hundred miles a week. He was also responsible for the design of the first post-box.

Once a private enclave, Bedford Square, to the west, remains the prettiest and least spoilt of all the Bloomsbury Squares. When it was first constructed, about 1775, its access roads were guarded by beadles who turned away all but the residents or those who could prove they had business with them. Whether the nature of that business was a will or a box of figs, the head of the company had always to bring it himself. Clerks were simply not admitted.

One of Bedford Square's most famous residents was Margot Asquith, the lively second wife of the Liberal prime minister, Herbert Asquith. The daughter of Sir Charles Tennant, Bart., she had proved a captivating if wilful débutante and there was much speculation concerning her possible choice of husband. At one point the spotlight fell on another future prime minister, Arthur Balfour, then secretary for Ireland. But Balfour prejudiced his chances by telling a newspaper reporter: 'No, that is not so. I rather think of having a career of my own.' Margot's announcement of her engagement to Asquith came as a shattering blow to her mother who 'sank upon a settee, put a handkerchief to her eyes and said: 'you might as well marry your groom!'

In spite of Lady Tennant's doubts, the marriage proved a happy one. Margot outlived her husband by seventeen years,

The Grand Staircase of Montagu House, a site now occupied by the
British Museum

dying at the age of eighty. Towards the end of her life, when
loneliness and dejection led her rather to neglect herself, she
told one visitor that she was existing on 'macaroni and
memorial services'. She predicted that her own memorial
service would be very well attended. In fact the church was
half empty, all her contemporaries having predeceased her.

The year in which Margot died – 1945 – was the year in
which her daughter, Princess Elizabeth Bibesco, also
breathed her last. Elizabeth had spent most of her life
involved in charitable work, but was such a chatter-box that
on one occasion her husband, Antoine, was driven to remark
that in his wife's care: 'the lame walk, the blind see and the
dumb *would* speak, if they could get a word in edgeways'.

Great Russell Street, which runs out of Bloomsbury Street to the east, houses the British Museum, arguably the finest collection of its kind in the world. It stands on the site of old Montagu House, erected in 1680 by Ralph, Duke of Montagu and paid for with his wife's 'galleon' money. The Duchess had previously been married to Christopher, Duke of Albemarle, who invested what little fortune he possessed in an expedition to look for sunken treasure. Nobody expected him to find any. He did, but died the very same day. His interest then passed to his wife, the so-called 'mad' Duchess, who soon contrived to get all the treasure for herself; the other investors never seeing a penny.

The Duchess used her ill-gotten gains to live in Imperial splendour, surrounded by a host of servants, all of whom were required to serve her on bended knee. She swore that unless the Prince of Tartary himself were to come to her door and beg her to be his wife by throwing himself at her feet, she would never remarry. Hearing of this, the unscrupulous Duke of Montagu dressed up as the Prince, prostrated himself before her and thus acquired both her hand and her fortune. The land in Great Russell Street on which he built his house with the 'galleon' money covered eight acres. Six years after it was finished the mansion burned down in just five hours. Ralph promptly had it rebuilt and lived here until his death in 1709. *Old and New London* records that he left the bulk of his fortune to his pets and that while he was writing his will: 'one of his cats jumped on his knee. "What!" says he, "have you a mind to be a witness, too? You can't, for you are a party concerned and therefore interested.'

The present building was erected to designs by Sir Robert Smirke between 1823 and 1852. In 1978 the cumbrous classical façade, with its forty-four Ionic columns, was scrubbed clean for the first time since it was built. The Victorian soot and grime which had become such an intrinsic part of our heritage was scraped off, leaving it looking like some sham antique, built yesterday. The facelift has proved not only in the worst possible taste, but very confusing: several elderly members of the staff are said to have been searching for the building ever since.

The scope of the treasures to be found within the four walls of the British Museum is so vast that it would be impossible here to give even the briefest catalogue. As Virginia Woolf noted: 'There is in the British Museum an enormous mind. Consider that Plato is there cheek by jowl with Aristotle; and Shakespeare with Marlowe. This great mind is hoarded beyond the power of any single mind to possess it.' Indeed many people feel there is too much here. If only, as J. B. Priestley has suggested: 'there was a little room somewhere in the British Museum that contained only about twenty exhibits and good lighting, easy chairs, and a notice imploring you to smoke . . .'

If Great Russell Street tends to be overshadowed by its eminent neighbour, it has had at least two other famous residents. The poet Shelley lived his last days in England at number 119, a house still extant; and from 1916 to 1922 the 'Super Tramp', W. H. Davies, had lodgings opposite what is now the YMCA. He lived in terror of cats and negroes and was kept awake at night by a piano-thumping Belgian prostitute who occupied the rooms above. He refused to complain because – in addition to his other phobias – he had the vagrant's deep dislike and distrust for the police. (As a youth he had been sentenced to twelve strokes of the cat for shoplifting.)

Born into a respectable middle-class family in Newport, Monmouthshire, Davies left home at the earliest opportunity and sailed for America. He remained there five years, developing into a classical hobo. He contrived to spend most of the winter in prison and existed in summer on what he could earn from strawberry-picking and driving cattle. In the Arizona desert he all but starved and saw the desert rocks turn into loaves of bread. In the Klondyke he panhandled for gold. He travelled about by jumping trains. On one of these journeys he was forced to leap from a freight car travelling at high speed, injuring his leg so badly that it had to be amputated. He was fitted with a heavy wooden one which ultimately killed him: the effort of dragging it around for forty years fatally weakened his heart.

The first London space to be called a 'square', Bloomsbury Square, which opens out of Great Russell Street, was the scene of a very strange duel in the spring of 1694. The circumstances which led to it were equally curious. A handsome but poor young man named Wilson came up to London from Leicestershire to seek his fortune. Within a short time he acquired all the trappings of prosperity: beautiful clothes and a grand style of living. Some people suspected that he was a highwayman; others that he was an alchemist blessed with the power to transform base metal into gold. In fact, he was neither.

Soon after his arrival in town he had been noticed by the beautiful Elizabeth Villiers, Countess of Orkney, the mistress of William III, who had fallen instantly in love with him. Through a third party she arranged a meeting, but in order to protect her identity, insisted that it take place at night. As an additional precaution she hid her features behind a mask. The couple quickly embarked upon a passionate liaison. The Countess made Wilson presents of large sums of money asking only in return that he should never attempt to remove the mask which, except in the dark, she continued to wear whenever they met.

Matters might have gone on in this way indefinitely had Wilson not one day happened to encounter the lady socially. Her face, of course, made no impression on him; but when their hands accidentally touched he instantly recognised the shape and form of the ring she was wearing. The Countess, who loved her good name a great deal more than her little man from Leicestershire, and realising that she stood on the brink of exposure and disgrace, immediately approached a well-known rake named John Law whom she bribed to challenge her lover to a duel. As Law was an expert in these matters, the outcome was never in doubt. But although Wilson now knew the name of his murderous mistress – a mistress whose face he was never to see – he refused to reveal it even as he lay dying in Bloomsbury Square. The story came out entirely by accident some fifteen years later when some letters which the two lovers had exchanged found their way into print.

As a boy, Benjamin Disraeli lived for twelve years at number 6 Bloomsbury Square; and there is a statue nearby to another politician, the great Whig, Charles James Fox. It is a muddled work, the sculptor, Sir Richard Westmacott, having dressed his subject in the robes of a Roman senator whilst placing in his hand a rolled-up copy of Magna Carta.

Charles James Fox was a fast-living man much addicted to gambling and to drink. On one occasion, an acquaintance looked in on him at Brooks's and found him in the dining-room, flanked by seven empty bottles of port. He asked if he had emptied them unassisted. 'No', said Fox. 'I was assisted by a bottle of Madeira.' On another occasion, Fox gambled at Almack's for nineteen hours without respite. Breaking off to deliver a speech to the House of Commons, he returned to the Club, gambled eight hours more and then jumped into a carriage, ordering the driver to take him to Newmarket races. He died at Chiswick House on 13 September 1806. His friends on that day had gathered there to await the end and, according to Samuel Rogers, the news of his passing was communicated to them by Lady Holland: 'in her own odd manner . . . she walked through the room with her apron over her head'.

The Great Debater was interred in Westminster Abbey with great pomp and so close to his old parliamentary adversary, William Pitt, that Sir Walter Scott wrote:

> Drop upon Fox's grave the tear,
> Twill trickle to his rival's bier.

An equally preposterous statue to be found nearby is that to George I. In a scanty-looking toga he perches on the spire of St George's church in Bloomsbury Way. A stolid unimaginative man – 'an honest blockhead' – who spoke only German, George I succeeded to the throne of England in 1714 on the death of Queen Anne. He took little part in the government of the country, leaving the administration of affairs almost entirely to his first minister, Sir Robert Walpole. His first loyalties were ever to Hanover, the country of his birth, and the nature of his emotional responses was exclusively Teutonic. In 1682 he married his cousin, the Princess Sophia Dorothea of Celle. But from 1694 until her death, thirty-two years later, he kept her confined at Ahlden Castle, in Hanover, for infidelity with Count Konigsmark.

Walking east along Bloomsbury Way we come to Southampton Place where, in 1671, the actor and poet laureate, Colley Cibber, was born. His entire career was bound up with the Theatre Royal, Drury Lane, and Cibber it was who first coined the phrase 'perish the thought'. As a producer he was often irascible; and when a bit-player persisted in fluffing his lines, he shouted: 'Fine him five shillings!' It was explained that the man was of so little consequence that he was working solely for his keep. Cibber roared: 'In that case give him ten shillings a week – and fine him five!'

11

Belgravia and Chelsea

Until 1826 Belgravia was 'a barren waste, a fetid swamp' known as the Five Fields. In that year a special Act of Parliament was passed to allow its landlords, the Grosvenor family, to drain it and raise the levels. They then sought out Thomas Cubitt, a former adventurer and journeyman-carpenter, to develop it. Cubitt transformed a difficult site simply by burning the top soil of clay into bricks and utilising the substratum of gravel for the foundations of the houses.

The western boundary of modern Belgravia is formed by Sloane Street, a long straight thoroughfare boarded on the one side by tall houses and mansion blocks and on the other by elegant leafy squares. In about 1786 the necromancer Count Cagliostro had rooms in Sloane Street. Opinion as to his powers was divided; but when a Frenchman publicly denounced him as a fraud, Cagliostro's reaction was immediate and emphatic. He wrote an open letter to him, published in the Public advertiser:

In physics and chemistry, Mr Joker, arguments go for little and sneers for nothing – experience is all. Permit me, then, to propose a little experiment, which will divert the public, either at your expense or at mine. I invite you to breakfast for the 9th November next, at nine o'clock in the morning; you will furnish the wine and the accessories; I will furnish one dish in my own style – a little sucking pig, fattened according to my method. Two hours before breakfast I will present him to you alive, fat and healthy. You will engage to have him killed and cooked and I will not go near him till the moment he is put on the table; you shall cut him yourself into four pieces, choose that which attracts you the most, and give me any piece you please. The day after this breakfast one of four things will have happened: either we shall be both dead or both alive or I shall be dead and you alive, or you dead and I alive. Out of these four chances I give you three, and I bet five thousand guineas that the day after the breakfast you will be dead and I shall be in good health. You will confess that no fairer offer could be made, and that you must either accept the wager or confess your ignorance and that you have foolishly and dully cut your jokes upon a subject beyond your knowledge.

Count Cagliostro, the necromancer, who had rooms
in Sloane Street

The Frenchman declined the challenge.

Cadogan Place, which occupies approximately half of Sloane Street's eastern boundary, has known many famous residents. Harold Macmillan was born here in February 1894; and the abolitionist, William Wilberforce, died at number 44 in 1833. According to Augustus Hare, a lady with a wooden leg was living somewhere in Cadogan Place in the 1870's. One day, walking in the park, she noticed that she was being followed. On a subsequent occasion her admirer pressed a letter into her hand. It was a proposal of marriage. The lady passed it to her solicitor and there the matter might have ended had the pair not encountered each other some months after at a country-house party. Forced acquaintance ripened into love and in due course they were married.

Six weeks after the marriage, the lady's new husband suddenly announced that he had been called to town on urgent business. He would be gone three days. Before he left he said: 'Where two lives are so completely, so entirely united as ours are, there ought to be the most absolute confidence on either side.' With that he handed her a bunch of keys, urging that she look into 'a cupboard in my dressing-room which contains certain memorials of my past peculiarly sacred to me'.

As soon as he had left, the wife rushed to the closet. Inside were two long canvas-wrapped parcels, each bearing a label. Each bore the name of a former wife and each contained a wooden leg.

Feeling that she was 'married to a Blue Beard – a monster who *collects* wooden legs', the wife decided to flee to France. Unfortunately, says Hare, 'she had not consulted Bradshaw and had some hours to wait in London before the tidal train started'. She decided to use the time to look up the friends who had introduced her to her husband and upbraid them for not informing her of his true nature. To her amazement, the couple entirely refused to hear a word against him. It was true, they said, that he had been twice-married; and indeed both wives had had wooden legs; but the marriages had been

sublimely happy, the wives extremely virtuous, and he had
suffered agonies of grief at their loss. They had refrained
from raking up the past not only because they were certain
that his character was above reproach, but because it was
perfectly clear that in her he had found an even greater love.
The wife was so completely won round by the obvious
sincerity of this explanation that she cancelled her plans to go
to France, caught the next train home and never left her
husband's side again.

Walking east down Pont Street – in fiction the home of
Bertie Wooster's Aunt Agatha, 'the Pest of Pont Street, the
human snapping-turtle' – we come by turns to Wilton Row.
At the tip of its north-western spur is the Grenadier public
house, one of London's most 'secret' taverns. It was once
patronised by George IV and more recently featured in the
film 'Around the World in Eighty Days'. Until cars were
permitted to rumble down the cobbles and park outside, the
landlord operated a rickshaw service from here to the top of
Wilton Crescent. Like so many of London's truly old buildings, it is said to be haunted. Each September – the month of
his death – the ghost of a former guardsman materialises in
the cellar, on the stairs to the rear of the bar, or in one of the
upper rooms. He is thought to be one of the Duke of
Wellington's men who used the Grenadier as a gambling den.
One night he was beaten to death in the back room (now the
restaurant) after being caught cheating at cards.

At the bottom of Wilton Crescent is Belgrave Square, still
one of the most exclusive squares in London. It was laid out
by the builder of Belgravia, Thomas Cubitt, who, unlike
other speculators, was a cautious man. He began with what
today would be called a show-house, building no more until
he received firm orders for them. He worked on the Square
with George Basevi who in 1845 fell to his death while
surveying Ely Cathedral.

In 1953 the present Queen's coronation was planned from
Belgrave Square, number 14 then being occupied by the Earl
Marshal of England, a hereditary official responsible for the

organisation of all State occasions. At that date the office was invested in the sixteenth Duke of Norfolk, a man of considerable ability but few words. One evening, at a dinner-party, he turned from the person on his left to the lady on his other hand and said: 'Now, I have only two topics of conversation: cricket and drains. Choose.'

Although an Earl Marshal must undertake many duties, a coronation is far and away the most demanding. He must not only appoint the officials, allocate tickets to the Abbey, supervise the erection of scaffolding and deal with all the problems of precedence, etiquette and dress, he must also live with the knowledge that almost no coronation in the last nine hundred years has passed off entirely without incident. Indeed the catalogue of disaster is almost endless. In 1189 the service for Richard I was reduced to a shambles by a dive-bombing bat; and two centuries later Richard II not only lost a slipper at a crucial moment but was so exhausted by the lengthy service that he had to be carried home in a litter. Charles I came clad in white satin – traditionally the colour of sacrifice – and his son, James II, had trouble balancing the crown. At the coronation banquet which followed, the King's Champion (a mounted knight whose role was to challenge to mortal combat anyone refusing to accept the new king's right and title) fell off his horse.

When the same Champion delivered his challenge at the coronation of William and Mary it was taken up by an old woman on crutches. Dimly suspecting a hoax, or that the old lady would turn out to be an expert swordsman in disguise, the Champion refused to fight. At the coronation of Queen Anne the Archbishop of Canterbury, seemingly unaware that the Queen had produced seventeen children, none of whom lived beyond infancy, expressed the somewhat tactless hope that she would 'leave a numerous posterity to rule these kingdoms'. In 1837, when Queen Victoria received the homage of the peers, the aptly named Lord Rolle fell over the step leading to the throne and had to be saved by the hand which he was proposing to kiss. Half a century later, when her son, Edward VII, came to the Abbey to be crowned, the Dean of Westminster drenched Queen Alexandra with the contents of the chalice and wandered off with the crown. This was eventually retrieved by the Archbishop of Canterbury who was so flustered that he jumbled his words and put it on the King's head back to front.

The year prior to Queen Victoria's coronation, Caroline, the eighteen-year-old bride of the Duke of Montrose, came to live at number 45 Belgrave Square. She was then a pretty and lively young woman with a strong sense of fair play. A year or two afterwards, at the height of the Flora Hastings scandal, she and Lady Sarah Ingestre booed Queen Victoria at Ascot. The Queen was so incensed by their behaviour that she is said to have enquired into the possibility of having them flogged.

In later life Caroline grew 'big and heavy with a very red face'. She became a leading racehorse-owner and, after the death of her second husband, nearly eloped with the jockey, Fred Archer. The relationship eventually foundered on mutual snobbery: Caroline could not bear the thought of marrying a common jockey, while Archer was mortified to discover that marriage to a Duchess would not automatically make him a Duke. In 1894, fifty-eight years after first coming here, Caroline died in Belgrave Square, married to a third husband forty-five years her junior. Montrose Place, which abuts on to the garden of her former residence, is named in her honour.

South of Belgrave Square is Grosvenor Gardens, once the home of F. E. Smith, Lord Birkenhead. Statesman, lawyer, orator and wit, 'F.E.' was a man of extraordinary ability and did everything on a grand scale. When Mr Justice Bigham was asked what role he envisaged for the monolithic Royal Liver building in Liverpool he said: 'Probably new chambers for F. E. Smith.' His library in Grosvenor Gardens held more than twelve thousand volumes and his study door was fitted with a special aperture through which he received his mail direct from the postman. An approachable father, when his son brought him a bad school report he kicked it round the library for twenty minutes. As a young girl, his daughter, Pamela, spent her holidays in Grosvenor Gardens sliding down the bannisters, a past-time forbidden her at boarding-school.

At the end of his life 'F.E.' became markedly eccentric. His fondness for drink damaged his liver beyond repair; and the smoke from his beloved cigars so impaired his eyesight that he could no longer read. His libido, however, was not effected. Shortly before his death he was found wandering up and down a hotel corridor, muttering: 'I must have a woman at once. I can't wait.' His shrewdness also remained intact to the end and he was one of the few men never taken in by the swindler, Horatio Bottomley. When the portly financier announced that he was off to attend the installation of a new Archbishop of Canterbury, 'F.E.' urged him to hurry: 'His Grace will need a crook.'

In 1928, shortly after his release from prison, Bottomley himself came to Grosvenor Gardens to found *John Blunt*, a magazine which he hoped would emulate the fabulous success of his earlier brainchild, *John Bull*. In fact, as Bottomley was by now totally discredited in the eyes of his former readers, the venture quickly foundered. The man, who in his hey-day had survived sixty-seven bankruptcy petitions and writs in just five years, died in poverty in 1933.

Joining the western side of Grosvenor Gardens is Ebury Street, the home until his death in 1933 of the Irish writer, George Moore. He lived at 121 with his three companions: two old maidservants (who doted upon him) and a pet python with a taste for guinea-pigs, which it swallowed alive. One can only hope that Moore was a better neighbour here than he had been in Dublin – where he went out of his way to annoy the Miss Beams by having his door painted a bilious green, by rattling their railings with a walking-stick to provoke their dog, and by hurling stones at their cat. They retaliated by hiring a hurdy-gurdy man to play under his window while he was trying to write.

George Moore, the Irish writer, who lived with his pet python at
121 Ebury Street

One day a young lady called on Moore at Ebury Street to
tell him of the death of a friend. She was ushered across the
Aubusson carpet, past the Manet portrait and into the study.
As gently as she could she broke the news. Moore rose from
his chair and holding his head in his hands began to walk
about the room, muttering to himself. This went on for some
time. At last he said: 'Life is dreadfully unfair. My dear
friend Edmund Gosse, dead.' The young lady was forced to
tell him that he had misheard: the dead friend was not

Edmund Gosse but Martin Rosse. At this Moore looked startled – then cross. 'My dear young woman', he said, 'you surely don't expect me to go through all that again.'

In the spring of 1941 Sir Henry 'Chips' Channon passed Moore's old home late one night. A bomb had blown out the windows and he could distinctly hear the telephone ringing inside. He was struck by the irony of this: Moore had always refused to have a telephone installed in order to deny one of his former mistresses the pleasure of ringing him up. Anyone wishing to contact him had to ring a local chemist who then sent an assistant round with a message. In a long life, Moore had many mistresses – although his conquests never quite matched his boastings. As Susan Mitchell said: 'Some men kiss and do not tell, some kiss and tell; but George Moore told and did not kiss.'

Crossing Ebury Street at its south-western boundary is Eccleston Street, once the residence of the nineteenth-century sculptor, Sir Francis Chantrey. The son of a poor Derbyshire carpenter, Chantrey established a thriving practice in the first quarter of the nineteenth century and was rewarded with a knighthood. On his death, in 1841, his fortune of £150,000 was bequeathed in trust to his wife, who, as soon as he was buried, 'went into the studio with a hammer and knocked off the noses of many completed busts, so that they might not be too common'. An equally odd lady who lived nearby was 'Grota', the wife of the historian, George Grote. From 1836 to 1848 the couple lived at 3 Belgrave Place. Possibly to escape his preposterous wife, Grote chose to be buried with his great friend and fellow historian, Connop Thirlwall, in Westminster Abbey. Sydney Smith, who maintained that Mrs Grote was the origin of the word grotesque, said of the Grotes: 'I like him, he is so ladylike; and I like her, she's such a perfect gentleman.'

North of Eccleston Street is Eaton Place, in 1922 the scene of a tragic murder. On 22 June Sir Henry Wilson, a former Chief of the Imperial General Staff, had just stepped from a taxi outside his home at number 36 after returning from unveiling a war memorial at Liverpool Street station when he was shot four times in the back by two Sinn Feiners. He appears to have put up something of a fight because when the butler from the house next door ran into the street he found Sir Henry's sword lying on the steps 'out of its scabbard'. Threatening to shoot the driver, his murderers commandeered the dead man's taxi and were driven into Ebury Street where they ran off. Fortunately, the sound of shots had brought several policemen to the scene. A running chase ensued, two officers being seriously wounded before the assassins were overpowered. At their trial they claimed to have marked out their victim for the assistance he had rendered the government of Northern Ireland. They were hanged in Wandsworth prison a few months later.

Parallel to Eaton Place is Eaton Square, formerly the home of 'the startled cab-horse', Neville Chamberlain. British prime minister from 1937 to 1940 and a prime appeaser of Hitler and Mussolini, Chamberlain was lonely, self-sufficient and utterly charmless. His fortune derived from the firm of Nettlefold and Chamberlain, manufacturers of patent screws, and his outlook was typical of the factory-owning classes of that period. None of the machinery at Nettlefold and Chamberlain's was fitted with safety-guards: they tended to hamper production. Their lack caused a number of serious accidents. In time it was found that this, too, restricted production, the cries of the maimed tending to draw other employees away from their benches. The directors overcame the problem by imposing a series of fines for workers inconsiderate enough to scream when injured.

Leaving Eaton Square and walking south-west we come to Sloane Square, the south-eastern boundary of Chelsea. On the east side is the Royal Court theatre, rebuilt in 1888. Further modernisation was undertaken in 1965, much of it long overdue. Until that date the lavatory in the gentlemen's cloakroom flushed with such a roar that it completely drowned out the dialogue on stage for as long as two minutes.

Next to the theatre is Sloane Square underground station,

chiefly remarkable for a conduit pipe which runs at little more than head height above the platforms. More than a hundred years old and made of cast-iron, it carries the waters of one of London's 'lost' rivers, the subterranean Westbourne, which has its source several miles away to the north in Hampstead. During the Blitz the station was reduced almost to rubble. Only this brave old conduit remained intact, defiantly watertight.

In the early 1920's, Donald, the hero of *England, Their England*, encountered an elderly gentleman on Sloane Street underground station. Sporting an 'elegant long white moustache and carrying a rolled-up silk umbrella' he was bemoaning the news of England's route in the second Test at Melbourne. Turning to Donald, he said: 'It all comes of treating it as a game. We don't take things seriously enough in this country, sir, damnation take it all.' With that 'he stepped heavily upon the toes of a humble clerkly looking person behind him'.

On the west side of Sloane Square is Peter Jones' striking department store, a fine example of curvilinear curtain work. Peter Jones first set up in business in nearby Draycott Avenue, then Marlborough Road. His shop soon after collapsed, temporarily burying his wife. In spite of this early setback he prospered; and after his death, in 1906, that other great store-owner, John Lewis, purchased the Sloane Street premises from his executors. Being a frugal sort of man, rather than take a taxi from his office in Oxford Street, he walked to Sloane Square with the purchase price of £22,500 stuffed in his pocket.

Another Draycott Avenue tradesman of the period was Thomas Crapper, a sanitary engineer whose name has become synonymous with his business. Several of the early water-closets which he manufactured were named after streets in this vicinity.

Running west out of Sloane Square is the Kings Road, once little more than a cart-track leading to Hampton Court Palace. A private thoroughfare in a rather sinister and desolate area, it was patrolled at night by royal troops. Until 1830, when it became a public highway, the only people allowed to pass down it were the King and holders of special passes. On one side these passes bore a crown and on the other the words: 'The King's Private Road'.

Tryon Street, the fifth turning on the right out of the Kings Road, commemorates Vice-Admiral Sir George Tryon. It was formerly named after another and equally luckless seaman, Admiral Keppel. On 22 June 1893 Sir George Tryon was on manoeuvres with the Fleet in the Mediterranean when he inexplicably issued an order which was certain to lead to disaster. This was immediately obvious to his subordinates but none had the courage to overrule him. His flagship, the 'Victoria', was rammed and sunk. Sir George and most of his crew perished. Shortly before the ship went down, the Admiral called out, accepting full responsibility for the disaster; and in the very moment the 'Victoria' plummeted to the bottom, his ghost appeared at his house in Eaton Place, fifteen hundred miles away, where his wife was holding an 'At Home'. Witnessed by several hundred people, it strode with grim visage and unseeing eyes across the room, turned – and vanished.

Beyond Tryon Street is Markham Square, the home in March 1946 of the poet, Dylan Thomas. He was lodging at that date in a basement flat owned by his brother-in-law, the artist, Anthony Devas. A Welshman to the core, Thomas loathed London and called living in it 'the capital punishment'.

West of Markham Square is Sydney Street, dominated by St Luke's church, built in the Perpendicular Gothic style and completed in 1824. Charles Dickens was married here in 1836 and a few years later the spire was responsible for the sad demise of M. de Groof, 'The Flying Man'. M. de Groof's heavier-than-air-machine was being towed one day towards Ranelagh Gardens when it began to drift in the direction of the steeple. The intrepid aeronaut cried out to be cut adrift as he was sure he could make a safe descent in the region of the churchyard. Descend he did, but neither as gently nor as accurately as predicted: the fall killed him.

Continuing westwards and turning into Paultons Square we come to Danvers Street, for many years the home of the Scottish bacteriologist, Sir Alexander Fleming, the discoverer in 1928 of penicillin. He made the discovery entirely by accident, a careless laboratory assistant at St Mary's hospital, Paddington, having allowed mould to develop on a culture in error. Fleming might never have been in a position to note this had he not been an excellent shot. It was his skill as a marksman which first drew the attention of the vaccine therapist, Sir Almroth Wright. On the strength of it he gave the young man a job at St Mary's as a researcher.

Walking to the bottom of Danvers Street we arrive at the Chelsea Embankment. A little to the east is Cheyne Walk with a cluster of Georgian houses more redolent with history than any others in Chelsea. The first of these is number 4, built in 1718, and once the residence of 'George Eliot' (Mary Ann Evans). She and her husband moved here on 3 December 1880. A few days later, Mary Ann attended a concert at the St James's Hall, Piccadilly, where she contracted a chill. Nineteen days after moving into her new house she was dead, aged fifty. Her married life had lasted for just seven months.

From 1765 to 1782 number 6 Cheyne Walk was occupied by Dr Dominicetti's Fumigatory Steam Baths. For a time very fashionable, the business eventually collapsed and its Venetian proprietor fled abroad owing money. His house later became a boarding-school for choristers of the Chapel Royal, one of the inmates of which was the young Arthur Sullivan. Half a century later, Noel Coward aspired to be one of the company but failed his audition.

With its fine lamps, its impressive iron-work gates and twenty-two front-facing windows, number 22 Cheyne Walk is a truly superb house. Sharing it at various times with Swinburne, Meredith and Hall Caine, Dante Gabriel Rossetti lived here during his widowhood and here painted 'Beata Beatrix', now in the Tate Gallery. He came to the house in 1862 and remained here until his death, twenty years later, dosing himself with whisky and chloral and growing ever more paranoid. At one time he even suspected the birds singing in the garden of plotting his downfall.

Rossetti populated his house in Cheyne Walk with a bizarre menagerie which would have driven lesser mortals mad. There was a white bull which, because it had Jane Morris' eyes, was allowed to reduce the garden to a wasteland; and a white peacock which was found dead under one of the sofas by a visitor. Another inmate was a kangaroo. Having killed its mother it was in turn killed by the racoon. The wombat, which was much admired by Lewis Carroll and is thought to have been the model for the dormouse in *Alice in Wonderland*, had a great fondness for floral hats, eating first the wax fruit, then the fabric. One lady complained bitterly at this treatment. Rossetti was all contrition; but after she had gone he picked up his pet and crooned: 'Poor wombat. So indigestible.' The creature is still remembered in Cheyne Walk and the landlords of number 22 continue to insert a clause in all new leases forbidding tenants 'to keep wombats'.

Rossetti's former home was later occupied by the legendary miser, John Campden Neild. Notwithstanding that he had inherited a fortune of a quarter of a million pounds, he dined each night on stale bread and a boiled egg. He hitched rides with the coalman rather than incur the expense of a cab and he refused to have his clothes cleaned in case the process wore them out. Although his housekeeper faithfully looked after him for twenty-five years, more than once saving his life, she received nothing in his will. He left his entire fortune to Queen Victoria.

Number 18 Cheyne Walk, rebuilt in 1867, was once a Coffee House owned by a former servant of Sir Hans Sloane. As a side-line, and in order to increase business, he exhibited a wide range of curiosities in his front parlour. Among these were: 'A Piece of Queen Catharine's Skin'; 'A Necklace Made of Job's Tears'; 'Pontius Pilate's Wife's Chambermaid's Sister's Hat'; 'The Pope's Candle'; and 'The Four Evangelists' Heads Cut on a Cherry Stone'.

The American artist, James McNeill Whistler, lived for twelve years at number 96 and here painted the famous portrait of his mother. He was a devoted disciple of the 'Matching' school and is said once to have dyed a rice pudding green in order that it should blend with the walls of his dining-room.

Towards the end of his life another artist, J. M. W. Turner forsook his grand house in Queen Street for lodgings in Cheyne Walk. Looking for rooms, he came one day to the door of number 118. The landlady, failing to recognise him, asked for references. 'References!' stormed Turner, thrusting a bundle of bank-notes in her face, 'these are my references'. The landlady was rather taken aback. 'Well, sir', said she in a somewhat kinder voice, 'but what is your name?' 'Name, Ma'am?' countered the artist. 'May I ask what is *your* name, Ma'am?' She said: 'Oh, I am Mrs Booth.' 'Well, then, Ma'am', said Turner, 'I am *Mr Booth*.'

With his telescope under his arm and his sketch-pad in his hand, Turner became a familiar figure along the shore of the Thames. Because he was short and fat and rather fierce-looking, the local urchins christened him 'Puggy'. In 1851, six days before Christmas, 'Puggy Booth' died at his lodgings in Cheyne Walk 'without a groan' and muttering 'the sun is God'. Shortly before he did so he was visited by a physician who announced that he must prepare for the end. Turner said: 'Take a glass of sherry and look at me again.' The physician did so: but the verdict remained the same.

In 1916 another great man, the novelist, Henry James, died at number 21 Carlyle Mansions, Cheyne Walk. In his last hours he was visited by a friend who came to tell him that he had been awarded the Order of Merit. Having whispered the good news in the novelists's ear, he waited for some response. None came. James' eyes remained closed. His face registered no emotion. The friend left believing that the writer had passed into his last sleep oblivious of the high

J. M. W. TURNER, R.A.

'Puggy Booth' (J. M. W. Turner) who lodged at 118 Cheyne Walk,
and died there in 1851 muttering 'The sun is god'

honour bestowed upon him. But some hours after, as the
maid was tidying his dresser, he suddenly stirred and in a
small polite voice asked her to switch out the light . . . 'to
spare my blushes'.

Beyond Cheyne Walk is Cheyne Row, once the home of
the essayist and historian, Thomas Carlyle. He moved into
number 5 in 1834, remaining there until the day of his death,

forty-seven years later. Here his wife Jane almost murdered a constable (with the pistol which she kept beneath her pillow when her husband was from home) when he came to warn her of an unlatched window; and here Thomas heard one night the 'short rap' of John Stuart Mill upon the door. Some weeks previously, Mill had borrowed the only manuscript of the first volume of Carlyle's *History of the French Revolution*. He had come now to confess that his maid had 'taken it for waste-paper' and burned it. It was a trying evening. 'Mill, whom I had to comfort and speak peace to, remained injudiciously enough till almost midnight, and my poor Dame and I had to sit talking of indifferent matters; and could not till then get our lament freely uttered.'

For Carlyle, the annihilation of his manuscript was a catastrophe. 'I had not only forgotten the structure of it, but the spirit it was written with was past.' Nonetheless, he sat down and within a matter of weeks wrote it over. It was a dispiriting task and at the end of it he confessed to feeling like a man who had 'nearly killed himself accomplishing zero'.

Oakley Street, which connects the Chelsea Embankment with the Kings Road, was formerly the home of the distinguished mathematician, Charles Sanger. An absent-minded man, he could never remember the number of his house (fifty-eight). He used as a mnemonic 'the Septuagint minus the Apostles'. Captain Scott lived next door with his mother and two sisters whilst writing the account of his 1904 expedition to the Antarctic; and the Duke of St Albans, a direct descendant of Nell Gwynne, also had a house here until recently.

Whilst on a public reading tour – a tour which lasted intermittently for four years – Mark Twain resided in nearby Tedworth Square, number twenty-three. The tour proved so successful that he was not only able to pay off the crippling debts incurred by his stock-market speculations but was even left with a small surplus.

By turns a printer and a Mississippi pilot, Twain took his pen-name from the wharfingers, or dockers, who used to count the cargo they unloaded by tolling: 'Mark one, mark twain' etc. A classical humourist, when an account of his death was published in error he described it as 'grossly exaggerated'. In later years his talent for 'debunking' acquired a rather malicious edge. He disliked the work of that other Chelsea resident, Turner, and once compared his paintings to 'a tortoiseshell cat floundering in a plate of tomatoes'.

South of Tedworth Square is Chelsea Royal Hospital, founded in 1682 by Charles II for the care of retired and invalid soldiers. The inspiration for the Hospital is said to have come from Nell Gwynne. Equally doubtful is the story that her mother drowned in one of the boundary ditches, having fallen into it one night dead drunk.

In the cemetery adjoining the Hospital there are several interesting graves, including one to a pensioner who lived to be over a hundred and was killed by a falling bomb during the Blitz. Buried nearby are two women, Christina Davis and Hannah Bell. Both formed attachments to men sent off to fight in the Crimea and both followed their lovers by passing themselves off as soldiers. The impostures were only uncovered when they were wounded in action. In some respects they were lucky. At the time in question the wearing of the King's uniform – or even the uniform of a Chelsea Pensioner – without authority was still a hanging offence.

The Hospital has always provided a degree of medical care for the Pensioners and there was until recently a Resident Physician. One of the most eccentric of these was Dr Monsey, whose method of extracting teeth was desperate. Taking a strong piece of cat-gut, he wound one end round the tooth: the other end he threaded through a hole drilled in a bullet which he then inserted into his revolver and fired.

Tite Street, to the west of the Hospital, counts two famous men among its residents. John Singer Sargent lived and died at number 31, keeping a hanging-basket in his hall from which the less well-off might help themselves to money; and for eleven years, until the day of his arrest for homosexuality,

Oscar Wilde occupied number 34. It was here in 1891 that Wilde was introduced to Lord Alfred Douglas; and it was from here, three years later, that he was forced to eject Lord Alfred's father, the bucolic Marquess of Queensberry, who had come to horsewhip him. Turning to his manservant, Wilde said: 'This is the Marquess of Queensberry, the most infamous brute in London. You are never to allow him to enter my house again.'

Some time later a man called Allen came to Tite Street bearing a rather compromising letter which Oscar had written to Lord Alfred. He was shown into the playwright's study where he handed the document over, saying rather darkly: 'A very curious construction can be put on this letter.' Oscar conceded that it could, adding: 'But art is rarely intelligible to the criminal classes.' Allen said he had been offered sixty pounds for it. Oscar advised him to take it: 'I myself have never received so large a sum for any work of that length, but I am glad to find there is someone in England who considers a letter of mine worth sixty pounds.' Allen's confidence beginning to falter, he now confessed, rather weakly, that the man in question was 'out of town'. 'Ah', said Oscar, smoothly, 'but he is sure to come back.'

Seeing that there was no advantage to be had from it, Allen presented the letter to Oscar. In turn, Oscar handed over ten shillings, adding: 'I am afraid you are leading a wonderfully wicked life.' At the door, where the two men shook hands, Allen said, rather apologetically: 'There is good and bad in all of us.'

'You are a born philosopher,' said Oscar.

12

The City

In 1922 George Santayana wrote that 'England is the paradise of individuality, eccentricity, heresy, anomalies, hobbies and humours.' This is nowhere more true than the City of London. Since 64 A.D., when the Romans erected a 'busy emporium for trade' on the site, its 677 acres have proved fertile soil, reaping a rich harvest of profligacy and profanity, wrongdoing and worth, loneliness and love. There is dignity here and high-toned humanity too. There is also a great deal of selfishness and self-seeking.

During the Elizabethan era, one of the greatest of the City's self-seekers was Sir Christopher Hatton, Lord Chancellor to Elizabeth I, who won favour with the Queen by his dancing. In 1576 Hatton Garden was in the possession of one Richard Cox, the Bishop of Ely. Elizabeth, desiring to make a gift of it to Hatton, wrote to Cox ordering him to relinquish it. This he refused to do – until Elizabeth wrote in a more vigorous vein. 'Proud prelate', said she, 'you know what you were before I made you what you are: if you do not immediately comply with my request, by God I will unfrock you.' The Bishop saw the sense of this argument.

According to the *Ingoldsby Legends*, the 'dancing' Lord Chancellor's wife, the redoubtable Lady Hatton, entered into a pact with the Devil in Hatton Garden. At the height of a ball at Hatton House he appeared to her as a dancer, dressed all in black, and carried her off. She was never seen again:

> But out in the courtyard – and just
> in that part

where the pump stands – lay
bleeding a *Large Human Heart.*

The encounter is commemorated by Bleeding Heart Yard,
which abuts on to Ely Place, a private cul-de-sac so called
from having once housed the London Palace of the Bishops
of Ely and the most perfectly preserved Georgian precinct in
London. The nineteen little houses and the land on which
they stand were until recently considered to form a part of
Cambridgeshire and in consequence the Metropolitan police
have no right of access or arrest here. In practice, anyone
causing a nuisance may be ejected by the beadles who have
ruled in Ely Place for centuries. Their cry has now been
silenced, but at one time they used to patrol the precinct, and
at midnight called out:

> 'Tis twelve o'clocke
> Look well to your locke,
> Your fier and your light,
> And so good-night.

eminently sensible advice to this day.

On the west side of the Place is the Roman Catholic church
of St Etheldreda's, built about 1290 but restored in 1935 and
again in 1952. It takes its name from a deeply venerated
Cambridgeshire Abbess, sometimes called St Awdry, who in
the seventh century founded a religious house on the site of
what is now Ely Cathedral. St Etheldreda died in 649, some
said of a throat tumour inflicted upon her as a judgement for
her love of devotional beads and necklaces. Known as St
Awdrys, and later simply as 'Tawdrys', these necklaces were
of such poor quality that the word 'tawdry' has entered the
language as a synonym for anything gross or shoddy. Every
year, on 3 February (the Feast of St Blaise) the ceremony of
the Blessing of the Throats is held in St Etheldreda's, the
priest intoning a blessing whilst holding two candles, fixed in
the shape of a cross, against the adam's-apple of those

petitioning for relief from afflictions of the throat. The ceremony commemorates St Blaise's miraculous cure of a young boy whom he found choking on a fish bone.

On a lighter note, number 20 Ely Place was once the home of Mary Howitt, the poetess, best remembered for the verses beginning:

> Won't you walk into my parlour?
> Said the spider to the fly.

As Ely Place is itself something of a spider's-nook, she may have had it in mind when writing the poem.

Bleeding Heart Yard, site of a sixteenth-century encounter with the Devil

In the seventeenth century, the comedian, Joe Hains, was strolling in the vicinity of Ely Place when he was taken up by the bailiffs for a debt of twenty pounds. He attempted to get free by claiming mistaken identity. He was in the process of giving a fictitious name and address when he spotted the Bishop of Ely driving up Holborn Hill in his carriage. Saying that here was a man who knew him well and would vouch for him, Joe ran up to the carriage and thrust his head in at the window. Being a quick-thinking sort of fellow, he represented the bailiffs as two atheists teetering on the brink of conversion. Would the Bishop help? The Bishop at once called out: 'My friends, if you will come presently to my house, I will satisfy you in this matter.' On the strength of this, the bailiffs allowed Hains to go. On discovering that he had been hoodwinked, the Bishop, far from being angry, laughed uproariously and paid over twenty pounds to the bailiffs out of his own pocket.

Passing out of Ely Place to the south, we find ourselves at the junction of Charterhouse Street and Holborn Viaduct. In 1945 one of the last V-2 rockets fell on London at this spot, killing more than a hundred people. A little to the east is the church of St Sepulchre's, founded here in 1290 but rebuilt in the fifteenth century and repaired by Sir Christopher Wren after the Great Fire of 1666. Near the east end of the aisle is buried Captain John Smith, who in 1605 joined an expedition to colonize Virginia and was captured by red indians. He was saved from death by the intervention of the chieftain's daughter, the Princess Pocahontas. After receiving a false report of Captain Smith's death, Pocahontas married a man called Rolfe, who brought her to London where she was presented to Queen Anne. Towards the end of this visit it is said that she encountered Captain Smith in the street and was so overcome with shock that she died. In fact, if any one thing killed the Princess, it was the damp English climate.

In the south wall of the church is a bricked-up doorway that formerly gave access to a 'secret' tunnel leading to the condemned hold of Newgate prison – which until 1901 stood a little to the south of here. The handbell which rests nearby is known as the Execution Toll of Old Newgate. It was carried down this passage on the eve of executions and tolled outside the cells of prisoners about to die.

In the eighteenth century the graveyard of St Sepulchre's was a favourite resort of grave-robbers, or 'Resurrection Men', who disposed of their wares to the surgeons of St Bartholomew's Hospital, a mere stone's-throw away on the far side of Giltspur Street.

Snow Hill, which leads west from St Sepulchre's to Far-ringdon Street, was once a boarding-point for the coaches which plied between here and the north. As the journeys were very long, and usually terminated late at night with most of the passengers asleep, the area became known as 'Snore Hill'. Nicholas Nickleby boarded a coach at the Saracen's Head in 'Snore Hill' when he first set out for Dotheboys Hall; and in 1688 John Bunyan died here of a cold which he caught while out evangelising. Snow Hill was also much favoured by bands of Mohocks – aristocratic ruffians – who amused themselves by rolling women down it in barrels.

Running east out of Snow Hill is Cock Lane, so called from having once been an area given over to the breeding of fighting-cocks. At the point where it junctions with Giltspur Street is Pie Corner, the spot where the Great Fire burned itself out in 1666. High on the wall is a stone cherub known as 'The Fat Boy of Gluttony'. It formerly bore the quaint inscription: 'This Boy is in Memory Put Up of the Late Fire of London, occasioned by the Sin of Gluttony, 1666'.

Walking south down Giltspur Street and turning east into Newgate Street, we come to Greyfriars Passage, covering in part the site of an ancient burial ground and one of the most haunted spots in London. Five queens were buried in the church which once occupied this land, including the 'she-wolf of France', Queen Isabella, who left instructions that the heart of her husband, Edward II, whom she callously had murdered, should be deposited under the breast of her effigy.

According to Timbs' *London Curiosities*, Isabella encountered here one day her husband's mistress, who was later also to poison her husband, also called Edward, a crime for which she was hanged at Tyburn. The two women fell to fighting. The contest proved so vicious that the churchyard's guardian ran away rather than attempt to separate them. Although there is no record of their having done so in recent years, their shades continued to re-enact the encounter on moonlit nights for many centuries. Other ghosts still to be seen here from time to time are a terrifying spectral hound; and the shade of Elizabeth Barton, 'The Holy Maid of Kent', buried in the churchyard in 1534 after her execution for opposing Henry VIII's divorce from Catherine of Aragon.

Newgate Street, which runs from Holborn Viaduct in the west to Cheapside in the east, takes its name from one of several gates which gave access to the City when it was still enclosed by a great wall. At that date, Newgate Street was populated by butchers. As a result of their unscrupulous practice of inserting air-filled sheep's bladders into carcasses in order to 'inflate' both the size and the price, the street was nicknamed 'Blow Bladder Lane'.

South of Newgate Street is Old Bailey, dominated by the Central Criminal Court. It stands on the site of the notorious Newgate Prison and is surmounted by a bronze-gilt figure of Justice. In the days before central London became a smokeless zone, the figure had to be cleaned approximately every six months. As it is situated some two hundred feet above the ground, and can only be reached by standing in the precariously balanced scales which the figure holds in one of its outstretched hands, it was not a task for the faint-hearted. One man who undertook it became so paralysed with fear, as the scales swayed back and forth in a high wind, that he had to be rescued by the fire brigade and sent on holiday to recover.

On the far side of Old Bailey is the Hall of the Stationers' Company. In the 1550's the Stationers were entrusted by the government with the task of checking all works of prose for

New Gate which formerly stood on the site of Newgate Street

seditious or heretical material. Those which they condemned were burned in Stationers Hall Court by the Public Hangman and Lady Jane Grey was only one of many who had their libraries depleted in this fashion. The Stationers were also, of course, printers of books. Most of their work was excellent. Unfortunately, they are remembered today for the one which was not. In 1632 they printed an edition of the Bible in which the seventh commandment was rendered as: 'Thou shalt commit adultery' – a sin of ommission which drew upon them the wrath of the Star Chamber and a heavy fine.

Bordering Stationers' Hall on its northern side is Amen Court. At its far end, and marking the boundary with what was formerly the graveyard of Newgate prison, is a ghostly wall dating back to Roman times. It was once a part of the old City wall. Amen Court was formerly known as 'Dead Man's Walk', from being the path along which executed felons were conveyed to the grave; and for many years there were reports of a dark indefinable shape seen crawling along the top of this wall. It progressed with a scraping noise and what sounded like the rattle of invisible chains.

At the top of Ludgate Hill, to the south, is St Paul's

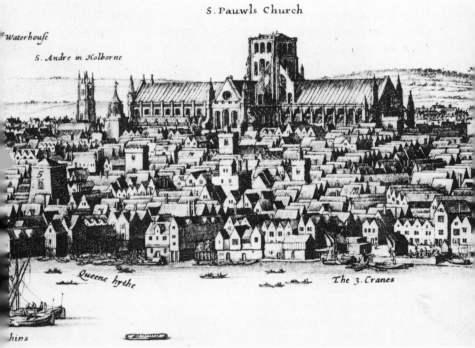

'A loathsome Golgotha' – the medieval church of St Paul's (1647) destroyed in the Great Fire. From an engraving by Wenceslaus Hollar

Cathedral, the masterpiece of Sir Christopher Wren. It was constructed between 1675 and 1710 to replace the medieval church of old St Paul's, destroyed by the Great Fire. Many people considered the devastation visited on old St Paul's as something of a divine judgement. It had deteriorated over the years into a 'loathsome Golgotha', frequented by cut-purses, whores, card-sharps, quack doctors, marriage-brokers and drunks. Its aisles and walkways were lined with the stalls of common tradesmen: costermongers and butch-ers, tanners and lawyers, bakers and water-carriers, vying each to outdo the other by touting for custom at the top of their voices. At one time the authorities even allowed the practice of archery to be carried on within the building, the target being the high-roosting pigeons.

As the wide walkway formed by the north and south transepts offered the public a literally God-given shortcut through the churchyard, most of the businesses here flourished. In the course of time the tradesmen, also, began to take advantage of it, leading their horses and heavily-laden carts through the building rather than make the lengthy journey around the perimeter. As the average horse voids a minimum of six tons of waste matter a year, the floor became almost impassable.

Such was the profanity of the times that in 1600 a man by the name of Banks rode his horse to the top of the Cathedral. He did so for a wager, watched by a vast crowd. One of the crowd was a young apprentice, who ran home to exhort his master to come and watch. 'Away, you fool,' countered the master. 'What need I go so far to see a horse on the top when I can see so many asses at the bottom.' Mr Banks and his clever little horse later visited Italy, repeated the stunt, and were burned as heretics.

If the common people abused St Paul's and treated it with contempt, they were nonetheless better behaved than some of the clergy who ran it. One monk even attempted to rape a young girl who had come to him to make her confession. She quickly escaped from him: 'up the stairs of the great clock tower, raised the clapper or hammer of the bell of the clock, just as it had finished striking twelve, and, by means of the roof, eluded her assailant and got away. On accusing him, as soon as she reached her friends and home, she called attention to the fact of the clock having struck thirteen at the time; and on those in the immediate neighbourhood of the cathedral being asked if so unusual a thing had been heard, they said it was so. This proved the story and the monk was degraded.'.

After its destruction in the Great Fire, old St Paul's was removed piecemeal. It filled in all some 47,000 carts. The present building cost £736,952 2s 3¼d, the money being raised by a special levy on coal. (Coal, it is said, ultimately got its revenge by blacking the Cathedral's face.)

Dominating the Cathedral's great western forecourt is a statue to 'Brandy Nan,' Queen Anne, 'with her face to the brandy shop and her back to the church'. It replaces a former statue to the Queen which in 1769 was disfigured by a drunken Lascar who mistook it for his mother. He broke off the nose and was decamping back over the railings with the stone orb and sceptre when he was arrested by the watchman, whom he attempted to stab. On 12 September 1940 an unexploded bomb came to rest at the foot of the present statue. Two Royal Engineers were later awarded the George Cross for successfully defusing it.

Immediately inside the Cathedral's west door, on the northern side, is a memorial chapel to Lord Kitchener. It contains a secret door leading up to the dome. This might never have been discovered but for the ghost of a clerkly little man who haunted the chapel. He mooched about, whistling to himself, until noticed, when he disappeared through the masonry in the vicinity of the door. When renovations to the chapel were undertaken, one of the Cathedral officials, remembering the strange little ghost, asked workmen to excavate the wall at the point where he habitually disappeared. The door was uncovered and the hauntings ceased.

Buried in the crypt of St Pauls is England's greatest sailor, Lord Nelson. He lies beneath a marble sarcophagus –

'Brandy Nan': Statue of Queen Anne outside St Paul's

originally intended for Cardinal Wolsey and later Henry
VIII – encased in the Aboukir Coffin.

The Aboukir Coffin was fashioned from the main-mast

of the French flagship, 'L'Orient', captured at the battle of Aboukir in 1798. The English cannon having set the 'L'Orient' on fire, Lord Nelson ordered the long-boats to be lowered to take up her crew. But the French captain, who had been wounded in the engagement, refused to leave his ship, as did his young son, Casabianca. As the long-boats receded, the fire ignited the ship's magazine and the 'L'Orient' was engulfed in a mass of flames. Casabianca was seen attempting to lash his father to a spar, with the intention of floating him free. At this point the ship exploded. Despite the intense heat and showers of sparks, Nelson at once ordered the long-boats back. But although the boy and his father were spotted in the water, they were swallowed up by the smoke and failing light before they could be rescued. This singular act of heroism later inspired Mrs Hemans' poem, 'Casabianca', familiar today for the line: 'The boy stood on the burning deck'.

After Nelson's death, at the battle of Trafalgar, his body was transported back to England preserved in a barrel of brandy. There is a story that the cask was placed on deck and that one enterprising sailor managed to stay drunk for the best part of the voyage by inserting a drill through the planks and syphoning off the contents. Although the story is almost certainly untrue, the phrase 'To Tap the Admiral' – obtaining a drink by devious or surreptitious means – has passed into naval terminology.

Walking through the churchyard of St Pauls – now an impersonal concrete wasteland – we come to Cheapside, once known as 'the Beauty of London'. It was formerly a street-market and takes its name from the old English word 'cyppan' – to barter. In 1461 a grocer named Walter Walker was living in Cheapside, carrying on his business at the sign of the Crown. One day, in a jocular mood, he boasted that he would make his son 'heir to the Crown'. This rather bad pun reached the ears of Edward IV, who, having been King for only eight days, failed to see the joke. He had poor Walter beheaded at Smithfield for treason.

At the eastern end of Cheapside is the church of St Mary-le-Bow, so called from the ancient bowed arches of its vault. To be born within the sound of Bow bells is said to be the true definition of a cockney. The same bells are said to have reached Dick Whittington as he trudged up Highgate Hill en route to seek his fortune and urged him to 'turn again'.

For all this, the church has a sinister and depressing history. In 1090 its predecessor lost its roof in a gale (the avalanche of timber causing considerable loss of life); and a hundred years later it was razed by fire when the authorities attempted to smoke out one Walter Fitzosbert, nicknamed 'Longbeard'. Fitzosbert was a political activist who seems to have been genuinely committed to righting the wrongs of the poor. He sought sanctuary in the church after publicly denouncing the crippling taxation imposed for the purpose of raising the ransom for Richard I. As soon as he and his followers emerged from the building they were summarily hanged.

In 1271 the tower of the church toppled into the street, and people were again killed. Soon after the tower was restored, one Lawrence Duckett was murdered in it. Seventeen men were later hanged for their complicity in this crime and a woman accessory burned at the stake. No satisfactory motive for it was ever established and several richer and more powerful accomplices were merely 'hanged by the purse'.

Dean Swift, in satirical mood, once forecast 'that when the Dragon on Bow church kisses the cock behind the Exchange, great changes will take place in England'. In 1832 both fell in need of repair and were removed to the same workman's yard. Remembering the prophecy, the workman saw to it that they duly kissed. In the June of that year the Reform Bill was carried by Earl Grey and the Whigs, and England reached one of the great crossroads of her history.

The third turning on the left out of Cheapside is Wood Street. Following it to its end, we come to Fore Street and the church of St Giles, Cripplegate, built in 1545 and marooned today in the Barbican sea. In 1790 extensive renovations were carried out to the church and these were made an excuse for looking into the grave of the poet, John Milton, who had been interred here (in 1674) not with one of his three wives but his father. A female grave-digger named Elizabeth prised off the coffin's outer coating of lead, exposing the poet's corpse to view. She next ripped open the shroud, caving in the ribs in the process. Milton's five upper teeth – still firmly embedded after a hundred and sixteen years – were knocked out and carried off as souvenirs by a local innkeeper. A pawnbroker removed a tuft of hair, together with a tooth from the lower jaw. Less interesting oddments were examined but contemptuously tossed back.

Being something of an opportunist, Elizabeth now instituted a charge for viewing the corpse, employing two brawny henchmen to bar the door against those unwilling or unable to pay. The coffin was shrewdly placed in the lea of a dark pew and briefly illuminated by the light of a tinder. The price of threepence allowed for only one strike, additional illumination costing extra. As demand decreased, so did the fee, first to tuppence, then to a penny. After a busy two days, the supply of sightseers dried up entirely and the corpse was mercifully reinterred. When the Vicar came to hear of what had passed he flew into a terrible rage – not at the sacrilege, but the loss of revenue to himself and the church. At one point he seriously considered suing Elizabeth for a tenth of her receipts, the traditional 'tithe'.

Progressing east down Fore Street and then into London Wall, we come to Moorgate, where in 1795 the poet Keats was born. His birthplace, number eighty-five, was then a tavern stable where his father worked and lodged. Keats spent his formative years in Moorgate, where he proved to be a child 'most violent and ungovernable' – at least according to Benjamin Robert Haydon: 'At five years of age or thereabouts, he got hold of a naked sword, and shutting the door, swore nobody should go out. His mother wanted to do so, but he threatened her so furiously, she began to cry, and was obliged to wait till somebody, through the window, saw her position and came to the rescue.'

Given Keats' character, the incident is more probably explained by Colvin, who states that on Keats' mother being ordered to rest, the child insisted 'on keeping watch at her door with an old sword, allowing no one to go in'.

Following Moorgate into Princes Street, we come to the Mansion House, 'sedate, severe, churchy' and 'a kind of Hallelujah Chorus in stone'. Built in 1739, it is the official residence of the Lord Mayor of London. As the Lord Mayor is chief City magistrate, it is also a police court, and as such the only private residence in London with cells.

One of the first Mayors of London known to us by name was Henry FitzEylwin, elected in the last years of the twelfth century. Since then, many hundreds of men have held the post. We can look at only a few.

In 1346 the honour fell to Sir Robert Knollys. During his term of office he built a small bridge across Seething Lane to connect his two properties, one on either side of the road. Unfortunately, he failed to obtain permission and was fined *in perpetuity* one freshly plucked rose which is still presented each year to the Lord Mayor by his descendants.

A second Alderman who fell foul of the law during his mayoralty was Lord Mayor Curtis. In 1795, in his role of magistrate, he fined himself five shillings for failing to keep the streets clean – adding the rider that he hoped it would be a warning to himself.

A very patriotic Lord Mayor was Sir Bartholomew Read. In 1502, at a banquet, he was shown a magnificent jewel by a foreign merchant. The merchant sneered that it was beyond the purse even of the King of England. The price was a thousand marks. Read examined the stone, called for pestle and mortar, and ground it to dust. He then poured the dust into his wine and drank it. Throwing the merchant his money, he said: 'Speak honourably of the King of England, for thou hast now seen one of his subjects drink a thousand marks at a draft.'

One of the poorest Lord Mayors in history was Sir Simon Eyre, who in 1445 at first refused the office, saying that he lacked the money with which to maintain it. At this, one of his Aldermen mentioned that he had often heard him remark: 'I have at home a table for which I would not accept a thousand pounds.' Eyre laughed and invited the gentleman home with him to inspect it. 'On their arrival Mr Eyre desired his wife to "prepare the little table and set some refreshment before our guest". This she would fain have refused, but finding he would take no excuse, she seated herself on a low stool, and, spreading a damask napkin over her lap, with a venison pasty thereon, Simon exclaimed . . . "Behold the table which I would not take a thousand pounds for."'

In 1611 the Lord Mayor was Sir William Craven. He seems to have spent his entire term of office cowering in fear of the plague and when he could stand it no longer: 'Took horse and galloped westward till he reached a lonely farm-house on the Berkshire downs, and there built Ashdown House. The local legend is that four avenues led to the house from the four points of the compass, and that in each of the four walls there was a window, so that if the plague got in at one side it might go out at the other.'

Sir James Bartholomew, Lord Mayor in 1479, also lived in fear of contracting the plague and once had his Sheriff fined £50 'for kneeling too close to him while at prayers in St Paul's'.

As far as is known, both Sir William and Sir James died peacefully in their beds. Only the luckless Sir John Shorter met a summary end. In 1688, on the way to a mayoral engagement, he reined in his horse at the gates of Newgate prison to drink a glass of spiced wine. The tankard was large, with a heavy ornate lid. As Sir John lowered it from his lips, the lid inadvertently clapped shut, making a noise which startled his horse. The horse threw him and he died from his injuries the following day.

East of the Mansion House in Threadneedle Street,

deriving its name from the three needles on the sign of the Merchant Taylors Company, situated at number 30. At the western end of the street is the Bank of England, founded in 1694. It moved to its present site in 1736 and has been known affectionately as 'The Old Lady of Thread-needle Street' ever since. The building, by Sir John Soane, covers an area of almost five acres. More than five hundred buses pass it every day and seven subterranean streams run beneath it. For many years it was protected at night by a detachment of soldiers: one officer, three NCO's, a drummer and a dozen men. The officer, and a guest of his choosing, were allowed the privilege of sending out for their dinner at the Bank's expense, other ranks bringing sandwiches. Since the practice was discontinued in 1973 the premises have been guarded at night by automatic scanners.

In the course of its long and distinguished history a number of interesting people have been associated with the Bank. One was Kenneth Grahame (who in 1908, and to amuse his son, Alistair, wrote a quaint riverside tale called *Wind in the Willows*); and another – a colleague of Grahame's – was Montagu Norman, elected Governor of the Bank in 1920. In 1950, six years after his retirement, Norman died a very bizarre death. Walking home one evening, in the dark, he tripped over a sitting cow, sustaining injuries which killed him.

One of the Bank's most curious directors was 'J.M.', who dressed at night as a navvy and scoured the streets of Whitechapel, carrying a pick-axe, in the hope of catching Jack the Ripper.

Its most memorable cashier was Abraham Newland. Newland slept every night at the Bank for a quarter of a century and signed every banknote in person. When he died, in 1807, the Bank entered upon a turbulent period in its history; and half a century later, following a series of panic withdrawals, narrowly avoided bankruptcy, having at one time barely sufficient reserves to cover the next day's transactions. It survived by paying out in farthings, the least valuable of coins, very slowly.

At that date banknotes could be issued for any sum and frequently were. In 1740 one of the Bank's directors, wishing to purchase a large country house, was issued with one for £30,000. He hurried home and was about to lock it away when he was called out of the room. On his return, he was unable to find it. It could not have been stolen and he eventually assumed that it must have floated from its resting-place on the mantelpiece into the fire. After some deliberation, the Bank issued a replacement note, asking only that if the original should be presented, the director would bear the loss. No more was heard of the matter and in due course the director died.

More than thirty years elapsed. Then, one day, a gentleman walked into the Bank and presented the note to the Assistant Chief Cashier. The astonished official refused to accept it, explaining that it was void. He referred the man to the late director's heir – who also refused to pay. The gentleman returned to the Bank and quietly pointed out that, whatever the circumstances which might have been entailed upon it, the note was made payable to 'Bearer' and he was entitled to the money. The Bank had no recourse but to pay.

After a great deal of investigation, it was discovered that the mysterious presenter was an architect. He had purchased the late director's house and in demolishing it in order to build another had found the banknote lodged behind the fireplace.

Although the Bank still possesses 'some banknotes for large amounts . . . including a single note for one million sterling, kept in a frame', notes today are issued only in denominations of £50, £20, £10, £5 and £1. With the introduction of decimal currency, the old ten-shilling note was phased out and replaced by a coin. In spite of this there are still some twenty-five million old ten-shilling notes unaccounted for. They are no longer legal tender, but can be redeemed on presentation at Threadneedle Street. Predictably, the circulation of banknotes reaches its peak during the summer holiday period and again shortly before Christmas. As a result of inflation, £5 notes now account for more than fifty per cent of all paper-money. Due to the public's increasing reluctance to accept soiled or torn ones, the average life of a one-pound note is now about eight months. New notes are transported to the Bank from its printing works in Essex by means of a two-tier armoured car manned by twelve guards. It is accompanied along the route by a convoy of armed police. Once safely delivered to Threadneedle Street, the money is distributed to the major clearing banks by means of a little-publicised underground railway.

The garden of the Bank of England is said to be haunted by two ghosts: the spectre of a black-habited nun (sometimes thought to be the *real* 'Old Lady of Threadneedle Street'); and by the tragic shade of Sarah Whitehead.

In about 1811, Philip Whitehead, Sarah's elder brother, was employed by the Bank. Although nothing was ever proved against him, he and his sister lived considerably beyond their means and the Bank eventually dispensed with his services. Philip kept this information from his nineteen-year-old sister, first by dipping into his savings and then, when these were exhausted, by forging cheques. In due course he was caught and hanged. On the day of his arrest, when he failed to come home, Sarah, who seems to have been a remarkably uninquisitive girl, assumed that he had been press-ganged. She only discovered the truth when she made the journey to Threadneedle Street, some years later, and enquired after him through one of the officials. The shock unhinged her mind. Every day for the rest of her life she came here to look for her brother. The officials always treated her with the utmost kindness and may even have helped her financially. On her death, she was buried in the churchyard of St Christopher-le-Stocks, now incorporated into the Bank's garden. She walks here yet, in a groping wavering manner, as if in great distress, but seldom remains visible for long.

To the north east of the Bank is Throgmorton Street, named after the Elizabethan courtier and Chief Butler of England, Sir Nicholas Throckmorton. In 1571, Throckmorton was poisoned, possibly by the Earl of Leicester, one of his rivals for the Queen's favour.

The principal building here is the Stock Exchange, founded in 1773 for the business of buying and selling shares. The present structure of twenty-six storeys stands three hundred and twenty feet high and was completed in 1972. As many people now have unwitting dealings with it – through Unit Trusts, Pension Schemes and Building Societies – admission to the floor of the Stock Exchange is an arduous business. Applicants must first work for not less than three years for a firm affiliated to and approved by the Stock Exchange. They must also pass a twelve-hour examination, set in four parts. They must be prepared to find a four-figure deposit to be held as a surety for their future good behaviour and a similar sum as an entrance fee. They must also find two current stockbrokers to propose and second them. Each must themselves have been members of the Exchange for at least four years and have known the applicant for not less than two. Having surmounted all these obstacles, prospective brokers must lastly purchase one share in the Stock Exchange itself.

Despite these strict procedures for admission, the Stock Exchange has produced a stock of colourful characters, not least John Rive, who lived to be 118. Another, Martin Coles Harman, a rugged bull-headed man, purchased for £16,000 the island of Lundy and took to issuing coins with a portrait of himself on the front. His fortune was founded on the Rock Investment Trust. This later went into liquidation and Harman ended his career in prison. In 1944, his son, John Harman, redeemed the family name by winning a posthumous Victoria Cross whilst fighting with the West Kents in Japan.

One of the great eighteenth-century businessmen associated with the Stock Exchange was the jobber, Alexander Fordyce. One night, at dinner, he turned to a lady, a

Sir Nicholas Throckmorton, Chief Butler of England, poisoned in
1571 by a rival for the Queen's favours. Throgmorton Street was
named after him. By an unknown artist

complete stranger, and said: 'Madam, if you will entrust me
with £1,000 for three years, I will employ it advantageously.'
Although the lady was a little taken aback at the abruptness
of his manner, she agreed. At the end of the term, Fordyce

returned her £10,000. He was less astute with his own money and ended his days a pauper.

Bishopsgate, to the east of Throgmorton Street, is one of the longest thoroughfares in the City. It commemorates Bishop Erkenwald, who in the seventh century was granted a licence to levy a tax on all wood passing into the City by way of the gate which then stood nearby. Sir Thomas Gresham, the founder of the Royal Exchange, had a house in Bishops-gate (the site of the modern Gresham House). On the morning of 21 November 1579, he left here to go to the Exchange. The door had hardly closed behind him, however, when he suffered an apoplectic seizure and dropped dead on the pavement.

An equally luckless resident was the eighteenth-century dandy, Nathaniel Bentley, who owned an ironmongery warehouse here. After the sudden death of his fiancée, he changed overnight from a merry extrovert to a miserable recluse. He allowed the merchandise in his warehouse to gather dust and rot; and was nicknamed 'Dirty Dick' from his refusal to wash. After his death, in 1809, a Bishopsgate publican purchased the warehouse (and the remainder of the grubby stock) and turned it into a tavern. It is now his only memorial.

Opening out of Bishopsgate to the east is the passage of Great St Helen's, another piece of 'secret' London. It gives access to what has sometimes been called 'the Westminster Abbey of the City', St Helen's church, dating for the most part from the thirteenth century. At that date the church was affiliated to a Benedictine nunnery, the inmates of which were mostly the daughters or widows of rich City merchants. They led gay and fashionable lives and more than once had to be chastised for giggling and dancing and waving at strangers over the top of a screen. Among the various interesting monuments and tombs to be found here is one to Fanny Gamble. Note the truncated and rather ambiguous inscription: 'Faithful over a few things.'

On the south wall is a canopied tomb to Sir John Spencer, a

wealthy City businessman who died in 1609. His daughter, who is shown kneeling at his feet, was an only child and therefore the heir to his vast fortune. When she fell in love with the penniless Earl of Northampton, Sir John was less than pleased and forbade the couple to meet. One day the Earl called at the house disguised as a baker. Sir John, who had never met him, was pleased to see such a well turned out and respectful tradesman and gave him a sixpence. The Earl repaid this kindness by eloping with his daughter, whom he wheeled away in his covered baker's cart.

When he discovered the deception, Sir John was outraged and swore that sixpence was all that his new son-in-law would ever see of his estates. Shortly afterwards the couple had a son. Queen Elizabeth, who was kindly disposed towards Northampton, tricked Sir John into going to sit with his little grandchild and thereby effected a reconciliation.

This later became a source of some irritation to the Earl: his bride had always had a great fondness for her father's house and now spent more time in it than she did in her own. She also proved to have expensive tastes. Addressing him as 'My Sweet Life', she wrote him a letter setting out her basic needs. First, she would have:

> my two coaches . . . also I will have two coachmen. Also, and for that it is indecent for me to crowd myself up with my gentleman-usher in my coach, I will have him to have a convenient horse to attend me either in city or country. And I must have two footmen. And my desire is that you defray all the charges for me. And for myself, besides my yearly allowance (£10,000) I would have twenty gowns of apparel. Also, I would have you put £2,000 and £200 in my purse, and so you to pay my debts. Also I would have £6000 to buy me jewels and £4000 to buy me a pearl chain . . .

And so it went on. In the fullness of time the poor harassed Earl even had to pay for his father-in-law's elaborate tomb.

Another dignitary who formerly had a tomb in the church was the City magistrate, Sir Francis Bancroft. He was also a member of the Drapers' Company and left them a great deal of money on condition that one of their number should lift the hinged lid of his last resting place once a year and place inside a loaf of bread and a bottle of wine, intoning: 'Good morning, Master Draper, I hope you are well.' In case the lid proved too heavy to lift unaided, a small door was cut in the side of the tomb. The inspections continued for about a hundred years. They were eventually discontinued when the decayed condition of the body rendered the ceremony obnoxious.

At its southerly end, Bishopsgate junctions with Leadenhall Street, named after the lead-roofed mansion erected here in 1309 by Sir Hugh Neville. The East India Company had offices in Leadenhall Street from as early as 1600 and it was here that the essayist Charles Lamb worked for thirty-three years as a clerk. He was often late for work, but when his superior reprimanded him for this, Lamb retorted: 'Ah, but see how early I leave.'

Another of 'John Company's' employees was Thomas Snodgrass who, when it was noticed that he was living a life of extravagance, was asked by the suspicious directors to produce his ledgers and accounts. When he failed to do so – claiming to have lost them 'in a shipwreck' – he was sacked and ordered to forgo his right to a pension. In order to gain revenge, Thomas donned his oldest clothes and took to sweeping the street-crossing outside the Company's entrance. He recounted his story to those who passed and in time this 'shameful dismissal' led to a public outcry. The directors refused point-blank to re-employ him, but were forced to reinstate his pension. The day after they did so, Thomas descended on Leadenhall Street in a magnificent coach and thanked them in a very satirical manner.

The church of St Katharine Cree, which stands at the eastern end of Leadenhall Street, is named after a virgin of royal descent who was beheaded after being tortured on a spiked wheel, later known as a 'catherine wheel'. In 1920 the glass in the church's east window was taken down to be cleaned. After the dust and grime had been removed a curious inscription was discovered, rudely cut, possibly with a nail: 'Thomas Jordan cleaned this window, and damn the job I say – 1815.'

A second church, but one long-gone, is commemorated by St Mary Axe, which links Leadenhall Street with Houndsditch. It was jointly dedicated to St Mary the Virgin and St Ursula. The latter was a daughter of a minor English king who, with her improbable band of eleven thousand virgins was beheaded at Cologne by a horde of Huns. Until the sixteenth century the church claimed to possess one of the axes used on this occasion – an axe which in 1222 strokes chopped through 3666 necks, the maidens being arranged on the block three abreast.

Beyond Leadenhall Street to the west is Cornhill. In 1716 the poet, Thomas Gray, was born at number 39 and there might soon afterwards have died of a fit had his mother not pinioned him to the floor and opened one of his veins with a pair of scissors. In 1749, when Gray was thirty-two, his birthplace burned down. This made a deep impression on the poet and he lived in dread of fire for the rest of his life. In order to sleep more easily, he always kept a rope ladder close at hand and had an 'iron machine fitted to his bedroom window'. This led mischievous passers-by to call out 'Fire!' when there was none in the expectation of seeing him jump through the window in his nightshirt.

According to John Timbs, Cornhill was also formerly the centre of the lottery trade. One day, a Spanish political refugee named Don Thomas Isturitz:

feeling an inclination to sport twenty pounds, went into the office of Martin and Co. in Cornhill, where, referring to his pocket-book, he counted the number of days that had elapsed (since) his providential escape from Madrid. He found them amount to 261, and then demanded to buy *that* ticket; but it was nearly half an hour before it could be obtained, and only after a strict search amongst the lottery-offices in the City. At length a half ticket of number 261 was procured at two o'clock; and at five it was drawn a prize of forty thousand pounds, the only one ever exhibited to that amount in England. The lucky Don lay down that night twenty thousand pounds richer than he had risen.

The quest for easy money at this period was almost insatiable and it was not only lotteries that flourished. Speculation abounded of every kind and one dubious entrepreneur even found backers for 'A Company For Carrying On An Undertaking Of Great Advantage But Nobody To Know What It Is.'

At the western end of Cornhill is St Peter's church, reputedly the oldest in London, its foundation being ascribed to King Lucius in A.D. 179. Whether or not this is true, Dickens once described the tombstones here as 'drooping . . . as if ashamed of the lies they told'. Opposite the church is White Lion Court, recalling the ill-fated White Lion tavern which in 1765 burned to the ground the day after being sold for £3000.

A little further west is St Michael's Alley where in the seventeenth century the first cup of coffee was sold in England by a man from Smyrna operating from a tent. The drink quickly became popular and by the middle of the century a number of coffee houses had sprung up to cater to the new fashion. Most of these sported a large oak box, for gratuities, the front being engraved with the initials 'T.I.P.' – 'To Increase Promptitude'.

The derivation of the word 'Alley' is less certain. It may have originated from the French word 'Allèe' meaning a walk, or from the days when the game of marbles was played in long narrow enclosures such as this, the largest and most prized marble being known as an 'Alabaster' or 'Alley'.

In Birchin Lane, which runs parallel to St Michael's Alley,

the great historian, Lord Macaulay, spent part of his child-hood. Looking out of the window one day, he spied a smoking chimney. He turned to his father and asked: 'Is that Hell?'

At its southern extremity Birchin Lane gives on to Lombard Street, so called after the Lombards of northern Italy who in 1290 replaced the Jews as the bankers of England after the latter were expelled from these shores on the orders of Edward I for extortionate usury. The early Lombardy bankers were also usurers and it was here, in Lombard Street, that the three golden balls of the pawnbroker were first exhibited. Then as now, one ball was suspended above the other two – said by some to represent the likely odds of a pledge ever being redeemed.

Returning by way of Lombard Street to the Mansion House, we come to Walbrook and the church of St Stephen. The architect of Blenheim Palace, Sir John Vanbrugh, is buried here in a spacious family vault; but other citizens are more tightly squeezed. When repairs were carried out in 1850 'four thousand coffins were found beneath the church and were covered with brickwork and concrete to prevent the escape of noxious effluvia'.

One of the former rectors of St Stephen's was a man called Pendleton, the original 'Vicar of Bray'. When the 'mild and timorous' Lawrence Sanders confessed 'that he had not the strength of mind to endure the persecution of the time', Pendleton blustered that '*he* would see every drop of his fat and the last morsel of his flesh consumed to ashes ere he would swerve from the faith then established'. However 'he changed with the times, saved his fat and his flesh, and became rector of St Stephen's, whilst the mild and diffident Sanders was burnt at Smithfield'.

Turning right into Cannon Street and walking west, we come on the right to Bow Lane, formerly the home of the prodigious walker, Thomas Coryat. In 1608 Coryat did the Grand Tour entirely on foot: nearly two thousand miles in five months. The shoes in which he covered the distance were later put on display to coincide with the publication of a three-volume account of his journey, entitled: *Crudities Hastily Gobbled Up In Five Months' Travels.*

Opposite Bow Lane is Garlick Hill and the church of St James's Garlickhythe. Resting in a glass-fronted coffin in the vestibule is the mummified corpse of a man believed to be at least five hundred years old. He was unearthed by workmen when renovations were carried out to the building in 1839. Known as 'Jummy Garlick', he was kept for many years in a small and narrow closet in the body of the church. In 1942, after his resting place was nudged by a bomb, his ghost became restless for a while and severely frightened an American lady and her young son when it materialised on the steps leading to the gallery. Since his body has been rehoused the manifestations have ceased.

In 1531 the rector of St James's, Garlickhythe, was Arthur Bulkley DD, who ten years later was promoted to the Bishopric of Bangor. There he 'sold five fair bells out of the steeple of his cathedral . . . and it is reported that going to the sea-side to see them shipped off, he had not set three steps on his way homeward before he was stricken with blindness, so that he never saw afterwards.'

On the far side of Upper Thames Street is the Hall of the Vintners' Company, rebuilt in its present form in 1671. Five kings once sat down to dinner here, an occasion still recalled by the Vintners' practice of giving five cheers when showing loyalty to the monarchy, rather than the customary three.

Bell Wharf Lane, a little to the east of the Hall, also has royalist associations – of a sort. At the Restoration, in 1660, Elizabeth Cromwell, the wife of the late Lord Protector, came here under cover of darkness to bury some of the treasures which she and her servants had removed from the Palace of Whitehall. The booty filled seventeen wagons.

Walking east along Upper Thames Street, and then into Lower Thames Street, we come to Pudding Lane. It takes its name not from the modern meaning of the word, but the entrails of cattle which once were dumped here from the

The Great Fire of London (1666) which began in Pudding Lane

nearby market of Eastcheap. It was at number 25 Pudding
Lane, then 'the shop of one Farryner, the King's baker', that
the Great Fire of London broke out in 1666. It is commemorated a little further north by a fluted Doric column of
Portland stone surmounted by a flaming urn – the Great Fire
Monument. It stands two hundred and two feet high, said to
be the distance from its base to the house in Pudding Lane
where the Fire started. The bas-reliefs were at least in part
the work of Caius Gabriel Cibber, then confined in the
King's Bench Prison for debt. He came from there each
morning, returning to his cell each night. The Monument
cost £14,000 and was erected on the site of the first church
consumed in the Great Fire. It is open to the public, although
the balcony, which is reached by way of 345 black marble
steps, has now been meshed over to deter suicides – of which
there have been many.

The first person to jump from the Monument was a weaver named William Green. He did so in 1750, having first deposited his pocket-watch with the keeper – although not the eighteen guineas in his pocket. A few years later, a man called Thomas Craddock accidentally fell over the balcony after straining out to get a better view of a caged eagle below. According to *Old & New London*: 'The last suicide was in August 1842 when a servant girl from Hoxton, named Jane Cooper, while the watchman had his head turned, nimbly climbed over the iron railing, tucked her clothes tight between her knees, and dived head-foremost downwards. In her fall she struck the griffin on the right side of the base of the Monument, and, rebounding into the road, cleared a cart . . .'

The Great Fire itself burned for almost five days. In the course of its progress it laid waste 436 acres, devouring thirteen thousand houses, eighty-nine churches and destroying one complete parish for every hour of its life. For all this, only a handful of people were killed. When the Lord Mayor, Sir Thomas Bludworth, was called to the scene early on the Monday morning, he uttered the understatement of the seventeenth century: 'Pshaw, a woman might piss it out.' Forty-eight hours later, when the conflagration had 'altogether vanquished all human counsel and resource', he was spied scuttling to and fro, holding his head in his hands and endlessly repeating: 'Lord, what can I do?'

Walking east from the Monument and turning left across Tower Hill, we come to Great Tower Street. The first turning on the right here is Seething Lane, which takes its name from the 'ceafen' or chaff which would have drifted here downwind from nearby Fenchurch Street when that area was a market for the sale of corn.

For some years the great diarist, Samuel Pepys, worked at the Navy Office in Seething Lane. He came here in 1660 as secretary to his cousin, Admiral Sir Edward Montagu. Although at the time of his appointment he knew little of maritime affairs, and less of administration and supply, he was eventually to change the whole aspect of the navy. He instituted unprecedented reforms – weeding out the corrupt officials within the establishment and cancelling the contracts of the rascally tradesmen who had waxed fat by bribing them, and refused to budge from his desk even for the plague. When he did eventually close the ledgers of an evening, he walked the few yards to his house and employed the remainder of his time in recording the day's events in his diary, a task which, as it was usually done by the light of a guttering candle, eventually ruined his eyesight.

Thanks to that diary, we know more of Pepys than any other seventeenth-century man. He poured his whole life into it – often employing a peculiar admixture of foreign and invented words when wishing to conceal something from his wife, Elizabeth.

Truth to be told, there was much to conceal: Pepys was a libidinous man with a wandering eye. He snatched kisses from every pretty female – Dutch waitresses, carpenter Bagwell's buxom lady, the barber's wench, captains' wives seeking promotion for their husbands, even his own servants – provided there was small chance of getting caught.

In spite of this philandering – and Elizabeth's tendency to refer to her husband as 'pricklouse', a reference to his father having been a tailor – the pair only once fell out seriously. The cause was Deborah Willet, Elizabeth's maid. In addition to her other duties, young Deb was expected to assist in her master's undressing. It was only a matter of time, of course, before the master was contriving at hers. One night, Elizabeth caught him with his hands inside Deb's clothing. Her reaction was violent, swift and terrible to behold. She cursed and ranted, she flew at him and tore his hair, she frightened him in the night by holding a pair of red-hot tongs so close to his face that the heat started him out of a dream in which he imagined he was roasting in Hell. She demanded four hundred, six hundred, a thousand pounds, in order to quit his house for ever.

In the end, of course, it was Deb who had to go. The

following day, Pepys searched her out (not without difficulty) and gave her twenty shillings. Even in this he was discovered and Elizabeth's fury intensified. It was many weeks before life returned to anything like normal; but in the summer of 1669 Pepys and Elizabeth were reconciled and set off for a stay on the continent. On their return to Seething Lane, Elizabeth who four years earlier had been passed over by the plague contracted a chill. From this a fever developed and on November 10, in her thirtieth year, she died.

Pepys survived his wife by some thirty years. He never remarried, and on his death in 1703 was buried beside her in the vault of the church of St Olave's, Hart Street, at the top of Seething Lane. In some respects it is an unbecoming last resting place for such a merry man – a sinister black-guardly-looking church, immortalised by Dickens in 'The Uncommercial Traveller' as 'St Ghastly Grim'. If anything, the business of worshipping here was even more daunting than the exterior. Dickens again:

The opening of the service recalls my wandering thoughts. I then find to my astonishment that I have been, and still am, taking a strong kind of invisible snuff up my nose, into my eyes, and down my throat. I wink, sneeze and cough. The clerk sneezes; the clergyman winks; the unseen organist sneezes and coughs (and probably winks); all our little party wink, sneeze and cough. The snuff seems to be made of the decay of matting wood, cloth, stone, iron, earth and something else. Is the something else the decay of dead citizens in the vaults below? As sure as death it is! Not only in the cold damp February day, do we cough and sneeze dead citizens, all through the service, but dead citizens have got into the very bellows of the organ and half choked the same. We stamp our feet to warm them and dead citizens arise in heavy clouds. Dead citizens stick upon the walls, and lie pulverised on the sounding-board over the clergyman's head, and when a gust of air comes, tumble down upon him.

Bibliography

ABSE, J., *The Art Galleries of Great Britain and Ireland*, Sidgwick & Jackson 1975.

ADAMS, H. B., *The Education of Henry Adams*, New English Library 1966.

ADBURGHAM, A., *Shopping in Style*, Thames & Hudson 1979.

ALTICK, R., *Victorian Studies in Scarlet*, Dent, 1972.

ARGYLL, MARGARET, Duchess of, *Forget Me Not*, W. H. Allen, 1975.

Art Journal, see Periodical Pub. London Art-Union etc. January 1849–February 1912.

ASQUITH, M., *Autobiography*, Eyre & Spottiswoode, 1962.

AUBREY, J., *Brief Lives* (2 vols.). Clarendon Press, 1898.

AYKROYD, P., *Evil London*, Wolfe, 1973.

BABINGTON, A., *The English Bastille: A History of Newgate Gaol etc.*, Macdonald, 1971.

BAILEY, C., *Harrap's Guide to Famous London Graves*, Harrap, 1975.

BAILEY, J. (ed.), *The Diary of Lady Frederick Cavendish*, Murray, 1927.

BAILY, L., *Gilbert & Sullivan & Their World*, Thames & Hudson, 1973.

BALFOUR, A. J., *The Foundations of Belief*, Macmillan & Co., 1879.

BALSAN, C., *The Glitter & The Gold*, Harper & Bros (New York), 1952.

BANKS, F. R., *The Penguin Guide to London*, Penguin Books, 1958.

BARROW, A., *Gossip: 1920–1970*, Hamish Hamilton, 1978.

BATEMAN, M. (ed.), *This England; Selections from the 'New Statesman' 1934–1968*.

BEADLE, J., *Today's the Day*, W. H. Allen, 1979.

BEBBINGTON, G., *London Street Names*, Batsford, 1972.

BEDFORD, Duchess of, *Nicole Nobody*, W. H. Allen, 1974.

BELL, W. G., *Unknown London*, John Lane 1920.

BENCE-JONES, M., *Clive of India*, Constable 1974.

BENNETT, A., *Memoirs of a Welch heiress* (4 vols) Privately printed, 1785.

BENSON, E. F., *As We Were*, Longman, 1930.

BENSON, E. T. R., *London Immortals*, Wingate, 1951.

BESTE, H. D., *Personal & Literary Memorials*, Henry Colburn, 1829.

BIERCE, A., *The Devil's Dictionary*, A. F. Bird, 1906.

BIRKENHEAD, LORD, *Rudyard Kipling*, Weidenfeld & Nicolson, 1978.

BIRKETT, LORD (ed.), *The Newgate Calendar*, Dent, 1974.

BLOOM, U., *The Duke of Windsor*, Hale, 1972.

BLUNDEN, E., *Shelley*, Readers' Union-Collins, 1948.

BLUNT, W. S., *Diary*, Martin Secker, 1919.

BONE, J., *The London Perambulator*, Jonathan Cape, 1925.

BORER, M. C., *A Week in London*, Pelham Books, 1973.

– *The British Hotel through the Ages*, Lutterworth, 1972.

BOSWELL, J., *Life of Johnson*, J. M. Dent & Co., 1901.

BRADLEY, E. T., *The Roll-Call of Westminster Abbey*, Smith & Elder, 1903.

BRAMAH, E., *Tea & Coffee*, Hutchinson, 1972.

BRENTNALL, M., *The Old Customs & Ceremonies of London*, Batsford, 1975.

BREWER, E. C., *Dictionary of Phrase & Fable*, Cassell, 1975.

BROOKE-LITTLE, J., *The British Monarchy*, Batsford, 1976.

BROWN, I., *Balmoral: A History of a Home*, Collins, 1966.

BROWN, J., *Amusements*, 1700.

BRYANT, SIR A., *Samuel Pepys*, Collins, 1933.

BUCHAN, J., *Sir Walter Scott*, Cassell & Co., 1932.

BURNEY, F., *Diary & Letters*, G. Routledge & Sons., 1931.

BURTON, E., *The Early Victorians at Home*, Longman, 1972.

BURTON, J. A., *The Naturalist in London*, David & Charles, 1974.

BUTLER, S., *The Way of all Flesh*, Grant Richards, 1903.

BUTLER, I., *Murderers' London*, Hale, 1973.

BYRON, LORD, *Curse of Minerva*, Galignani (Paris), 1818.

CAMP, W., *The Glittering Prizes*, Macgibbon & Kee, 1960.

CUNNINGHAM, J. (ed.), *100 Great Kings & Queens & Rulers of the World*, Souvenir Press, 1973.

CARLYLE, T. *Reminiscences*, Dent, 1932.

CECIL, LORD DAVID, *Lord Melbourne*, Constable, 1965.

CHANCELLOR, E. B., *Lives of the Rakes* (6 vols), P. Allen, 1924.

– *Memorials of St James's Street*, Grant Richards, 1922.

– *The Private Palaces of London*, Kegan Paul & Co., 1908.

CHANNON, SIR HENRY, *Diaries*, Weidenfeld & Nicolson, 1967.

CHARTERIS, E., *Life of Gosse*, Heinemann, 1931

CHESTERTON, G. K., *The Man Who Knew Too Much*, Cassell & Co., 1922.

CHISHOLM, A., *Nancy Cunard*, Sidgwick & Jackson, 1979.

CLUNN, H., *The Face of London*, Simpkin Marshall, 1932.

COBB, I. G., *Of London & Londoners*, Williams & Norgate, 1951.

COHN, N., *Today There Are No Gentlemen*, Weidenfeld & Nicolson, 1971.

COLBY, R., *Mayfair: A Town Within London*, Country Life, 1966.

COLLIS, M., *Raffles*, Faber, 1967.

CONGREVE, W., *The Double Dealer*, 1693.

COOKRIDGE, E. H., *From Battenberg to Mountbatten*, Barker, 1966.

CORBETT, F. J., *Fit for a King*, Odhams, 1956.

CROCKER, W. C., *Tales from the Coffee House*, Hale, 1973.

CULLEN, T., *Maundy Gregory*, Bodley Head, 1974.

CURTIS, G., *Queen Anne*, Weidenfeld & Nicolson, 1972.

DARWIN, B., *British Clubs*, Collins, 1943.

DAVIS, D., *A History of Shopping*, Routledge, 1966.

DE CORNUEL, A. B., *Lettres de Mlle Aisse*, 1728.

DEFOE, D., *A Journey Through England* (8 vols), 1722.

DE MARÉ E., *London 1851*, Folio Society, 1972.

DICKINSON, V. (ed.), *Miss Eden's Letters*, Macmillan & Co., 1919.

Dictionary of National Biography

DOBBS, D., *Drury Lane*, Cassell, 1972.

DONALDSON, F., *The Actor Managers*, Weidenfeld & Nicolson, 1970.

DOWNES, M. P., *At the Pines: Swinburne & Watts-Dunton in Putney*, Hamish Hamilton, 1971.

DRURY, E., & BRIDGEMAN, H., *The British Eccentric*, Michael Joseph, 1975.

DUNHILL, M., *Our Family Business*, Bodley Head, 1979.

DUTTON, R. S., *London Homes*, Wingate, 1952.

EDEN, SIR ANTHONY, *Another World: 1897–1917*, Allen Lane, 1976.

EGREMONT, LORD, *Wyndham & Children First*, Macmillan, 1968.

EHRLICH, B., *London on the Thames*, Cassell, 1968.

EMERSON, R. W., *Essays* (2nd series), The Catholic Series, 1844.
– *Representative Men*, George Routledge, 1850.
Encyclopaedia Brittanica
EPTON, N., *Milord & Milady*, Oldbourne, 1962.
– *The English in Love*, Cassell, 1960.
ERRAND, J., *Secret Passages & Hiding Places*, David & Charles, 1974.
ESDAILE, K. A., *English Monumental Sculpture Since the Renaissance*, S.P.C.K., 1927.
– *Roubiliac*, O.U.P., 1928.
ESHER, VISCOUNT, *Journals & Letters*, 1934.
ESTEROW, M., *The Art Stealers*, Weidenfeld & Nicolson, 1967.
EVANS, B., *The Natural History of Nonsense*, Michael Joseph, 1947.
EVANS, HOWARD, *Our Old Nobility*, Reprinted from the Echo newspaper, with additions, 1879.
FANE, LADY AUGUSTA, *Chit-Chat*, Thornton & Butterworth, 1926.
FEDDEN, R., & KENWORTHY-BROWNE, J., *The Country House Guide*, Cape, 1979.
FIELDING, H., *Jonathan Wilde the Great*, (in 'Miscellanies' 3 vols), 1743.
FIRBANK, R., *The Flower Beneath the Foot*, Grant Richards, 1923.
FITZGIBBON, C., *The Blitz*, Macdonald, 1957.
– *The Life of Dylan Thomas*, Dent, 1965.
FRANKLIN, B., *Works* (2 vols) G.G.J. & J. Robinson, 1794.
FREMANTLE, A., *Three Cornered Heart*, Collins, 1971.
FREWIN, L., (ed.), *The Café Royal Story*, Hutchinson Benham, 1963.
FRITH, W. P., *My Autobiography & Reminiscences* (2 vols), R. Bentley & Son, 1887.
FULFORD, R., *The Prince Consort*, Macmillan, 1949.
FURNESS, LADY, & VANDERBILT, GLORIA, *Double Exposure*, Frederick Muller, 1959.
GAMMOND, P., *Your Own, Your Very Own*, Ian Allan, 1971.
GAY, J., *Trivia*, London, 1716.
GEORGE, D., (ed.), *A Book of Anecdotes*, Hulton Press, 1957.
GIBBS, P. H., *The Journalist's London*, Wingate, 1952.
GIRTIN, T., *The Abominable Clubman*, Hutchinson, 1964.
GLADSTONE-SMITH, P., *The Crime Explosion*, Macdonald, 1970.
GODWIN, WILLIAM, *Essays on Sepulchres*, London, 1809.
GRAVES, C. P. R., *Leather Armchairs*, Cassell, 1963.

GREEN, A., *Our Haunted Kingdom*, Wolfe, 1973.

GREEN, J., *Famous Last Words*, Omnibus Press, 1979.

GREEN, V. H. H., *The Hanoverians*, Arnold, 1966.

GREENWALL, H. J., *Northcliffe*, Wingate, 1957.

GRIBBLE, L., *More Famous Historical Mysteries*, Muller, 1972.

GRONOW, H., *Reminiscences*, Bodley Head, 1964.

GUEDALLA, P., *Selected Essays*, Harrap & Co., 1926.

GUNNIS, R., *Dictionary of British Sculptors*, Abbey Library, c. 1978.

HALLAM, J., *Ghosts of London*, Wolfe, 1975.

HANKINSON, C., *My Forty Years with Debretts*, Hale, 1963.

HARBEN, H. H., *A Dictionary of London*, 1919.

HARDWICK, M. & M., *Dickens's England*, Dent, 1970.

HARDY, J. G., *The Rise and Fall of the British Nanny*, Hodder & Stoughton, 1972.

HARE, A., *Walks in London* (2 vols), Dalby, Isbister & Co., 1878.

– *The Story of My Life*, Allen & Unwin, 1900.

HARINGTON, SIR J., *Epigrams*, 1615.

HARPER, C. G., *Queer Things About London*, Cecil Palmer, 1923.

HARRIS, F., *My Life and Loves* (4 vols), Obelisk Press (Paris), 1945.

HARRIS, L., *The Fine Art of Political Wit*, Cassell, 1965.

HARRIS, M., *The Dilly Boys: Male Prostitution on Piccadilly*, Croom Helm, 1973.

HARRISON, M., *London Growing*, Hutchinson, 1965.

– *London Beneath the Pavement*, Peter Davies, 1971.

– *The London of Sherlock Holmes*, David & Charles, 1972.

HAWKINS, SIR JOHN, *Life of Samuel Johnson*, Cape, 1962.

HAYDON, B. R., *Correspondence & Table-Talk* (2 vols), Chatto & Windus, 1876.

HAZLITT, W., *Conversations with James Northcote R. A.*, 1830.

HEPPNER, S., *Cockie*, Frewin, 1969.

HEWSON, G., *The Unfortunate Doctor Dodd*, Hutchinson, 1973.

– *Thief-Taker General*, Hutchinson, 1970.

HIGHAM, C., *The Adventures of Conan Doyle*, Hamish Hamilton, 1976.

HILL, B. J. W., *Windsor & Eton*, Batsford, 1957.

HILL, C. P., *Who' Who in History*, Blackwell, 1965. *Historical Register*

HOFFER, E., *The True Believer*, Harper & Bros. (New York), 1951.

HOLCROFT, T., (Wm. Hazlitt. ed.), *Memoirs of the Late Thomas Holcroft*, London, 3 vols, 1816.

HOLLAND, LADY, *A Memoir of the Reverend Sydney Smith by his daughter*, Lady Holland, 1855 (2nd edition), London.
HOLLOWAY, S., *London's Noble Fire Brigades 1833–1904*, Cassell, 1973.
HOLME, T., *Chelsea*, Hamish Hamilton, 1972.
HOLT, E., & PERHAM, M., *Kids' London*, Abelard-Schuman, 1972.
HOPE, A., *Why Didn't I Think of it First?*, David & Charles,

HORN, P., *The Rise & Fall of the Victorian Servant*, Gill & Macmillan, 1975.
HORNUNG, E. W., *Raffles: The Amateur Cracksman*, Methuen & Co., 1899.
HOSKINS, T., & MACKENZIE, F., (eds), *The Daily Mirror Old Codgers Little Black Book Number 4*, Mirror Books, 1979.
HUDSON, D., *Martin Tupper: His Rise & Fall*, Constable, 1949.
HUDSON, K., *Food Clothing & Shelter*, Baker, 1978.
HUGGETT, F. E., *Life Below Stairs*, Murray, 1977.
HUGHSON, D., *London*, (6 vols), London, 1809.
HYDE, H. M., *The Londonderrys*, Hamish Hamilton, 1979.
HYMAN, A., *The Rise & Fall of Horatio Bottomley*, Cassell, 1972.
JACKSON, S., *The Savoy*, Muller, 1964.
JENKINS, A., *The Stock Exchange Story*, Heinemann, 1973.
JOHN, E., *Charles I*, Arthur Barker, 1933.
JOHNSON, R. F., *The Royal George*, Knight, 1971.
JOHNSON, S., *Lives of the English Poets* (3 vols), 1905 edition.
JUDD, D., *The Life & Times of George V*, Weidenfeld & Nicolson, 1973.
"JUNE," *The Glass Ladder*, Heinemann, 1960.
KELLY, *London Street Directory*, John Murray, 1922.
KENNEDY, A. L., *Old Diplomacy & New*.
KENT, W., *Encyclopaedia of London*, Dent & Sons, 1937.
– *Walks in London*, Staples Press, 1951.
– *London for the Curious*, Clarke & Co., 1947.
– *London for Everyman*, Dent, 1931.
– *London Mystery & Mythology*, Staples Press, 1952.
KIPLING, R., *The Betrothed*, (from 'Departmental Ditties'), Mansfield & Wessels, New York, 1899.
KLAPPER, C., *London's Lost Railways*, Routledge & Kegan Paul, 1976.
LATHAM, J., *The Pleasure of Your Company*, Black, 1972.

LAVER, J., *Between the Wars*, Vista Books, 1961.

LEECH, J., *Funeral Sermon for the Princess Mary*, 1607.

LEJEUNE, A., & LEWIS, M., *The Gentlemen's Clubs of London*, Macdonald & Janes, 1979.

LESLIE, A., & CHAPMAN, P., *Madame Tussaud*, Hutchinson, 1978.

LEVINSON, M., *Taxi!*, Secker & Warburg, 1963.

LIVERPOOL, LORD, *Caroline: The Unhappy Queen*, Hale, 1967.

LLOYD, A., *The Wickedest Age*, David & Charles, 1971.

LOFTIE, W. J., *A History of London*, (2 vols), E. Stanford, 1884.

LONGFORD, LADY, *Wellington* (2 vols), Weidenfeld & Nicolson, 1972.

LOWNDES, B., *A Passing World*, Macmillan, 1948.

LUCAS, E. V., *A Wanderer in London*, Methuen & Co., 1906.

LUCAS, N., *The Lucan Mystery*, W. H. Allen, 1975.

LUDOVIC, L. J., *The Itch for Play*, Jarrolds, 1962.

LUKE, M. M., *A Crown for Elizabeth*, Michael Joseph, 1971.

LUSTGARTEN, E., *The Illustrated Story of Crime*, Weidenfeld & Nicolson, 1976.

MACAULAY, LORD, *Critical & Historical Essays Contributed to the Edinburgh Review*, Longman & Co., 1843.

MACKWOOD, N., *In & Out*, Debrett Books, 1979.

MACQUEEN-POPE, W., *Goodbye Piccadilly*, David & Charles, 1972.

– *Ghosts & Greasepaint*, Hale, 1951.

– *Give Me Yesterday*, Hutchinson, 1957.

MAITLAND, W., *London*, 1739.

MALLET, D., *The Greatest Collector*, Macmillan, 1979.

MALLETT, M., *Life with Queen Victoria*, Murray, 1968.

MANDER, R., & MITCHENSON, J., *The Theatres of London*, New English Library, 1975.

MANKOWITZ, W., *Dickens of London*, Macmillan (New York), 1977.

Manual of Rank and Nobility, 1832.

MARGETSON, S., *Regency London*, Cassell, 1971.

– *Leisure & Pleasure in the 19th Century*, Cassell, 1969.

MARSDEN, P., *In Peril Before Parliament*, Barrie & Rockliff, 1965.

MARSH, SIR E., *A Number of People*, Heinemann, 1939.

MASON, F. K., & WINDROW, N., *Know Britain*, George Philip, 1972.

MASSEREENE, VISCOUNT, *The Lords*, Frewin, 1973.

MASTERS, B., *The Dukes*, Blond & Briggs, 1975.

MAUGHAM, R., *Conversations with Willy*, W. H. Allen, 1978.

MAY, D. C., *Picture Book of London*, Hamlyn, 1977.

Bibliography

251

MAYER, T., *La Vie Anglaise*, Gollancz, 1960.

MEE, A., *London: The City & Westminister*, Hodder & Stoughton, 1975.

MILLS, J. F., *The Guinness Book of Art Facts & Feats*, Guinness Superlatives, 1978.

MINNEY, R. J., *The Tower of London*, Cassell, 1970.

MITCHISON, N., *Small Talk*, Bodley Head, 1973.

MITFORD, N., (ed.), *Noblesse Oblige*, Hamish Hamilton, 1956.

MORGAN, T., *Somerset Maugham*, Cape, 1980.

MORRIS, THOMAS, *The Napoleonic Wars*, Longmans, 1967.

MOSLEY, L., *Curzon; The End of an Epoch*, Longmans, 1960.

MOUNTFIELD, D., *The Coaching Age*, Hale, 1976.

MUGGERIDGE, M., *The Thirties*, Hamish Hamilton, 1940.

MUIR, F., *The Frank Muir Book*, Corgi Books, 1978.

NELSON, M., *Nobs & Snobs*, Gordon & Cremonesi, 1976.

NEVILL, R. H., *London Clubs*, Chatto & Windus, 1947.

NICOLSON, SIR H., *Diaries & Letters* (4 vols), Collins, 1966.

NORRIE, I., *The Book of the City*, High Hill Books, 1961.

NOORTHOUCK, J., *A New History of London*, 1773.

NORTON, G., *London Before the Blitz*, Macdonald, 1970.

PAIN, N., *George III at Home*, Eyre Methuen, 1975.

PARKINSON, C. N., *Jeeves: A Gentleman's Personal Gentleman*, Macdonald & Janes, 1979.

PATMORE, B., *My Friends When Young*, Heinemann, 1968.

PEARSALL, R., *The Worm in the Bud*, Weidenfeld & Nicolson, 1969.

– *Night's Black Angels*, Hodder & Stoughton, 1975.

PEARSON, H., *Hesketh Pearson by Himself*, Heinemann, 1965.

– *The Smith of Smiths*, Hamish Hamilton, 1934.

– *Dizzy: The Life & Times of Benjamin Disraeli*, Methuen, 1951.

PENNANT, T., *Some Account of London*, 1790.

PEPYS, S., *Diary*, Everyman's Library, 1906.

PERROTT, R., *The Aristocrats*, Weidenfeld & Nicolson, 1968.

PETRIE, SIR C., *Scenes of Edwardian Life*, Eyre & Spotiswoode, 1965.

– *The Four Georges*, Chivers, 1973.

PEVSNER, SIR N., *London*, Penguin Books, 1957.

Philosophical Transactions

PIPER, D., *The Companion Guide to London*, Collins, 1964.

POCOCK, T., *London walks*, Thames & Hudson, 1973.

POPE-HENNESSY, J., *Queen Mary*, Allen & Unwin, 1959.

PORTLAND, DUKE OF, *Men Women & Things*, Faber, 1937.

POTTER, J. D., *Fatal Gallows Tree*, Elek Books, 1966.

POUND, R., *Harley Street*, Michael Joseph, 1967.

PRIESTLEY, J. B., *The English*, Heienmann, 1975.

PUDNEY, J., *Crossing London's Rivers*, Dent, 1972.

PULLAR, P., *Frank Harris*, Hamish Hamilton, 1975.

REES, N., *Quote . . . Unquote*, Allen & Unwin, 1978.

REID, T. W., *The Life & Letters & Friendship of Richard Monckton Milnes, First Lord Houghton*, Cassell & Co., 1890.

RICKARDS, M., *Where They Lived in London*, David & Charles, 1972.

ROGERS, S., *The Table-Talk of Samuel Rogers*, Richards Press, 1952.

ROWSE, A. L., *The Tower of London in the History of the Nation*, Weidenfeld & Nicolson, 1972.

– *The Early Churchills*, Macmillan, 1956.

ROYAL COMMISSION ON HISTORICAL MONUMENTS, *An Inventory of the Historical Monuments in London*, H.M.S.O., 1925.

RUMBELOW, D., *The Complete Jack the Ripper*, W. H. Allen, 1975.

RUSH, P., *The Book of Duels*, Harrap, 1964.

RUSSELL, G. W. E., *Collections & Recollections*, Smith, Elder & Co., 1904.

SAMPSON, A., *Anatomy of Britain*, Hodder & Stoughton, 1965.

SCOTT, J. M., *The Book of Pall Mall*, Heinemann, 1965.

SERVICE, A., *London 1900*, Crosby, Lockwood & Staples, 1979.

SETH, R., *The First Time it Happened*, Odhams, 1965.

SHELLEY, P. B., *Anarchy*, 1819.

SHERIDAN, T., *Life of Jonathan Swift*, 1785.

SIMON, G. L., *A Place for Pleasure*, Harwood Smart, 1975.

SITWELL, O., *Noble Essence & Courteous Revelations*, Macmillan, 1950.

– *The People's Album of London Statues*, Duckworth, 1928.

SMITH, A., *Dictionary of the City of London Street Names*, David & Charles, 1970.

SMITH, J. T., *Nollekens & His Times* (2 vols), London, 1828.

SMYTH, SIR J., *The Victoria Cross*, Muller, 1963.

SOYER, A., *The Modern Housewife*, Simpkin Marshall & Co., 1856.

SPARROW, G., *The Con-Men*, Barkers, 1975.

– *The Great Defamers*, Long, 1970.

– *The Great Assassins*, Long, 1968.

SPEAIGHT, R., *The Property Basket*, Collins and Harvill Press, 1970.

Spectator, The

SPENCE, J., *Anecdotes*, Centaur Press Edition, 1964.

STEWART, W., *Characters of Byegone London*, Harrap, 1960.

STOW, J., *Survey of London*, 1603.

STRYPE, J., *Stow's Survey (revised)*, 1720.

SUTHERLAND, D., *Raise Your Glasses*, Macdonald, 1969.

SUTHERLAND, J. (ed.), *The Oxford Book of Literary Anecdotes*, Clarendon Press, 1975.

SWINNERTON, F., *Figures in the Foreground*, Hutchinson, 1963.

SYKES, C., *Nancy: The Life of Lady Astor*, Collins, 1972.

TANNER, L., *Recollections of a Westminster Antiquary*, Baker, 1969.

TAYLOR, J. R., *Dictionary of the Theatre*, Penguin Books, 1966.

TENNYSON, C., *Alfred Tennyson*, Macmillan, 1949.

THOMAS, F., *Last Will & Testament*, David & Charles, 1972.

THOMPSON, C. J. S., *The Quacks of Old London*, Brentano's, 1928.

THOMPSON, G., *London's statues*, Dent, 1971.

THOMSON, G. M., *Lord Castlerosse*, Weidenfeld & Nicolson, 1973.

THORNBURY, W., *Old & New London* (6 vols), Cassell, Petter & Galpin, 1873.

THRALE, H., *Thraliana* (2 vols), Clarendon Press, 1942.

TIBBLE, J. W. & A., *John Clare: A Life*, Cobden-Sanderson, 1932.

TIMBS, J., *Curiosities of London*, Virtue & Co., 1855.

— *English Eccentrics & Eccentricities* (2 vols), Richard Bentley, 1866.

TOYNBEE, A. J., *Acquaintances*, O. U. P., 1967.

TRENCH, C. C., *The Royal Malady*, Longmans, 1964.

TRENCH, S., *Bury Me in My Boots*, Hodder & Stoughton, 1968.

TRENT, C., *Greater London*, Dent, 1965.

TSCHUMI, G., *Royal Chef*, William Kimber, 1954.

TURNER, E. S., *Amazing Grace: The Great Days of Dukes*, Michael Joseph, 1975.

— *What the Butler Saw: Two Hundred And Fifty Years of the Servant Problem*, Michael Joseph, 1962.

— *All Heaven in a Rage*, Michael Joseph, 1964.

UDEN, G., & YGLESIAS, R., *Cabbages & Kings*, Kestrel, 1978.

UNDERWOOD, P., *A Gazetteer of British Ghosts*, Souvenir Press, 1971.

— *A Host of Hauntings*, Frewin, 1973.

— *Haunted London*, Harrap, 1973.

WAKEFORD, G., *Three Consort Queens*, Hale, 1971.

WALL, C. J., *The Tombs of the Kings of England*, Sampson, Low Marston, 1891.

WALLECHINSKY, D., & WALLACE, I. & A., *The Book of Lists*, Corgi Books, 1978.

WALPOLE, H., *Marginal Notes*, Philobiblon Society, 1854.

– *Walpoliana* (2 vols), Phillips, 1804.

WARD, M., *Gilbert Keith Chesterton*, Sheed & Ward, 1944.

WHEATLEY, H. B., *London Past & Present* (3 vols), Murray, 1891.

WILDE, O., *The Picture of Dorian Gray*, Ward Lock & Co., 1891.

WILLIAMS, LORD F., *Nothing So Strange*, Cassell, 1970.

WILLIAMS, G. G., *Guide To Literary London*, Batsford, 1973.

WILLIAMS, G. R., *The Hidden World of Scotland Yard*, Hutchinson, 1972.

WILLIS, F., *A Book of London Yesterdays*, Phoenix House, 1960.

WILSON, H., *Memoirs*, W. Dugdale, 1839.

WINDSOR, DUCHESS OF, *The Heart Has Its Reasons*, Michael Joseph, 1956.

WINSTEN, S., *Days with Bernard Shaw*, Hutchinson, 1951.

WOOD, A., *The True History of Lord Beaverbrook*, Heinemann, 1965.

WOOLF, L., *The Journey Not the Arrival Matters*, Hogarth Press, 1969.

WRIGHT, L., *Warm & Snug: The History of the Bed*, Routledge & Kegan Paul, 1962.

YARWOOD, D., *The Architecture of Britain*, Batsford, 1976.

YOUNG, J. C., *A Memoir of Charles Mayne Young*, (2 vols), London & Oxford, 1871.

ZEIGLER, P., *William IV*, Collins, 1971.

Index

Mountbatten, Lord and Lady, 8
Mountford, Lord, 128
Mulgrave, Earl of, 96–7
murders, 29, 31, 43, 47, 62, 68, 71, 72, 73, 75, 76–7, 86, 90, 95, 148–50, 156–8, 162, 163, 164, 178–9, 201–2, 216–17, 224
Murray, Major, 148–50

'Nancy', origin of, 110–11
Nash, John, 99, 140
Nash, Richard 'Beau', 128
National Gallery, 91, 118
National Theatre, 146
Naval and Military Club, 22
Navy Office, 241–2
Naylor, Georgiana Hare, 57
necromancy, 193–5
Neild, John Campden, 206
Nelson, Lord, 117, 135, 221–3
Nettlefold and Chamberlain, 202
Neville, Sir Hugh, 235
New Compton St, 45–6
New Exchange, 86
New Palace Yard, 113
Newcastle, Dukes of, 72
'Newgate Calendar', 68
Newgate Prison, 162, 215–16, 217, 219, 227
Newgate St, 216–17, *218*
Newland, Abraham, 228
Newton, Sir Isaac, 176–7
Nicholas Nickleby (Dickens), 216
Nicholson, Aileen, the Highland Piper, 165
Nicols, Daniel, 27
Nicolson, Sir Harold, 159
nightingale, Berkeley Square, 16
Nightingale, Florence, 2, 12, *13*, 23
Nil Desperandum Mining Company, 139
Nithsdale, William Maxwell, Earl of, 169–70
Niven, David, 38
No Sex Please – We're British, 73
Nollekens, Joseph, 51–2, 67
'Noodle, Lord' (Duke of St Albans), 23–4
Norfolk, Dukes of, 197
Norman, Montagu, 228
Northampton, Earl of, 234
Northcliffe, Lord, 96, 137
Northumberland, 1st Duke and Duchess of, 146–7
Northumberland Avenue, 146–8, 149
Northumberland House, 146–8
Northumberland St, 148–50
Notorious Mrs Ebbsmith, The, 45
nun, ghost of a, 230
nurse, ghost of a, 182

Oakley St, 209
O'Connell, Daniel, 44
Of Alley (York Place), 151
Oh! Calcutta, 75
Oklahoma, 75
Old Bailey, 217
Old Bond St, 27
Old Curiosity Shop, The (Dickens), 44
Old Kentucky Palace, 31
Old Palace Yard, 114
Old Park Lane, 14
'Old Q', *see* Queensberry, 4th Duke of
Old Shades public house, 116
Oldfield, Nan, 110–11
opium, 30, 31, 81
organist, All Hallows by the Tower, 166–7
L'Orient (French flagship), 223
Orkney, Elizabeth, Countess of, 190–1
Ormond, Dukes of, 126–7
Otway, Thomas, 164
owl, Florence Nightingale's, 2, 13
Oxford, Edward, 93
Oxford St, 31–2, 46, 51, 178, 203

Pachmann, Vladimir de, 35
Paget, Lady Florence, 32
Palace Theatre, 45
Pall Mall, 133–7; origin of name, 95
Palmerston, Lord, 22, 103–4
Panton, Colonel Thomas, 40
Panton St, 40
'Panton's Land', 40
Park Lane, 8, 12–14
Park St, 10
Parker, Dr, 111
Parker, Richard, 55, 56
Parliament, Houses of, 103. 111–13, 114
Parliament Square, 103–15
Parliament St, 115
parrot, Cheshire Cheese, 64
Patent Office, 59
Paul's Cross, 160
pavements, 59
Pawle, Leonard, 28
pawnbrokers' sign, 238
peacock, Rossetti's, 206
'Pedlar's Acre', 145
pedometer, 14
Peel, Sir Robert, 1, 93
pell-mell, 95
Pendleton, Vicar, 238
'Pendrell, Unparallel'd', 47
penicillin, 205
Penn, William, 166
Pepys, Samuel, 2, 61, 109, 117, 151–2, 165–6, 168, 241–3
Percy St, 178–9
Persian cat, ghost of a, 166–7

Ryder, Captain Richard, 125
Ryder St, 125

Sablonière Hotel, 41–2
Sacheverell, Lucy, 77
Sackville St, 27
St Albans, Dukes of, 23–4, 209
St Alban's House, 142
St Awdry, 213
St Bartholomew's Hospital, 216
St Blaise, 214
St Christopher-le-Stocks, 230
St Dunstan's-in-the-West, 59–61
St Edward's Crown, 174
St Etheldreda's, 213–14
Saint-Evremond, Charles, 99
St George's, Bloomsbury, 191
St George's, Hanover Square, 29
St George's Hospital, 91–2
St Giles, Cripplegate, 224–5
St Giles in the Fields, 47–8
St Helen's, Bishopsgate, 233–5
St James, Garlickhythe, 237
St James's, 124–42
St James's, Piccadilly, 139, 205
St James's House, 139
St James's Palace, 125–7
St James's Park, 94, 95, 98–100
St James's Place, 125
St James's Square, 138–9
St James's St, 125, 127–32
St Katharine Cree, 235–6
St Luke's, Sydney St, 204–5
St Margaret's, Westminster, 105, 114–15
St Martin-in-the-Fields, 121–2
St Martin's Lane, 78–80
St Mary Axe, 236
St Mary-le-Bow, 224
St Mary's, Lambeth, 145
St Mary's Hospital, Paddington, 205
St Michael's Alley, 237
St Olave's, Hart St, 243
St Patrick's, Soho, 49
St Paul's, Covent Garden, 84, *85*, 164
St Paul's Cathedral, 143, *219*-23, 227
St Peter ad Vincula, 173
St Peter's, Cornhill, 237
St Sepulchre's, 215–16
St Stephen, Walbrook, 238
Sala, George Augustus, 63
Salisbury, Countess of, 171, 173
Salisbury Square, 160
Sandwich, Earl of, 76–7
Sanger, Charles, 209
Sankey, Sir Heiron, 27
Santayana, George, 212
Sargent, John Singer, 210
Sassoon, Sir Philip, 2, 12–14
Savage Club, 18, 180

Savile Row, 28, 29
Savoy, Count Peter of, 89
Savoy Chapel, 153–4
Savoy Court, 89
Savoy Hotel, 12, 80, 89–90
Savoy Place, 153
Savoy Theatre, 89
Saward, James, 155
Schomberg House, 133–5, 136
Scotland Yard, 118, 148
Scott, Captain Robert, 209
Scott, Sir Walter, 191
secret tunnel, St Sepulchre's, 215
'seething', meaning of, 241
Seething Lane, 226, 241–3
Sellis (a ghost), 126
Seven Dials, 80
severed hands, 50, 82–3
sewers, 36, 59
Seymour-Hicks, Sir Edward, 35
Shaftesbury, Earl of, 35
Shaftesbury Avenue, 35–6
Shakespeare, William, 109, 110
Shaver's Place, 39–40
Shaw, George Bernard, 77, 152
Shaw, Norman, 19
sheep, stuffed, 19
Sheffield, John, Earl of Mulgrave, 96–7
Shelley, Clara and William, 47
Shelley, Percy Bysshe, 29, 47–8, 189
Sheridan, Richard Brinsley, 28–9
Sherlock Holmes public house, 148, 149
ships'-chandler, 165
shirt-makers, 140
shoes for nudists, 31
Shore, Jane, 160–1
Shorter, Sir John, 227
Shrewsbury, Countess of, 47
Siddons, Sarah, 135, *136*
Sinn Feiners, 202
Sitwell, Sir George, 27
Sitwell, Sir Osbert, 27, 93–4, 105, 125
sleepwalking butler, 18
Sloane, Sir Hans, 206–7
Sloane Square, 202–3
Sloane St, 193–5, 203
Smirke, Sir Robert, 188
Smith, F. E., Lord Birkenhead, 137, 198–9
Smith, George Joseph (bigamist), 29
Smith, Captain John, 215
Smith, Pamela, 199
Smith, Sydney, 2, 7, 201
Smithfield, 223, 238
Smithson, James, 147
Snodgrass, Thomas, 235
Snow, John, 53
Snow Hill 'Snore Hill', 216
Soane, Sir John, 70, 228